The Genius of Lisp

Cees de Groot

Typeset with LaTeX using Tex Gyre Patella, Liberation Sans, Latin Modern, and other open source fonts.

ISBN:
978-1-0698864-0-8 (paperback)
978-1-0698864-1-5 (e-book)
978-1-0698864-2-2 (hardcover)

First edition: January 2026
First revision, 21 February 2026

Berksoft Publishing
RR #1, Berkeley N0H 1C0, Ontario
`https://berksoft.ca/gol`

berksoft

John McCarthy passed away at his home in Stanford on October 24, 2011, long before I started on this book. I hope that it does his legacy some justice.

Contents

Foreword

The past is a foreign country; they do things differently there.
–L.P. Hartley, "The Go-Between"

Wow, this book is full of stuff. Stuff about the past—how we did things back when; more precisely: how some of us programmed computers, how computers were, how the older ideas about Artificial Intelligence pushed some of us in a programming direction not so in-vogue today. Cees de Groot—we've been friends for decades—has put together a masterpiece of scholarship which should make you wonder about the nature of creative making, especially programming. I lived through most of the era he writes about.

A foreword is supposed to make you want to read the book, and I'll do that by telling you about the (perhaps) strange way those of us doing old-style AI thought about programming and the kinds of places we did those explorations; these might explain why Lisp seems so bizarre.

We were trying to write programs we had no idea how to write, to do things many thought programs—and computers—could not do. This was so unlike most programming tasks as to render those others nearly unrelated—aside from all of them looking like typing source code into a computer and running that code. And the languages that emerged from these different sorts of tasks were as different as could be: Fortran, COBOL, and Algol on one side and Lisp and its derivatives on the other. Let's look at this a few ways.

In the old days, we were trying to write programs in a programming language; the current AI systems—Large Language Models—are masses of neural-net-like things, trained on a gazillion texts, using vectors and matrices to represent stuff, and depending on a cleverly devised (not designed in the usual sense) representation of words and a mysterious and mysteriously named *attention mechanism.* Aside from programming all the math and orchestration of the training and "execution" of the neural nets, there is no programming at all to address the problem of sentience.

Programming and training are completely different. To see how, let's look at two representations of the English word "rug," one from my mostly symbolic (Lisp coded) natural language generation system named InkWell and one from a neural-net-style system which uses a vector representation called Word2Vec:

```
GLOSS "floor covering consisting of a piece of thick heavy fabric (usually with nap or pile)"
HYPERNYM (("furnishing" NOUN 3405265) ("floor_cover" NOUN 3366823) ("floor_covering" NOUN 3366823))
HYPERNYM-CHAIN ("carpeting" "rug" "carpet" "furnishing" "floor_covering" "instrumentality" ...
HYPONYM (("broadloom" NOUN 2904233) ("brussels_carpet" NOUN 2908773) ("drugget" NOUN 3248835) ...
PART-MERONYM (("edging" NOUN 3265479))
PRIMARY-SYNONYMS ("spread_over" "cover" "edging" "furnishing" "floor_covering" "broadloom" ...
```

People can understand this representation—it resembles what an elaborate (paper) dictionary might contain. This next one is the start of a 300 element vector; ChatGPT (last I looked) uses a similar representation using 12,000+ element vectors:

```
#(0.49859 -0.13689 -0.065173 -0.12382 0.22354 -0.31371 -0.69246 0.086646 0.1844 -0.24845
  0.34194 0.19392 0.50211 0.039492 0.35557 0.44126 -0.24031 0.16172 0.033318 0.30486
 -0.38023 -0.25019 0.52148 0.34716 -0.24813 -0.38764 -0.3566 -0.28372 0.32065 0.2928
 -0.29343 0.24823 -0.34043 -0.5566 -0.58753 0.35852 -0.36568 -0.20364 -0.16413 0.55994
 -0.13701 -0.49386 0.44324 -0.91781 0.51201 0.22886 0.45647 -0.66312  ... )
```

Well, a person can read the numbers, but taken as a whole they don't mean a thing to people. This representation has some interesting properties. One is that if you compute the offset vector `woman` − `man` and then add it to the vector representing `king` you get (close to) the vector representing `queen`. LLMs use this property to seem smart and follow a thread of narration.

Old-style—symbolic—AI folks and deep-learning folks seem to agree that it is indeed very hard or even impossible to write programs to exhibit sentience. The deep-learning crowd holds that the right way to make something sentient is to emulate a rough model of what nature / evolution put together and train it with lots of data, creating a *being* that "knows" a pile of stuff in the form of many numeric parameters (hundreds of billions of them)—and to hell with understanding how it works aside from how the orchestration code works and the attention mechanism kind-of works.

But Lisp was designed in a world where people still believed it was possible to write programs that exhibit intelligence.

Here is one way to feel the strangeness of the pursuit of symbolic AI using Lisp. Imagine a reality where no one is sure how to write programs to help businesses with financial issues, such as how to keep books. It is such a mystery that philosophers routinely weigh in with reasons for why writing such programs is possible or impossible. There are international conferences presenting research on progress figuring out how to write what in our reality is called a *spreadsheet*. Nuts, eh? Software engineers and developers likely cannot fathom a situation like this; their issues include making such programs run fast, making them correct, and making them useful, not worrying whether making them is fundamentally impossible.

For AI researchers using Lisp, the process was something like this: Dream up an approach to making a computer exhibit some aspect of human intelligence, come up an idea how to program that approach, write the program, run it to see what it does, and finally judge whether the approach and program "worked"; otherwise, adjust the program, adjust the approach, or have another dream. In many cases, the approach might be out of feasible reach and the researcher needs to invent a new programming technique or language to realize the approach in a program. Such programming languages and techniques I know of include pattern matching, constraint solving, frame systems, societies of agents, perceptrons, Planner, Microplanner, Programmar, KRL, Conniver, resolution, blackboard systems, rule systems, theorem proving, unification, alphabeta search, counterinduction, circumscription, resource limited computation, Elephant, meta programming, Flavors, mixins, heterarchy, futures, aspects, method combination, multiple inheritance, planning, and some machine learning algorithms. Many of these are either full programming languages or domain-specific programming languages. I and others on many occasions have written programs that write programs that are compiled and executed as part of the routine operation of the system.

Creating new programming languages on top of Lisp is easy. For one thing, the question of parsing is off the table. Before there were parser generators (before the early 1970s), creating a new programming language required writing a parser *by hand*. When you're hot on the trail of a new idea for what a programming language can do, writing a parser is a distraction. And if you can "compile" your language into Lisp, then you also have a compiler for your language.

In this realm, the software being written is more like a colleague than a built tool. Such programs help the researcher explore a mystery rather than solve a problem—writing programs is a way to understand a domain's landscape. Cees reports the story of the origin of Scheme, but I'd like you to read Guy Steele's telling of the crux:

> *Then came a crucial discovery—one that, to us* [Steele and Gabriel], *illustrates the value of experimentation in language design. On inspecting the code for* `apply`, *once they got it working correctly, Sussman and Steele were astonished to discover that the codes in* `apply` *for function application and for actor invocation were identical! Further inspection of other*

> *parts of the interpreter, such as the code for creating functions and actors, confirmed this insight: the fact that functions were intended to return values and actors were not made no difference anywhere in their implementation. The difference lay purely in the primitives used to code their bodies. If the underlying primitives return values, then the user can write functions that return values; if all primitives expect continuations, then the user can write actors. But the lambda and alpha mechanisms were themselves identical, and from this Sussman and Steele concluded that actors and closures were the same concept.*
> –Steele & Gabriel "The Evolution of Lisp"

Design imperatives for Lisp weren't what you'd normally think of. Early approaches to thinking about what Lisp should be included proposing sample programs, writing possible code for them, and judging how the code looked. Doing this, John McCarthy set the stage for including beauty and elegance into the design of programming languages. Sometimes limitations like this can lead to important breakthroughs, like garbage collection:

> *The recursive definition of differentiation made no provision for erasure of abandoned list structure. No solution was apparent at the time, but the idea of complicating the elegant definition of differentiation with explicit erasure was unattractive.*
> –John McCarthy "History of Lisp"

People writing Lisp code to do old-style AI are engaged in a creative act of discovery, an attempt to understand; it is not software engineering, which can be defined this way: "constructing software to satisfy all stakeholder requirements so as to maximize value." To discover requires a different sort of language, and it requires a different approach, captured well by the writer Joan Didion:

> *I write entirely to find out what I'm thinking, what I'm looking at, what I see and what it means.*
> –Joan Didion, "Why I Write"

Beyond the task of writing impossible programs using Lisp was the nature of the places where this all happened. I will describe only the Stanford AI Lab; other AI labs did similar things. Cees's book talks about the origins of timesharing; at SAIL the "sharing" part was taken to an extreme. It was not possible to password protect directories or files; this meant that anyone who could log into the PDP-10 could read (and write!) any file in any directory. The terminal system was based on the Data Disc display system, which held 32 video images on a disk. The Data Disc had a DMA interface which enabled the timesharing system to put out a full screen display in $1/30^{th}$ of a second. Each of the 32 video outputs could be attached to any terminal in the Lab using a video switch; this meant that anyone could look over the shoulder of anyone else while they worked. Moreover, any keyboard could be tied to the job being displayed. While *you* were working, *I* could not only (secretly) watch, but I could type into your workspace. It was not possible to hide a channel from prying eyes. The way we looked at it was that people could learn by watching people work and by reading others' files. I was the so-called "Lisp Wizard" at SAIL; many learned how to program Lisp by reading my files, and I could help people by attaching to their video channels along with my keyboard and using the interoffice phone system. And if ideas spread, all the better.

While sitting in front of our video terminals in the early 1970s on the SAIL PDP-10 system, we could listen to a dozen different radio stations, watch a couple of TV stations, get news alerts from two news feeds, send email to anyone on the ARPANET, instant message folks, and exchange thoughts on community "bulletin boards." The Lab was also home to a computer music research group complete with computer-driven synthesizers and monthly concerts put on by composers in the Lab. Oh, and let's not forget the volleyball court, showers, and sauna. It was a garden of open and varied intellectual cross-pollination. At the MIT AI Lab, similar ideas led to Free Software, which later led to the idea of Open Source. Of course we programmed in Lisp and invented new ways to program while trying to make computers aware, perceptive, and chatty.

When the mind confronts the strange and unfamiliar, it tends to open up, to seek new thoughts to help grasp the oddness—"defamiliarization" has a long history in literary circles. Described by Viktor Shklovsky in 1917, defamiliarization is the technique of presenting common objects, scenes, or concepts in an unfamiliar or strange way to disrupt habitual, automatic perception. Making the familiar seem "strange" forces the observer to stop, think, and perceive reality with renewed, intense awareness. Confronted by the strangeness of the workings of the mind and how to realize it in software, coupled with working in an unconventional research setting, a researcher could very well dream up something new, wonderful, and (yes!) strange in response.

I've set the scene—Cees will finish the story. I hope you never again think of programming the same way.

I'm always delighted by the light touch and stillness of early programming languages. Not much text; a lot gets done. Old programs read like quiet conversations between a well-spoken research worker and a well-studied mechanical colleague, not as a debate with a compiler. Who'd have guessed sophistication bought such noise?
–Steele & Gabriel, "50 in 50"

Richard P. Gabriel
Redwood City, California

Acknowledgements

I started thinking about this book a couple of years ago, triggered by conversations with interns at various places where I worked and with other young people. (Nearing the completion of my sixth decade on this clump of rock, I think I'm now finally allowed to say "young people".) It seems to me that the teaching of the history of the relatively young profession that some millions of us have taken up is somewhat lacking, and I thought that a pity.

The stories of the origins of programming are interesting in themselves and much can be learned from them, so I decided to start writing about computer history. Thanks, all you co-op students and junior hires at the places I worked, for humoring this old fart's prodding; for better or for worse, it was what got this book started.

I sent a proposal to a publisher, and to my surprise, they accepted. So I responded in the most logical way: I panicked. I guess that this is the natural reaction: "Hey, I have this great idea for a book, let's send a proposal out to my favorite publisher!" "Oh, darn, they accepted. Now I have to write the thing."

We started work and the people at the publisher were great. But when we were preparing for an initial beta release of the book, a bombshell dropped: the publisher had to downsize to make ends meet. Publishing books is not a get-rich-quick scheme, and this small and dear publishing house struggled in the rise in popularity of self-publishing, people getting their content from Youtube, etcetera. Running a business means making hard decisions, and the hard decision here was to halt all development work. It was a disappointment, to say the least. Still, we got quite a bit of work done before it happened, and the professional feedback on outline, style, and voice has been invaluable. You know who you are, and thanks from the bottom of my heart for the trust and support.

A couple of decades ago I had the pleasure of running into one of the household names in Lisp, Richard P. Gabriel. Over the years we met a couple more times. Dick was the closest link I had to the whole Lisp world, so I reached out to him repeatedly and he generously obliged me with pointers to good sources, personal anecdotes of his time working with John McCarthy, and some very thorough reviews, esepcially of the parts of this book he is best acquainted with. They were "frank" reviews, but that is exactly what I needed. On top of that, he collected some stories as background material that I liked so much I asked his permission to include them verbatim. Permission was granted and you'll find them as unnumbered chapters at somewhat relevant positions in the book. Thank you, Dick, I hope that this book comes somewhat close to meeting your exeedingly high standards in writing. And thanks for a great foreword, it really does set the stage.

Finally, the most important person in my life, my wife Millie, not only accepted with good grace my announcement that I was going To Write A Book, she also brought me tea when I was sitting in my home office typing away instead of spending time with her. Thank you so much for your support, I promise to maybe do this again.

Preface

Welcome to The Genius of Lisp, in which we will explore one of the oldest and most revered of all programming languages. We'll discover its roots in the theoretical work of Alan Turing and logician Alonzo Church. And together we'll uncover the deep simplicity and remarkable power that is the genius of Lisp.

Lisp's creator was himself a genius: mathematician and computer scientist John McCarthy. When he invented Lisp, McCarthy introduced concepts at an early stage of computing that programmers take for granted today, like symbols, garbage collection, and higher order functions. McCarthy created Lisp specifically for Artificial Intelligence research, and for decades it was the language of choice for AI researchers.

But the genius of Lisp transcends any single application area. Lisp is in the bones of every programming language in use today. And it holds an almost mythical status among developers. You'll hear stories of amazing feats that Lisp programmers accomplished, often "with only a couple of programmers." It is still a rite of passage among coders to work through the textbook of MIT's introductory course "Structure and Interpretation of Computer Programs," taught for over three decades at that institution using the Scheme dialect of Lisp.

But Lisp is not just an influence and a legend, it is still in use today—though not always under that name.

In short, Lisp is everywhere: its essence runs throughout computing today. This is why it is worthwhile to learn how it came to be, why it came to be, and how the essence of Lisp is encoded in the DNA of today's programming paradigms.

The Strangeness of Lisp

We can't avoid it, there is this thing we have to address at the outset. Lisp code looks strange. If you've never encountered Lisp, you will find its syntax peculiar, even hard to read. Most programming languages manage to make at least some sense to laypeople. Not so much pure Lisp. Take this simple Basic program that prints "Hello, world!" a bunch of times:

```
10 I = 10
20 PRINT "Hello, world!"
30 I = I - 1
40 IF I > 0 GOTO 20
50 END
```

In Lisp, that might be written:

```
(defun hello (count)
  (print "Hello, world!")
  (if (> count 0)
    (hello (- count 1))))

(hello 10)
```

That's a lot of parentheses! See those four right parentheses in a row? Whew. And what is it with that syntax for comparisons and subtractions? That minus sign means subtraction, which is almost always expressed in infix notation: `count - 1`. Strange. My hope is that in the course of this book, all will be made clear and even reasonable. In Lisp, strangeness and expressive power go hand-in-hand, and you have to accept the one to unlock the benefits of the other.

This Book Is for You

The Genius of Lisp is not a Lisp tutorial. If it were, we might analyze those two blocks of code to determine whether they print their message exactly ten times, or maybe commit an off-by-one error. We don't care. That's not what this book is about.

The Genius of Lisp is a story. You'll get the most out of it if you read the chapters in order, not skipping around. Although some knowledge of programming is assumed, I've written the book to appeal to a broad audience, not just professional software developers. But if you come away from it wanting to learn Lisp—which I hope you do—you will readily find material on the internet that suits your particular knowledge level and learning preferences. The book and its appendices have plenty of pointers to get you started.

Whether you know something about Lisp or not, learning the story of Lisp should be enlightening. I think you'll find the language much more approachable and I hope you'll be more forgiving of its quirks, because you recognize that they are a necessary and appropriate component of the genius of Lisp.

Online Resources

A book these days is not complete without an online presence, and this book is no exception. While we're liberal with adding URLs (especially handy if you are reading the eBook version of this book), you don't need to bother copying them: a full list of links from this books, code, and other assorted resources is available at `https://berksoft.ca/gol`. That is also why for the print edition we moved all URLs to the back into the bibliography. If you are reading this on paper and want to visit resources, no need to type them, just go to the website and the bibliography is there, with clickable links.

Chapter 1

What is Lisp?

This is a book on Lisp.

But it takes some detours to get there. Those that don't know their history are bound to repeat its mistakes, etcetera, so we will take a bit of a dive into some history and background before we get to the meat of the book. It makes sense, therefore, to start with "What is Lisp?" and "Why should I care?"

First, let's get typography out of the way: "LISP" is how the name of this programming language was written originally, and it stands for *List Processor*. Somewhere along the way, people invented lowercase on computers and writing everything fully capitalized got out of fashion, so "Lisp" became the preferred writing style, and is still the most common way to spell the name of this language today. The book tries to be consistent but historically accurate, so we will refer to old versions as LISP, especially when the implementation's manual spells it that way. In general, though, the modern way of writing is used. However, while Lisp's name got modernized, internally lots of Lisp implementations still ignore (most) typecase and its functions and variables are typically spelled in all capitals, partially because "that is how things work internally" and partially to help function and variable names stand out in plain text comments. We will follow this convention in this book.

Seeing is believing, they say, so using SBCL [70], a free and open source implementation of the Common Lisp standard, let's dive in for a bit. Note, this is not a tutorial, at best this is a tasting flight. But do feel free to download SBCL, start it in a terminal window using `sbcl`, and follow along.

A program that prints "Hello, World!" is a must have these days. There are various options to print, let's use `FORMAT`:

```
☞ CL-USER> (format t "Hello, World!~%")
Hello, World!
```

```
NIL
```

(The typographic convention we will follow in this book is that user input are on lines marked with "☞" and the bit that you're supposed to type is in **boldface**, anything else is computer output like a prompt.)

FORMAT is a built-in function to format strings, the T (which stands for "true") tells FORMAT to send whatever it is about to format out to the standard output (your terminal), and then what follows is the string, with squiggly-percent being code for "print a newline here").

This happens, but then it also prints NIL. This is what FORMAT returns in this case, and it stands for "nothing". Every piece of Lisp code must return a value, and "nothing" is an acceptable value if there is nothing to return.

So far, so good. It's a bit odd that you have to use parenthesis though, but try this:

```
☞ CL-USER> '(format t "Hello, World!~$")
(FORMAT T "Hello, World!~%")
```

Spot the difference. Just one little single quote character got inserted, and indeed, this character means "quote what follows." Instead of the Lisp implementation interpreting the "stuff between parenthesis" as a program, a piece of code to execute, it is interpreted as a literal thing and returned as-is.

The "literal thing" here is a list, in this case with three elements: FORMAT, T, and "Hello, World!~%". Lists are usually pieces of data in computer programs and they are useful in many circumstances: a list of numbers to take the average value of, for example, is something that will cost you a lot of time with a desk calculator but a programming language will make short work of it. A list of names and telephone numbers, a list of things to do, a list of things that lists are good for, the list goes on and on. Lists are everywhere.

And in Lisp, code is lists and lists can be code.

```
☞ CL-USER> (eval '(format t "Hello, World!~%"))
Hello, World!
NIL
```

In most Lisps, EVAL is the name of a routine or function that takes a list and evaluates it as if it were a program (and returns the results of that program). In this case, the list was created directly by the quotation operator, but it could have come from a variable, read in from a file, and–most importantly–could have been constructed by some code. In the next bit of code, SETQ is how you assign a variable in Lisp, essentially tagging a piece of data with a name. Note that the code style here is considered "dirty" and SBCL will give warnings if you type along, Ignore these, everything will work just fine.

```
☞ CL-USER> (setq x 'format)
  FORMAT
☞ CL-USER> (setq y "Hello, World!~%")
  "Hello, World!~%"
☞ CL-USER> (setq program (list x t y))
  (FORMAT T "Hello, World!~%")
☞ CL-USER> (eval program)
  Hello, World!
  NIL
```

And that right there is the essence of the power of Lisp, and what makes it such an interesting programming language. We constructed "a program" from pieces and ran it. Lisp manages to make the line between what is "code" and what is "data" extremely blurry, and has developed some powerful constructs that allow Lisp programmers essentially rewrite the language: everything written in Lisp (with few exceptions) is malleable by treating it as data, operating on it as data, and finally interpreting the result as code again.

Blurring the boundary between code and data is made easier in Lisp by the decision to always have a function name first and then its arguments. It is called "prefix notation" and sets Lisp apart from pretty much all other languages, which have "infix notation". Infix notation is what we're used to when doing arithmetic:

```
1 + 2
3 * 4
2 * 3 + 4
```

But in Lisp, the "function name" always goes first, whether it is `FORMAT` or +:

```
+ 1 2
* 3 4
* 2 + 3 4
```

Note that for the third example, the infix notation needs a special list of "precedence rules" to say that multiplication comes first and thus the answer is 10, but in prefix notation this is not really needed and in fact we have written things here so that the answer is 14 (how do we write it so that it becomes 10?). There are a couple of advantages here:

- Everything is a function invocation. `IF`, `FORMAT`, `QUOTE`, `+`, all look the same in Lisp. This makes it simple to parse for a computer and simple to do things like generating code as not many special rules need to be taken into account.
- It is trivial to extend things to more than two arguments. Even though we see + typically as an operation that takes two numbers to sum, in Lisp `(+ 1 2 3 4 5)` does what you would expect it does.

It does take some getting used to, though. People sometimes make a big thing about the differences, but they're superficial and once you're used to it, it's quite natural. Some things are easier to write in infix notation, some are more suited for prefix notation, but on the balance, the difference is small. What remains, though, are the powers of prefix notation: unifying everything that is a function in the same format, which makes it easy to take apart, change, and reconstruct code and pass functions around by name and invoke them later in a straightforward way. It is, in fact, such a powerful approach that many, if not most, programming languages takes the format that the programmer types (in the "programming language syntax") and transform it immediately in an internal representation called an "Abstract Syntax Tree" which more often that not uses prefix notation for conciseness, precision, and expressive power. The big difference between such languages and Lisp is that Lisp does away with that extra layer (or, as we will see, it never added it) and what you type is what the system internally works with.

Lisp's powers were unique when it was born and to a large extent, they still are. While some programming languages picked up some of its ideas, none picked up on all of them (if they did, they would be called "Lisp" these days, so that is maybe not entirely fair).

Lisp's powers are what unleashed the AI revolutions, because it is just as simple in Lisp to express concepts as it is to express a list of numbers. Most current AI work still owes a large debt to the language, as most of the current AI work traces back directly to the golden age of AI where optimism was high, Lisp was the language of choice, but computers were, alas, nowhere near where they needed to be.

Last but not least, Lisp is a story of some of the best and brightest minds working over what is an incredibly long span of time to lay the foundations for the language, develop it, and influence pretty much every programming language invented since then.

This book will tell the story of all of that, and in more technical detail than the average book on "computer history". It will try to challenge you with puzzles and deep details, will not shy away from some math, in the hope that it'll will leave you with a deep understanding of how the magic works and why it matters.

Part I

Origins

Chapter 2

Inventing Computing: Church and Turing

To understand the genius of Lisp, we need to go back in time nearly a century, because Lisp is built on mathematical concepts developed in the 1930s.

Programming the earliest computers meant hewing close to the hardware: you worked in numbers, did operations on numbers, and you had access to just enough logic to do simple branching. John McCarthy's mind was operating at a very different level: he wanted to use a computer to manipulate functions and symbols. These are the objects logicians and mathematicians actually work with, far removed from the flipping of ones and zeroes that goes on inside computers. If we are to understand what McCarthy was trying to create, we need to start where he started: with some mathematical logic.

The concepts that underlie the genius of Lisp are rooted in the work of Alonzo Church and Alan Turing, who together laid the foundation for computing as we know it. So let's take a look at the aspects of their work that are most relevant to McCarthy and his brainchild Lisp.

Come with me now back to the 1930s, when computers did not yet exist. The *idea* of computing was in the air, though, and some deep thinkers were wondering about the potential limits of these hypothetical machines.

In 1930, a mathematician named Kurt Gödel caused some consternation in certain circles by showing that a grand project to "complete mathematics" as proposed by mathematician David Hilbert was doomed to fail: he proved that a complete and consistent set of axioms and theorems is impossible, and thus that a complete and consistent description of all mathematics could not exist [28].

Though this was a strictly mathematical development, it had ramifications for the as yet nonexistent field of computing. Something called the "Entscheidungsproblem" was raised: could a hypothetical machine decide whether a (mathematical) statement was valid? Could these hypothetical machines compute "everything"? What was "everything" anyway? And what, really, was a computer? It was in this atmosphere that Church and Turing did the groundbreaking work on which McCarthy erected Lisp. So it's time for Church.

> ENTSCHEIDUNGSPROBLEM? — Literally: "decision problem." It seems that Germany ruled mathematics in that era. Turing published the paper we will discuss in this chapter in the very British *Proceedings of the London Mathematical Society*. That volume has two articles in German, everybody apparently understood that "Entscheidingsproblem" meant "decision problem", and in Turing's paper we see a lot of writing in German's "fraktur" script where today's mathematicians usually prefer to use Roman or Greek scripts.

Alonzo Church Creates the Machinery of Computation

Born in 1903, Alonzo Church studied mathematics at Princeton, receiving his PhD in 1927. As a pure mathematician, his contributions to mathematical logic received wide acclaim during his lifetime, earning him multiple honorary doctorates, a fellowship with the British Academy, and memberships with both the American and National Academies of Arts and Sciences. His published papers span seven decades, and both mathematicians and computer scientists use multiple concepts that bear his name.

Here we'll focus on his invention that was the direct cause for Lisp: his Lambda Calculus. Introduced in his monograph *The Calculi of Lambda-Conversion* [12], this laid the foundation for not only Lisp, but for most modern programming languages. It was his attempt to define a style of mathematics around functions much in the way that Euclid defined a set of axioms around geometry: a simple basis to serve as a foundation on which arbitrarily complex structures could be built. The book deals with the concept of a function, which he defines as:

> [...a] rule of correspondence by which when any thing is given (as argument) another thing (the value of the function for that argument) may be obtained.

This is pretty much the description of "function" we give to beginning programmers today. The Lambda Calculus is all about functions. Functions are simply things that map one set of values (say, the set of all integers) to another set of values (say, the set of all irrational numbers—the square root function would be such a function). Here is a typical function as normally written:

$$f(x, y) = 2x + 3y$$

This function f takes two arguments, x and y, and returns a value based on those arguments:

$$\begin{aligned} f(x, y) &= 2x + 3y \\ f(3, 4) &= 2 * 3 + 3 * 4 \\ &= 6 + 12 = 18 \end{aligned}$$

Church borrows from existing work in the field to both restrict and expand his definition of functions: notice that his functions can only take one argument, but what is not so obvious is that the argument can be anything, even a function.

Currying

The one-argument restriction is easy to circumvent using a technique called "Currying." Currying is named after mathematician and logician Haskell Brooks Curry. His importance to the field of logic and programming is probably best illustrated by the fact that his first, middle, and last name have each been used to name a programming language, of which the purely functional language Haskell is the most widely known. Let's look at that function of two variables:

$$f(x, y) = 2x + 3y$$

You can replace this with two nested functions of a single variable, where one returns a function:

$$f(x) = (f(y) = 2x + 3y)$$

We now call $f(3)$, which returns a function!

$$f(3) = (f(y) = 2 * 3 + 3y)$$

This function we can call again with the "second" argument:

$$f(3)(4) = (f(y) = 6 + 3y)(4)$$

And now you can substitute 4 for y and get 18 again.

This trick accomplishes two things: it is much simpler to reason about functions if they have only one argument, and, by induction, it is easy to see that if you can curry a function of two arguments, you can curry a function of any number of arguments. This let Church apply his work universally, to anything that would fit this strict, but universal, definition of a function.

* * *

With the argument count restriction out of the way, Church also needed to make sure that really everything—all mathematics—fit in this domain, and therefore numbers were not part of Church's notation.

That's right, no numbers. They too are expressed as functions, so that "functions" is all that is left. The idea is that if you can describe all of mathematics with functions, then you have an exceptionally simple but universal bit of mathematical machinery to work with. We'll get there, but let's start with the basics so we can do a bit of a deep dive later into how this works.

Church's notation, now more commonly known as the "Lambda notation," distinguishes between a "form":

$$x^2 + x$$

And a function:

$$f(x) = x^2 + x$$

A "form" is what you might call a formula. It has "free variables" - that x in there has no context at all, it is a placeholder, but for what, we don't know. A function says something about these free variables—it "binds" them to the arguments of the function. The free variable x in the *form* has become a function argument x in the *function*. You can call a function, it's a packaged thing, and everybody would expect $f(4)$ to be 18 here. A form does not have that context. Remember these two terms: the distinction between form and function is important and we will return to the notion when discussing Lisp.

In Church's notation, a function is indicated by the Greek letter lambda (λ) and any function arguments directly follow it, without the parenthesis of the more common $f(x)$ notation. A dot separates arguments from form, so that the form $x^2 + x$, wrapped in a function in Church' notation, becomes:

$$\lambda x.x^2 + x$$

This is for all purposes the same thing as the $f(x)$ notation, with the important distinction that in the common case, we also "name" the function as f, and in this notation we merely say "this is a function accepting a single argument x." It doesn't have a name, it is literally "anonymous."

Applying this function, say, with the number 4, would be written as

$$(\lambda x.x^2 + x)(4)$$

However, this illustration is not really correct, as Church's notation is too restricted to handle complex concepts like "squared", "plus", or even "four."

The Rules of the Game

Forms and functions together are called "terms," and here are the full rules of the game to create a valid term in this notation:

- You can only use *symbols* (from the infinite list a, b, c, ..., z, a', b', ..., z', a'', ..., a''', ...) and the special characters λ, (, and). The dot is often used as a separator between variables and the form in lambda notation (and we will use it) but it is strictly not necessary: $\lambda x.x$ is the same as λxx.

- A symbol by itself, like x, is a well-formed term. The x is called a variable and here it is considered to be "free," as nothing says what role it plays—this kind of a term is a form, not a function.

- If M is well-formed and contains at least one free occurrence of x, then $\lambda x.M$ is well-formed. All occurrences of x in M are now *bound*. Say that M stands for the term xx, then this is a term with one free variable, x. We can turn this into $\lambda x.xx$ by this operation (called "abstraction"), binding the free variable with the Lambda operation. Note that M is just a placeholder for "any term" and not part of the notation itself—such capital letters just make it simpler to talk about "any valid term" and give examples.

- If terms F and A are well-formed, then (FA) is well-formed and stands for function application—the function F is invoked with the argument A. Variables in either part stay free or bound as they were in their respective part. For example, if F stands for

$\lambda x.x$ and A for y, then $\lambda x.xy$ is a valid term. Note that this does not change the status of "free" or "bound" variables: what was free stays free, and what was bound similarly stays bound. In the example, x is bound both before and after application, and y is and remains free.

That's it: only terms you can generate with these rules are valid terms, and they contain free or bound variables depending on their appearance as arguments in lambda operators. Anything else is invalid and not part of the lambda calculus.

Next, we have two rules that allow us to operate on terms:

Substitution In a term M, you can replace all variables x by y without changing anything. This is easy to see in normal function notation: $f(x) = 2 + x$ and $f(y) = 2 + y$ are essentially one and the same thing. Likewise, $\lambda x.x$ and $\lambda y.y$ are the same, as are $\lambda x.y$ and $\lambda y.x$.

Application Say you have a function $\lambda x.xyyx$ then you can *apply* this function with an argument. If the argument is b, then application means substituting all occurrences of x with b. This will give you the result $byyb$. Function application is essentially a search and replace operation.

A third rule, "extensionality," exists but is often skipped in treatments of the lambda calculus and that is what we will do as well.

Now You're Talking My Language

If you followed all that, congratulations. The official Church lambda notation is strange if you're not a logician who actively studies this particular field. The purpose of this book is not to torture you with arcane notation, so let's switch to a hopefully more familiar notation, JavaScript. This has the advantage that you can follow along in the browser (just go to your browser's developer tools which has a JavaScript console), but you can also install and use a stand-alone Javascript implementation like *NodeJS*.[1] The example responses we show in the rest of this chapter are for NodeJS; your browser may print out results in a slightly different format but that does not make a material difference. And you don't need to be fluent with JavaScript as we will use only the tiniest subset of it, just the bits we need to define valid Lambda Calculus terms. Function definitions will be single-argument functions using the JavaScript notation:

```
<arg> => <function body>
```

[1] https://nodejs.org/en/download

For example,

```
x => 2 * x
```

Will double it's argument.

We will *assign* these functions to "helper" Javascript variables which we type in all uppercase, to make clear that they're strictly not part of the Lambda Calculus, they are just placeholders to help us save some typing, just like the M, A and F before:

```
<FUNCTION_NAME> = <arg> => <function body>
```

To continue the example:

```
DOUBLE = x => 2 * x
```

Which makes `DOUBLE` the name of a function we can call, meaning that executing `DOUBLE(2)` would give us 4.

In JavaScript, variables can hold anything: numbers, strings, web pages, but here we stick to just the bits that we need for the Lambda Calculus. so they will hold just functions. One extra detail is functions with multiple arguments, which we will split up inot multiple nested functions of one argument (See "Currying" on page 11 for how this works). This takes some effort to get used to and is strictly not necessary in JavaScript (which, of course, supports functions with multiple arguments) but leaves us with the minimum amount of syntax needed and lets us stay close to the original. So, a function with three arguments will be written as:

```
<FUNCTION_WITH_THREE_ARGS> =
    <arg1> => <arg2> => <arg3> => <function body>
```

As in Church' paper, not much else is allowed, just function invocation, and from there we can build up pretty much everything we need. JavaScript's built-in helpers like `+` or `and` are therefore off-limits.

Let's start with the simplest possible function, $\lambda x.x$:

```
I = a => a
```

This expression has no free variables: the `a` in the function body appears as an argument which makes it bound, so the expression we are calling `I` is what is known as a *"closed expression"*. This simplest of all functions is named the "identity function": whatever you feed it, the identical thing comes out.

A couple more functions that are similarly simple are often called M, or "self application", and K, or "constant":

```
M = a => a(a)
```

```
K = a => b => a
```

But that first one is maybe not so simple. Try this: type in that definition for M and then enter M(M). We've found a quick way to cause an endless loop, with M calling itself. When we would run this in Node, for example, this happens:

```
☞ $ node
Welcome to Node.js v22.14.0.
Type ".help" for more information.
☞ > M = a => a(a)
☞ > M(M)
Uncaught RangeError: Maximum call stack size exceeded
    at M (REPL4:13:10)
    at M (REPL4:13:10)
    at M (REPL4:13:10)
    at M (REPL4:13:10)
    at M (REPL4:13:10)
    at M (REPL4:13:10)
    at M (REPL4:13:10)
    at M (REPL4:13:10)
    at M (REPL4:13:10)
>
```

Applying the self application combinator to itself never ends; a theoretically endless loop starts and is only terminated by practical limitations like the amount of memory set aside for bookkeeping that NodeJS calls the "call stack." But computers are not pure mathematics, and pure mathematics is where Church operated. So we'll ignore mere physical limitations for now and remain firmly rooted in theory: M(M) is perfectly valid, it just expands infinitely.

Note that we stay true to the original notation of the lambda calculus in the case of K: it is a function accepting one argument (a) that returns a function accepting one argument (b) that returns a. We can read this just as well as a function that takes two arguments (and returns the first argument) and for understanding how things work, this is our preferred interpretation.

With these simple tools in hand, we can start making a dent in the question "how do you express everything, *anything*, as a function?"

Everything as a Function

Let's start with Boolean operators, the essential building blocks of logic and computers. Keep in mind the mantra of the Lambda calculus: everything is a function. So our immediate challenge is: "What function could stand for the concept of *true*? Which one for *false*?"

> Boolean Logic — Named after George Boole, boolean logic operates on just two values: true and false. The three functions we will implement here are "and", which is true if (and only if) all its arguments are true; "or", which is true if at least one of its arguments are true, and "not" which is true if its only argument is false. In all other cases, these functions return false. More complete descriptions and more functions can be found on Wikipedia [83]

The answer depends on what you need them for, of course, but what they are used for most often is for decision making: *if* something is true, *then* we do this *else* we do that. It makes sense, therefore, to have *true* as a function that returns its first argument, and *false* as a function that returns its second argument:

```
T = a => b => a
```

```
F = a => b => b
```

So far so good, or is it? Just to be sure, and for this one time, we'll compare to how this looks in the original notation and then we'll stay with JavaScript exclusively. True is defined as:

$$\lambda x.\lambda y.x$$

And false as:

$$\lambda x.\lambda y.y$$

To test our Boolean functions, we're going to need a full set of logic operatoins, so let's get the essential ones defined. "Not" is the next one, and here it is:

```
NOT = p => p(F)(T)
```

Not is, again, a function and just as in any programming language, it is a unary one: it takes just one argument. The argument gets called with `(F)(T)` (or `(F, T)` if we'd allow multiple arguments). It is relatively simple to see how this works. For *not true*, we say `NOT(T)`:

```
NOT(T)
=> T(F)(T)
=> F
```

(Check the definition of the function F for the second step). Conversely, if the argument is (or, indeed, expands to) false:

```
NOT(F)
=> F(F)(T)
=> T
```

As you can see, this simple function does what we need: *true* becomes *false* and the other way around. Entering these definitions in a JavaScript console lets you play around with our simple logic engine:

```
☞ > NOT(T)
[Function F]
☞ > NOT(F)
[Function T]
```

Magic. We just convinced a modern and complex programming language that you can have Booleans with just some trivial functions. Let's quickly wrap up with the "and" and "or" operations:

```
AND = p => q => p(q)(p)

OR = p => q => p(p)(q)
```

To figure out how they work, look at how NOT is defined and try to reason through it. It works, that's for sure:

```
> AND(NOT(F))(T)
[Function T]
```

We can make decisions! Next comes counting, so we need to learn how to work with numbers, at least the natural numbers—if we can do that, we can begin to believe that, with enough patience, we could build up all of mathematics this way.

Numbers are simple as long as you're happy to accept that this abstract form of counting indeed represents the concrete thing that most of us call "numbers." Again, the start is simple—counting starts at zero:

```
ZERO = f => x => x
```

Zero is defined as a constant function that returns its second argument. This only makes sense as a starting point if you look at the next two integers:

```
ONE = f => x => f(x)

TWO = f => x => f(f(x))
```

The first argument for these "number" functions is a function that we apply as often as the number's magnitude. Zero times for zero, one times for one, two times for two, and so on, so we can generalize a "next," or "successor" function:

```
SUCC = n => f => x => f(n(f)(x))
```

The successor of a number `n` is just another application of the function `f`. This is probably best explained with an example that steps through the expansion of the successor of two:

```
SUCC(TWO) ->
SUCC(TWO, f, x) ->
f(TWO(f)(x)) ->
f(f(f(x)))
```

Three applications of `f` stand for three, and now we can define four, then five, and so on.

Where we can count up by one, we can do sums, and when we can do sums, we can do multiplications:

```
PLUS = m => n => f => x => (m(f)(n(f)(x)))

MULT = m => n => f => x => (m(n(f))(x))
```

Here we will content ourselves with just showing that it works; figuring out what goes on is a fun exercise and I invite you to pause here and grab some paper and a pencil to work through these examples (because we sort of cheated here: you don't really need a computer and a programming language to work through these examples, pen and paper should do fine. It just takes a bit longer).

In our JavaScript implementation keeping track of things is starting to become hairy. We don't have two nice "landing points" like we had with `T` and `F` when discussing Booleans, therefore the built-in printing is letting us down here:

☞
```
> PLUS(ONE)(TWO)
[Function (anonymous)]
```

All that JavaScript can tell us is that `PLUS(ONE)(TWO)` equals some function, but given that everything is a function here, that is hardly helpful. It would be neat to be able to have it tell us which "number-equivalent" function we're looking at—ideally by printing that equivalent number. For that, we define some helpers to convert between these numbers-as-functions (called "Church numerals") and regular numbers:

```
church_to_int = c => c((x) => x + 1)(0)
int_to_church =  n =>
    n === 0 ? ZERO : SUCC(int_to_church(n - 1))
```

and we're back on track:

```
☞ > church_to_int(PLUS(ONE)(TWO))
3
```

And with this little translation layer, we can show that we can do simple computations with just functions and that these computations "do the same thing" as if we would have just added the numbers one and two. We could continue: sutraction and division are begging for attention, for example, but let's agree that if we can do multiplication and addition, then the rest is, in theory, doable as well (and, of course, feel free to challenge yourself and attempt these two operations!). It would be easy to fill the rest of the book with it and suffice it for now to say that these books have been written and are plentiful. We can leave Church's Lambda Calculus with the belief that it can, indeed, represent all of math and therefore all possibile computations. Out of merely the simplest of mathematical ideas, the one-argument function, Church built a universal computing machine.

Well, abstractly anyway. It took one of his students to write the spec for a realizable computer. And that student would become more famous than his teacher.

> THE MOCKINGBIRD — If this topic interests you beyond the brief discussion above, logician Raymond Smullyan wrote a delightful book that should keep you busy for a while, *To Mock A Mockingbird: and Other Logic Puzzles* [76]. A good part of this work is dedicated to puzzles around the Lambda Calculus.

Alan Turing Creates a Virtual Computer

Alan Turing was born nine years after Alonzo Church and studied with him at Princeton. Turing's work with British intelligence during World War II has been the material for at least one movie. We will focus here, though, on the parts of his life's work that are most relevant to the creations of computer languages in general and to

Lisp and Artificial Intelligence in particular: Turing machines, the Turing Test, and his thinking about machines, brains, and what it all means.

Turing played around with a related challenge closely related to Church's work. He, too, wanted to devise a mathematics that could compute anything. But his approach landed him in the fast lane towards receiving the title of "Father of Modern Computing"–rather than starting with abstract functions, he built his edifice on top of a (still abstract) computing machine, a device that *in princple* could be built. It was that machine that he then elegantly used to make statements about the halting problem, where his collaboration with Church culminated in the Church-Turing thesis. Essentially, that thesis says that anything that can be computed by an algorithm can be computed on the device we're about to explore. It showed that all computers are, in effect, equivalent in terms of their limits and is one of the foundational ideas of computer science.

First described in his 1936 paper *On Computable Numbers, With an Application to the Entscheidungsproblem* [85], the "Turing Machine" is a simple device that runs off an endless tape. While Church's sleight of hand was elegant in theory but complicated in practice as a way of representing mathematics, Turing's brainchild was something that one could build and which merely needed a large amount of tape—infinite in theory, but usually well short of that in practice. Turing machines have indeed been constructed, albeit mostly for the fun factor by hobbyists. Turing never envisioned his computer as an actual physical machine: to him it was just another vehicle of the mind to help logicians reason about computation.

A Turing machine is, in principle, quite simple:

- There is an internal "state table", which tells the machine what to do. The states are numbered, and the action to execute is defined by the current state number, and the symbol under the read head on the tape.
- The machine reads a symbol at the current location of the tape.
- Based on its internal state and the value of the symbol, it can perform a limited number of actions: it writes a potentially new value at the current location of the tape, and then either moves one position to the left on the tape, one position on the right on the tape, or it stops computing ("halts"). If it doesn't halt, it then starts over.

Symbols and state can be as simple as a single character or bit, and the state table is typically similarly limited. Having warmed up our

JavaScript skills in the previous section, let's try to build a Turing machine.

A Turing Machine in JavaScript

First, we need an endless tape and a machine that has a little bit of internal state and knows where on the tape we are (an actual physical machine would have the tape "just there" under the read/write head, but we need to keep track of our virtual tape). In JavaScript, the easiest representation of a tape is as an array (these can grow as needed in the language), and the whole machine can be represented as a JavaScript "object" with `pos` and `state` fields for the two components we need to track.

```
tape = []

machine = {
  pos: 0,
  state: undefined
}
```

Now, all that this machine needs to be able to do is the following: read the current location, use that and its internal state to look up what to do and what state to move to, execute the actions, and then move to the new state. We closely follow Turing in two respects:

- The machine can execute multiple actions in one go. This is just a convenient optimization: you could split all these actions up with their own private machine states chaining them and nothing would change;
- We use alternating "output" and "working" memory cells on the tape. Turing himself did this as an optimization. You could designate separate sections of tape, but that would mean a lot of moving back and forth.

Let's define the lookup table that determines the next action as a simple JavaScript object. Its keys are the state and current tape symbol, and its values a two-element array: first the actions, then the new state. The actions are a set of simple functions that operate on the machine and the tape:

```
e =  () => tape[machine.pos] = undefined
p0 = () => tape[machine.pos] = 0
p1 = () => tape[machine.pos] = 1
r =  () => machine.pos++
l =  () => machine.pos--
```

Five simple functions that can erase the tape, print a 0 or a 1, and move the tape one position left or right. That is all that we need for now to define a simple machine, say one that writes alternating zeros and ones:

```
states = {
  'b/any': [[p0, r], 'c'],
  'c/any': [[r], 'e'],
  'e/any': [[p1, r], 'f'],
  'f/any': [[r], 'b']
}

machine.state = 'b'
```

We use any to stand for any symbol on the tape (0, 1 or undefined) and the slash to separate state and symbol—this is merely for readability. The machine state starts at 'b', where it will print a 0 and move one right, then set the machine state to 'c'. The rest should be simple to follow: it does indeed endlessly fill up a tape with alternating 0s and 1s on the output cells, leaving all the working memory (interleaving cells) untouched.

Turing had to work with pencil and paper to verify that this machine did, indeed, do the job. We can do better, this bit of code will implement something that can "run" the above "program":

```
turing_step = () => {
  state_key = machine.state + '/' + tape[machine.pos]
  any_key = machine.state + '/any'
  action_items = states[state_key] || states[any_key]
  functions = action_items[0]
  next = action_items[1]
  functions.forEach(f => f())
  machine.state = next
}

dump = () => console.log('tape', tape, ', machine', machine)

turing_run = (n) => {
  for (i = 0; i < n; i++) {
    turing_step()
    dump()
  }
}
```

For the sake of this discussion, this is probably the least interesting bit of code—the point of Turing's argument is not whether you implement it using a human following the steps, build a machine that can do this, or write a small bit of code in JavaScript. The point is that Turing was discovering universal truths about computing in general. Actually implementing the machine was merely the proverbial exercise left for the reader. In fact, when a co-worker after the war started talking about implementing the machine and showed optimizations and errors in his paper, Turing was annoyed—that was not relevant (as recalled by Donald W. Davies in *The Essential Turing* [17]).

Let's follow his advice and focus on *what* the machine does, not *how* it does it, as it is the more interesting part:

```
> turing_run(10)
tape [ 0 ] , machine  pos: 1, state: 'c'
tape [ 0 ] , machine  pos: 2, state: 'e'
tape [ 0, <1 empty item>, 1 ] , machine  pos: 3, state: 'f'
tape [ 0, <1 empty item>, 1 ] , machine  pos: 4, state: 'b'
tape [ 0, <1 empty item>, 1, <1 empty item>, 0 ] ,
  machine  pos: 5, state: 'c'
```

As you can see, the system indeed does what we thought it would do: fill up the tape with alternating ones and zeroes. We should shorten it a bit though. Earlier we said that we would follow Turing in allowing any number of actions, and it is easy to verify that the following machine is equivalent:

```
states = {
  'b/undefined': [[p0], 'b'],
  'b/0': [[r,r,p1], 'b'],
  'b/1': [[r,r,p0], 'b']
}
machine.state = 'b'
```

It won't hurt to check though. Erase the tape, reset the machine, and off we go:

```
> machine.state = 'b'; machine.pos = 0; tape = []; turing_run(4)
tape [ 0 ] , machine  pos: 0, state: 'b'
tape [ 0, <1 empty item>, 1 ] , machine  pos: 2, state: 'b'
tape [ 0, <1 empty item>, 1, <1 empty item>, 0 ] , machine  pos: 4,
        state: 'b'
tape [ 0, <1 empty item>, 1, <1 empty item>, 0, <1 empty item>, 1 ],
  machine  pos: 6, state: 'b'
```

We can now run everything through a single state that does different things depending on what the value of the cell under the reader is. And conveniently enough, these two short examples display all there is to know about Turing machines.

Here is a slightly more complex example from the paper. We now also will use the scratch cells that are so annoyingly in the way in the output above. Can you figure out what this will do?

```
pe = () => tape[machine.pos] = 'e'
px = () => tape[machine.pos] = 'x'

states = {
  'b/undefined': [[pe, r, pe, r, p0,
                   r, r, p0, l, l], 'o'],
  'o/1': [[r, px, l, l, l], 'o'],
  'o/0': [[], 'q'],
  'q/any': [[r, r], 'q'],
  'q/undefined': [[p1, l], 'p'],
  'p/x': [[e, r], 'q'],
  'p/e': [[r], 'f'],
  'p/undefined': [[l, l], 'p'],
  'f/any': [[r, r], 'f'],
  'f/undefined': [[p0, l, l], 'o']
}
machine.state = 'b'
```

This is starting to look like a proper computer program, albeit in a low level programming language. We could go on and on and devise ever more complex machines to do things like addition and subtraction, and these are all possible—if you want to play with it, using unary notation (where 0 = '1', 1 = '11', 2 = '111', and so on) works best.

Note that all your "programming" will happen in these state tables. The actual JavaScript program we wrote–the mechanics of the Turing machine—doesn't need to change. A Turing machine's behavior is fully defined by this state table: it can become arbitrarily complex but will always completely define what the corresponding machine can do.

Inventing Software

If we think about a Turing machine a bit like Alan Turing might have thought about it, in terms of physical machines instead of convenient JavaScript state tables, this constant rewiring of your hardware as you change the state tables would get old pretty quickly. We have it easy, just another table to copy and paste, but think of this machine implemented with '30s technology, with wires, relays, and switches. Changing the machine to behave differently becomes a nightmare. Can we do better? Turing figured out a way to do better, and that way is the crux of his argument.

What if we *encode* these Turing machines somehow, building a sort of higher level Turing machine that could read a definition of a Turing machine from tape and then start to behave like the Turing machine encoded on the tape? Would that work?

Turing set out to work and devised a two-step encoding, where first the state table gets simplified—instead of states 'b', 'c', ... we have states 'q1', 'q2', ...; instead of "print 0" or "erase", we just use symbols 0, 1, 2, as many as we need. The "print alternating zeroes and ones" machine would then have a state table as follows:

State	Current Symbol	Actions	New State
q1	s0	ps1,r	q2
q2	s0	ps0,r	q3
q3	s0	ps2,r	q4
q4	s0	ps0,r	q1

A next, intermediate step of encoding then replaces states by the letter "D" followed by a number of "A"s corresponding to its index, and symbols similarly by the letter "D" followed by a number of "C"s. After compacting every row in the table (leaving out the "print" as that now always happens), we're back at the simple machine that does a print and move every round, where the move "N"—unused here—stands for "don't move": Finally, we join every-

Row	Encoding
q1s0s1rq2	DADDCRDAA
q2s0s0rq3	DAADDRDAAA
q3s0s2rq4	DAAADDCCRDAAAA
q4s0s0rq1	DAAAADDRDA

thing with semicolons between then and then replace letters with numbers according to the somewhat arbitrary mapping A = 1, C = 2, D= 3, L = 4, R = 5, N = 6, ; = 7 to translate:

```
DADDCRDAA;DAADDRDAAA;DAAADDCCRDAAAA;DAAAADDRDA
```

into

```
31332531173113353111731113322531111731111335317
```

With this last step, every possible Turing machine can be described by a single number, which he calls the Standard Definition (or "S.D."). Note that this number is large—Turing machines that can do more interesting things will have mindbogglingly large numbers, but that is to be expected. Take a simple program on a modern computer, for example a program that just prints out "Hello, world!": expressed as a single number it will have close to 35,000 digits on the Linux operating system.

The next step that Turing takes is the sort of thing that is logical with 20/20 hindsight and brilliant if you think about where we were in the development of computers:

> It is possible to invent a single machine which can be used to compute any computable sequence. If this machine U is supplied with a tape on the beginning of which is written the S.D. of some computing machine M, then U will compute the same sequence as M. [85]

Of course, merely stating that something is possible doesn't count in a paper that is to be published in a prestigious journal, so he then goes on to describe an actual machine which we now call a Universal Turing Machine. It will take in any of these numbers that express a standard definition and then will start to operate as the exact Turing Machine that that number describes. Pause there for a bit, if you will. A Universal Turing Machine is a machine that:

- Has internal state;
- Can read data from tape to reconfigure its behavior;
- Can reconfigure itself to *any* Turing machine we can think of.

Basically, what he describes is a computer driven by software. And, like Church before him, he does that using only some basic concepts to bootstrap himself to that level. The paper becomes a lot more technical from this point on, but using this machinery, Turing showed that two things must hold true:

- Any computation that we can execute can be expressed as a Turing machine;
- We can never predict, from looking at the number representing a program, whether a machine will halt or not.

For Turing, that second result was the more important one—he was working on the problem in logic that asks for an algorithm that can decide whether a statement is universally valid or not. All the work above was a setup to cast this problem into a different problem—can we predict whether an algorithm halts or not?—so he could give a negative answer to that question. For us, however, the more important result is the universality of his machine. While it was equivalent to Church's lambda calculus, what Turing described was a universal computing machine.

[2] `https://commons.wikimedia.org/wiki/File:Turing_Machine_Model_Davey_2012.jpg`

Figure 2.1: A physical Turing machine
(Source: *Rocky Acosta, via Wikipedia*[2])

Turing was right in concluding that his invention was purely a vehicle to express mathematical logic. Regardless, people attempted to build Turing machines, mostly for fun or to make a point (for example, Penrose in *The Emperor's New Mind* [63], or the model in Figure 2.1). It took a long time for one of his former co-workers, the one who got chastised by Turing for wasting his time on implementing a Universal Turing Machine, to actually implement a working version. Davies' article in *The Essential Turing* [17] is worth a read if you want to see just how complex the thing is.

The Turing Test

In 1950, Turing wrote an article titled *Computing Machinery and Intelligence* for MIND, a philosophy journal published by Oxford Press on behalf of the philosophical society Mind Association[84].

This was a time where computers barely existed—Turing himself famously wrote a chess program but could not find a computer powerful enough to run it on, so the first game the program played consisted of Turing flipping back and forth through his code, executing the program on paper, and taking half an hour per move.

Still, the absence of actual computing machines didn't stop him from thinking big and in this paper he explored the idea of computers that could think, and could think well enough indeed to pass as humans. How would we decide when a computer indeed operated at a human-level intelligence? His solution was what we now call the Turing test: let an operator interact with a human and a computer, and if said operator (a human) cannot tell the difference, the computer has achieved human-level thinking.

We now know that computers can actually be much less smart than a human and still trick humans into thinking they are "real persons," but with this paper, Alan Turing pretty much kicked off the field of Artificial Intelligence.

Doing math on computers in such a way that they could eventually exhibit behavior we'd call intelligent, that was the goal of John McCarthy's work, leading him to the naming of the field of Artificial Intelligence, the creation of Lisp, and subsequently a rich career in academia. In the next chapter, we'll take a closer look at the person who bestowed all these blessings on computer science and software engineering.

THE HALTING PROBLEM — While not in scope of the book, it is still interesting to briefly touch on how Turing showed that a computer can never decide whether a program will halt. Envision a program for a Turing Machine that reads the Turing number for a random program and emits "Yes" or "No" depending on whether said random program will eventually halt. Call this program M.
Now, create a program G that does the following:

- It calls M with its own (G's) Turing number.
- If M says that G halts, it will keep running forever.
- If M says that G won't halt, it will immediately exit.

By constructing this one bad apple, Turing showed that there was no way to create M and crushed the hopes and dreams of a lot of logicians in one brief proof-by-paradox.

Chapter 3

McCarthy Invents Lisp

John McCarthy was born in Boston, Massachusetts, on September 19, 1927, on the eve of the Great Depression, the child of immigrants. His father, John Patrick McCarthy, was a Roman Catholic from Ireland, his mother, Ida Glatt, a Lithuanian Jew.

Like many immigrants, the McCarthys saw education as the road to success in their adopted society. Though John Senior had only a fourth-grade education, he made sure that the McCarthy household had a well-stocked library, and every evening the dinner table was the site of discussions of everything from politics to poetry to science.

John Junior particularly loved to read about science. The McCarthy library had titles like *100,000 Whys: A Trip Around the Room*, *The Boys' Book of Electricity*, and *New Background of Science*. John met all the stereotypes of the nerd: bright, cocky, physically clumsy. He knew from early childhood that he was going to be a scientist.

And he was bright. After graduating from high school two years early, he got accepted as an undergraduate at the (already) venerable California Institute of Technology, aka Caltech. The academic curriculum posed no problem for him; he had already taught himself most of their coursework. His problem was the physical education requirement: Ultimately, Caltech kicked him out for failing PE, and as it was wartime, this ended his student deferment for military service, and the Army drafted him.

Maybe military service helped him mature; in any case, Caltech re-admitted him, and he proceeded to complete his Bachelor's degree and start work on his PhD.

During this time, he attended a conference sponsored by Caltech's biology division on "cerebral mechanisms in behavior," where one of the speakers was John Von Neumann, then at the Institute for Advanced Study in Princeton, New Jersey, where he held a lifetime tenured professorship. Everyone who ever met Von Neumann was impressed by his intellect, and John McCarthy was no exception.

John Von Neumann — On the off chance that this name does not ring a bell: Von Neumann was a mathematician, engineer and computer scientist and already very famous in his days. Born in Hungary, he is one of the people who worked during World War II on the Manhattan Project to develop the first nuclear bomb, and during his career made contributions in close to a dozen different scientific fields, ranging from biology to economics.
In the field of Computer Science, he is probably best known for the "Von Neumann Architecture," which specifies a style of computers that have one unified working memory both for code and data. It is the most common form of computer design and always has been, with its biggest competitor, the "Harvard Architecture," which has separate memories for code and data, only being common in smaller, "embedded," devices. Note that he did not invent the architecture, he merely described it in a paper for the first time and thus got his name attached to it.
Given that Lisp intentionally obfuscates the boundaries between code and data, only Von Neumann style computers are well suited to run the language, so without his contribution to at least popularizing the concept, this book might never have been written.

Shortly after, McCarthy moved to New Jersey to complete his PhD at Princeton, and he stayed on at Princeton for two years as an instructor.

At Princeton, McCarthy had begun exploring finite automata, a mathematical framework for modeling and studying the properties of machines in the abstract. Could it be instructive to model the human brain through the lens of finite automata? He ran the idea by Von Neumann, who encouraged him to write a paper on it.

There was a general sense that connecting biology, psychology, and engineering could lead to understanding the nature of intelligence. Scientists were moving into each other's fields, with engineers trying to figure out how the brain worked and biologists considering the brain as a machine. People were writing programs to make the early computers mimic human thinking, or at least trying to. One important person he met around this time was Marvin

Minsky, who would later go on to start MIT's Artificial Intelligence Laboratory.

McCarthy wanted to understand all this research. A summer job at nearby Bell Labs offered him the opportunity to work with Claude Shannon, now known as "the Father of Information Theory," and Shannon and McCarthy decided that it was time to bring all these people together. They put together and published a volume of papers under the title of *Automata Studies* [75]. The idea that the human brain was somehow like a machine was controversial, and they chose that title to be not too outrageous. But McCarthy was disappointed with the papers. He had hoped for more ground-breaking work. Maybe the somewhat uninspiring title was the problem.

FINITE AUTOMATA — Finite automata are, like Turing machines, members of a class mathematicians call abstract machines or automata, models for analyzing how systems (may) work; these concepts span a huge field containing pretty much every conceivable kind of machine, operating deterministically or not, being finite or infinite in certain characteristics, and so on. Finite automata are essentially restricted Turing Machines. They have a single state they are in (but no other internal memory), and they can't rewrite tapes: they strictly read from an input "tape" and write to an output "tape". Therefore, they can't use tape as a sort of working memory. They are much more akin to a simple function except that (pure) functions don't have state. A lot of things that a Turing machine has no problem expressing can't be done with finite automata. But on the upside, such restrictions also make them a simple building block for more complex systems. And as they were quite well-known to mathematicians, it was only to be expected that McCarthy would consider them as the starting point for AI. But subsequent research exploring finite automata as the basis for Artificial Intelligence ended up as a series of dead ends.

The Dartmouth Conference

A couple of years later, McCarthy took another shot at bootstrapping the new field he was about to name. Now an adjunct professor at Dartmouth College, he got Minsky, Shannon, and an IBM scientist named Nathaniel Rochester together to propose a summer workshop at Dartmouth to continue the work started with the book. This time, however, he did not take any chances with uninspiring naming. The workshop was to be called the "Dartmouth Summer Conference on Artificial Intelligence."

The idea was modeled after how he heard the Department of Defense did some of its groundbreaking work: round up the smartest people in the field, throw them in a room, and get results. While the DoD was successful in this approach (Pentagon-level funding probably helped), for the Dartmouth conference, this never really materialized. The participants came and went at different times and never properly worked together. Nevertheless, some important papers were presented.

One of the groups that was farthest ahead in artificial intelligence was a team from the RAND Corporation. They were developing a program called Logic Theorist that, that same year, managed to create proofs for thirty-eight out of the fifty-two theorems in the second chapter of Russell and Whitehead's *Principia Mathematica* [87], a seminal work on mathematics. Most of the proofs would otherwise require a college student's level of proficiency, and some of the proofs even improved on the ones given in the book. This and some other quick wins generated a lot of optimism around the young field of Artificial Intelligence. It was 1956, and computers were still primitive, but it was widely felt that with the huge advances already made, the problem of general artificial intelligence would be cracked in a matter of a few years.

As mentioned earlier, one busy area of AI focus was writing computer programs to play chess or checkers. Indeed, Turing himself had implemented a chess program dubbed "Turochamp"—on paper, because computers were not able to execute the algorithms he penned in the late '40s. Chess is an extremely complex game, where each position on the board can lead to an amount of future positions that is truly astronomical. From the starting board with the 32 pieces on their predetermined squares, it only takes a handful of moves to reach billions of possible positions. Not even today's computers are capable of dealing with the combinatorial explosion—if you see all possible future moves, responses to moves, and so on as branches of a tree, then a method for pruning the tree was needed.

McCarthy helped formulate one such method, called the "alpha/-beta heuristic." It let the computer focus on the moves most advantageous to the player and stop evaluating moves that gave the opponent a powerful counter. The idea is simple: analyze the board position and give it a score. If it's lower than one value (alpha—

the minimum score for the computer player) or higher than another value (beta—the maximum score for the opponent), don't consider any further moves. While this may in theory exclude risky gambits that only pay off much later, it was a pure necessity: computers could (and can) not cope with even a small part of the complexity of chess, and this heuristic could remove most of the search space, making looking ahead practical.

While developed in the context of chess, McCarthy found ideas like these applying to a much larger set of problems. After all, most real-world situations are far too complex to analyze, and "real" intelligence, he reasoned, must therefore use similar heuristics to avoid spending endless amounts of time on useless ideas. He felt that most solutions we've come up with, like language when viewed as a solution to the problem of how to communicate, similarly got shaped by the problem and weren't innate or genetic as others believed.

THE FIRST CHESS PROGRAM — Chess was an early interest of AI researchers. Games are an excellent sandbox to try out ideas, and it should be no surprise that Alan Turing shared this interest and created a chess program before computers existed that could run it.

Turing played his Turochamp executing the algorithm on paper, much like how he operated his Turing machines when he wrote the paper on that topic. His exact algorithms got lost, but later attempts to reconstruct it from notes and recorded games he played this way seem to indicate that it was not really good at playing the game. The notes also showed that Turing regularly ignored the advice given by the algorithm, playing moves that were better in his own judgment instead. Still, it marked the beginning of a journey that only ended some five decades later, in 1997, when the computer chess program Deep Blue defeated grandmaster Gary Kasparov. Today, chess engines outperform humans by a large margin and have ELO ratings that humans can only dream of.

Inventing AI in the Punch-Card Era

I probably haven't made something clear, and it is significant: Up to this point, McCarthy hadn't had access to a computer. He'd played with finite automata and developed heuristics, but he had never used a real computer. Remember Nathaniel Rochester, the IBM scientist who helped Shannon and McCarthy set up the Dartmouth Conference? Rochester now deserves additional attention for the role he played in furnishing McCarthy with access to his first actual computer.

An electrical engineer by training and a computer scientist by trade, Rochester co-designed the first mass-produced scientific computer for IBM, the 701. From there, he became chief architect of the whole 700 series. When he met McCarthy, he was also leading a group to simulate abstract neural networks—which emulate how the brain operates on the level of neurons—on IBM's latest and greatest entry in that model line, the IBM 704. The 700 series computers were IBM's products for science and engineering, and one of Rochester's responsibilities was to make one of these machines available for research purposes, placing it at MIT but also reserving computer time to the other institutions in New England. IBM would keep a third of the machine time to itself, a third would be allocated to MIT, and the remaining third was for the rest of the schools involved in the program.

With its powerful vacuum tube processing unit (specializing in floating-point calculations, important for science and engineering) and plentiful magnetic core memory, it was a true state-of-the-art workhorse. It was also the machine on which McCarthy would create Lisp, so let's see what he had to work with.

The central processing logic had, by this time, progressed from mechanical to electronic (one of the first computers had a camshaft running along its impressive length to synchronize operations!). Vacuum tubes, an invention from the late 19th century, were the device of choice. Tens of thousands of them formed complicated circuitry, switching electrons at high speed and collaborating to execute up to 12,000 floating-point calculations each second (and even more regular integer/logic operations—the 704 could do around 40,000 of them each second).

Vacuum tubes failed all the time, and finding the one that broke was a complicated task, but still, it could achieve on average a whole day of work before a failing tube ended a run. Despite these shortcomings, vacuum tubes were a well-known technology, and the IBM 704 was well-built. All in all, the 704 was regarded as a reliable computer.

Memory was state-of-the-art core memory. Before this, technologies like delay lines and stored charges on cathode ray tubes called Williams tubes were used, but the 704 used magnetic core memory—tiny ferrite donuts arranged with wiring in stacks of matrices that, when maximal hardware was installed, could hold over a million bits, arranged in 32,000 words of 36 bits that served as the processor's working memory.

The IBM 704's permanent storage was a bit more mundane: it used punch cards to feed the machine instructions, and magnetic drum and tape which served as slow, long term bulk data storage. The whole contraption weighed close to 9 tons and cost over two million dollars, or roughly twenty million dollars in today's money. The records are silent, alas, on the monster's power draw.

Give Me Recursion!

Computing was in its infancy when McCarthy got his hands on the 704. Compilation of high-level ideas/procedures into actual machine code that the computer could execute was still very much a manual activity. Higher-level programming languages were needed, and some early efforts were driven by scientific computing. dnd For example, Information Processing Language (IPL) was a low-level assembly-style language that focused on list processing. It was created by the researchers at Rand Corporation that joined the Dartmouth summer program, and they used it to implement their Logic Theorist program. It was well known that representing knowledge as lists was a flexible option: most data structures can be represented by lists, so if your programming language is good at handling them, you can use all sorts of data structures for storing and manipulating knowledge. IPL contained a lot of new and useful concepts (that Lisp later heavily borrowed from), but it was extremely low-level, somewhere between machine code and assembly, and, like these, hard for humans to read.

McCarthy wanted something better, and that something better at the time was what we can probably view as the first higher-level programming language that was actually implemented, FORTRAN. (Today it's written as Fortran). Developed by IBM specifically for scientific and technical computing, Fortran was a standard language for the IBM 704.

FORTRAN was a simple language: 32 statements including a basic arithmetic-only IF statement, but it already came with an optimizing compiler and was extensible by creating libraries with new statements. A young PhD employed at IBM, Herbert Gelernter, was tasked with implementing some ideas from Minsky on theorem proving and, with McCarthy as a consultant, added a list processing library to that first Fortran implementation.

When McCarthy wanted to use it to differentiate algebraic expressions, however, he noticed that FORTRAN-plus-lists fell well short of what he needed. What he needed first and foremost was recursion, and that was something that FORTRAN could not provide.

"Recursion" is a complicated term for a simple approach: break down a problem in smaller bits and look at these first (breaking these down again, and so on, until you have a problem that is so easy you can just solve it.) Differentiation is a task that screams recursion. To differentiate a complex function, you break it down into simpler parts and differentiate these. If you have to take the derivative of this function, for example:

$$f(x) = x^4 - 3x^3 + 2x^2 + x$$

Then you recall that the derivative of a sum is the sum of the derivatives, so you calculate the derivatives for x^4 ($4x^3$), $-3x^3$ ($-9x^2$), $2x^2$ ($4x$), and x (1), and then put them all back together to get:

$$f(x) = 4x^3 - 9x^2 + 4x + 1$$

For even more complex formulas, these steps might repeat, so you keep breaking down the function into ever smaller units that you can actually take the derivative of, and then you end by putting it all together.

Once you start looking, recursion appears everywhere: a tree structure is easiest represented by recursion, whether you talk about the computer science concept or a real tree: they both consist of the same pattern nested, as it were, in itself, where each branch is a mini-tree of sorts. A lot of basic algorithms like sorting, the factorial function, or finding the greatest common denominator, trivially succumb to recursion. FORTRAN's lack of support for recursion would not cut it, and McCarthy decided that only a new language would do the job. And something like Church's lambda calculus would provide just the tools needed: expressive, functional, and with recursion built in.

Recursion in the Lambda calculus

"Recursion built in" is something that warrants some explanation, because the attentive reader will have noticed that we did not talk about recursion when discussing Church's work. Recursion with regularly named functions is easy enough. We will pick a simple example, the factorial function $x!$. In case you have never encountered it, x! tells you to multiply all numbers $1, 2, ..., x$ together:

$$
\begin{aligned}
1! &= 1 \\
2! &= 1 * 2 = 2 \\
3! &= 1 * 2 * 3 = 6 \\
\cdots 6! &= 1 * 2 * 3 * 4 * 5 * 6 = 720 \\
69! &= 1 * 2 * 3 * 4 * 5 * 6 * 7 * \cdots * 69 \approx 1.71122452 * 10^{98}
\end{aligned}
$$

Sixty-nine factorial is the largest factorial under 10^{100}, so this shows how quick this function grows. The factorial function can be defined using recursion as:

$$
\begin{aligned}
\mathtt{factorial}(x) &= 1 && \text{if } x = 0 \\
&= x \cdot \mathtt{factorial}(x-1) && \text{if } x > 0
\end{aligned}
$$

Note that we call the function itself by name, which is easy to do if you, well, named it in the first place. But as you recall, lambda functions are anonymous and this "trick" does not work. Luckily, after Church published his idea other logicians went to work and found a way around it which got named the "Y combinator," and this is the trick:

$$Y = \lambda f.\ (\lambda x.f\ (x\ x))\ (\lambda x.f\ (x\ x))$$

Using this magic incantation of the Lambda Calculus, you can create a recursive function by a) rewriting it so that it takes the function to recurse into as its argument, and b) then passing that function to this combinator. In Lambda-ish notation, factorial becomes:

$$\mathsf{FACTORIAL} = \lambda f.\lambda x.\ \text{if } (x = 0) 1 \text{ else } n \cdot f(n-1)$$

and we can then "call" it as $Y(\mathsf{FACTORIAL})(5)$. And yes, we took some shortcuts here. The biggest shortcut is that the whole point is that the Lambda Calculus does not have named functions, so Y and FACTORIAL are just notational conveniences. The actual expression would have the FACTORIAL text replaced in the Y body and that would then be the lambda expression to call, but usually, it's simpler to skip that step and use these "combinators" as if they were named functions and, well, combine them without writing them out. For details on how the sleigh of hand around the Y-combinator works, we'll refer to the many sources on the Internet, like Wikipedia [22]; for our purposes suffice it to say that this trick was well-known at the time.

* * *

Starting with a blank slate, concepts like recursion, functions, and symbolic manipulation would be the cornerstones of a new language. Of course, this new language was Lisp, and in the next chapter, we will dive into its origins.

Chapter 4

The Birth of Lisp

Work on Lisp started piecemeal as McCarthy worked through research problems, mostly connected with the IBM 704 computer and IBM establishing a New England Computation Center at MIT which would have one of these machines. A new programming language called FORTRAN was just out and as it was extensible, McCarthy got busy fixing some of the shortcomings he saw in the language.

Two projects drove the development of ideas around what a programming language required to support Artificial Intelligence research. The first was Marvin Minsky's work at IBM on developing a program that would prove theorems in plane geometry, for which McCarthy was a consultant. The second was McCarthy's own work on a program called The Advice Taker, a proposed system that would use logic to reason about a knowledge base and, importantly, could be enhanced at run-time. While AI work already was being done by the group at Rand in their custom IPL language, McCarthy thought that the language was too low level and too specific to the computer that they used; FORTRAN was higher level, had a nice and familiar algebraic notation, and could be extended with subroutines for things like list processing. List processing was quite high on the list of requirements: lists provide a natural format for storing arbitrary knowledge that a computer could operate on, and that pretty much was the whole idea behind the Advice Taker proposal. So he initially focused on extending FORTRAN.

Hacking List Processing in FORTRAN

One major stumbling block that McCarthy hit was early FORTRAN's `IF` statement. It was primitive, to say the least:

`IF` (*expression*) *label_if_negative*, *label_if_zero*, *label_if_positive*

Or, in English: if the expression results in a negative number, jump to the code marked by the first label; if it is zero, to the second label; if it is positive, to the third. For example, a (pseudo-ish) FORTRAN function to take the absolute value of a number:

```
   FUNCTION ABS(X) DO
   IF (X) 10, 20, 20
10 X = X * -1
20 RETURN X
   END
```

Essentially this was a conditional "GO TO" statement. There are two things to note here: it is an *arithmetic*, not a *logical*, `IF`, and it is a *statement*, not an *expression*. Statements get called for their side effects, like printing something on a screen or paper, while expressions get called for their results, like taking the sum of two values. In this case, the `IF` statement has the side effect of letting the computer jump around in the code, to the lines marked with `10` and `20` depending on whether `X` is negative, zero, or positive.

The if statement working on numbers rather than booleans is easily solved by convention: declare 0 as "false," 1 as "true," and you can use numbers as logic (this is how programmers using the widely used "C" Programming Language are still operating 70 years later). The second drawback, however, having `IF` as a statement instead of an expression, meant weaving a lot of jumps and GO-TOs through the code, which obviously made things hard to follow. Luckily, the language by now (FORTRAN II) supported subroutines, so McCarthy could add his own version of `IF`, which he named `XIF` and looked like this:

`XIF` (*condiitional_expression*, *non_zero_expression*, *zero_expression*)

This would return the result of *non_zero_expression* if *conditional_expression* was non-zero, and *zero_expression* otherwise. The first version of an `IF` expression was born. Still, this was not good enough because the way things were implemented around subroutine calls is that first, all three arguments would be computed, and only then the system could look at the first value for the conditional expression. If either `non_zero_expression` or `zero_expression` were expensive to compute but not often the branch chosen, this could slow down the system with doing unnecessary computations, potentially by a lot. Say we want to either compute the sine or the cosine of an angle and use the above function:

```
XIF(DO_COMPUTE_SINE, SIN(ANGLE), COS(ANGLE))
```

The order that things happen here is that `SIN(ANGLE)` is computed, then `COS(ANGLE)` is computed, and both values are passed together with `DO_COMPUTE_SINE` as arguments to the `XIF` subroutine. If either of these two functions had side-effects, then the situation got worse beyond just wasting precious computer time:

```
XIF(IS_TRUE, PRINT("Hello"), PRINT("'Bye'))
```

Think about the order of execution - this would just always print "Hello" and "Bye" before `XIF` even gets called! Clearly, FORTRAN could not be extended they way McCarthy wanted. He proposed a true conditional expression in a short paper that got published as a letter in *Communications of the ACM* in 1958. That form would "short-circuit" its logic, and only evaluate either branch expression depending on what the conditional expression evaluated to. But FORTRAN was not expressive enough to have this done as a subroutine, only as a language extension.

* * *

In the meantime, work on adding list processing to FORTRAN proceeded. As computer resources were scarce, formats were optimized to fit the computer rather than the human. One such optimization was to format lists in prefix notation, rather than the more customary infix notiation. Say we want to represent that person *A* knows person *B*, we would write:

```
A "knows" B
```

In prefix notation, this becomes:

```
"knows" A B
```

This prefix notation ensures that the code branching on the data can look at the first element, then figure out what kind of data it is so it knows what to do with the arguments that follow. This allows for optimization (like parsing the arguments differenly based on whether, say, a logical or arithmetic operation is needed) and allows for simpler design of complex expressions. Prefix notation has some advantages for both computers and humans alike, too. For example, taking the sum of a list of numbers:

```
A + B + C + D + E + ...
```

Becomes:

```
+ A B C D E ...
```

Another important decision was how to structure lists in memory. Lists are naturally implemented as pairs of *pointers* to locations in memory. A pointer, in diagrams, is just an arrow between boxes; in a computer, it is just a number. The number represents the memory location of the element being pointed at, its *address*, and usually, in a computer, memory is just a flat list of basic computer "words" with the first one having the address 0, the second one the address 1, and so on until you reach the end of the memory. So when we say that lists are naturally implemented as pairs of pointers, schematically it will look like this structure:

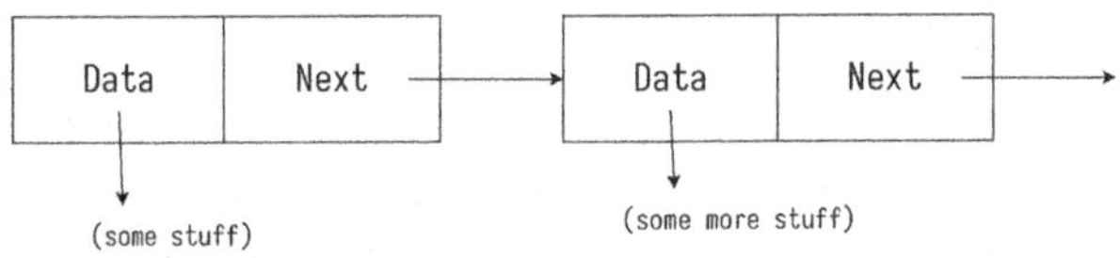

Where the `data` pointer points at the data (the contents of the first element of the list), and the `next` pointer points at the next element of the list. In the computer, see this as two computer words, where the first one has the address of wherever the data lives, and the second one the address of wherever the two-word-cell for the next element in the list can be found.

The data pointer can point at other lists as well, which allows you to implement tree structures (lists of lists) for example:

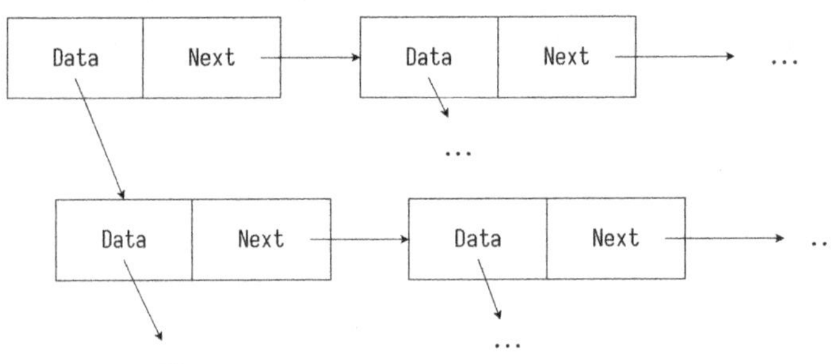

With that knowledge, we can construct the list with the numbers 1, 2, and 3 as follows:

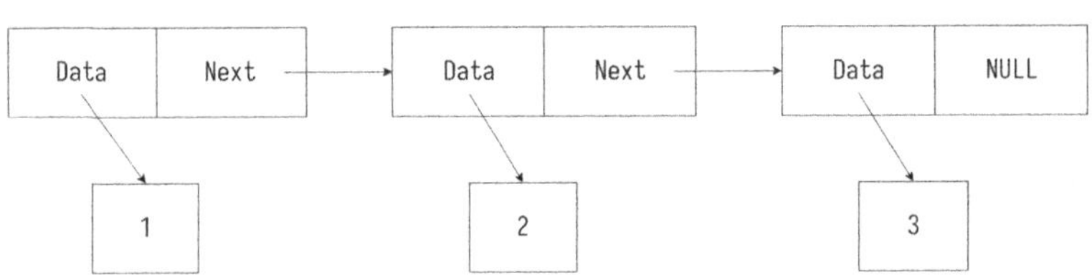

The `NULL` in the slot for "next" in the last cell signals that there is nothing else to follow, it marks the end of the list. As implemented here, we use 3 computer words for the list structure and 3 computer words for the values; more than if we would have stored them as an

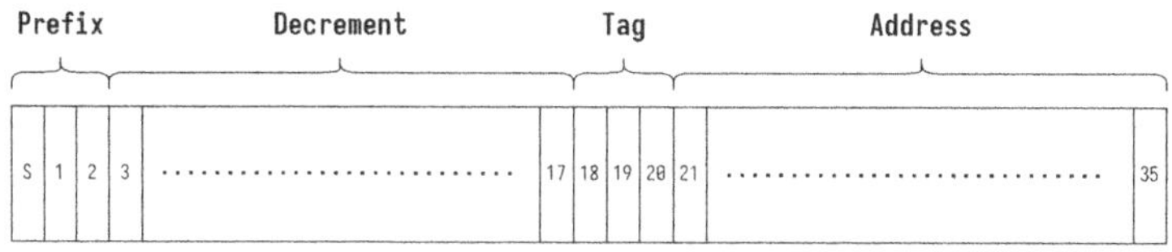

Figure 4.1: IBM 704 machine word layout
(Reproduced from [35])

array but also way more flexible: appending a number simply means allocating a new cell to point at the number:

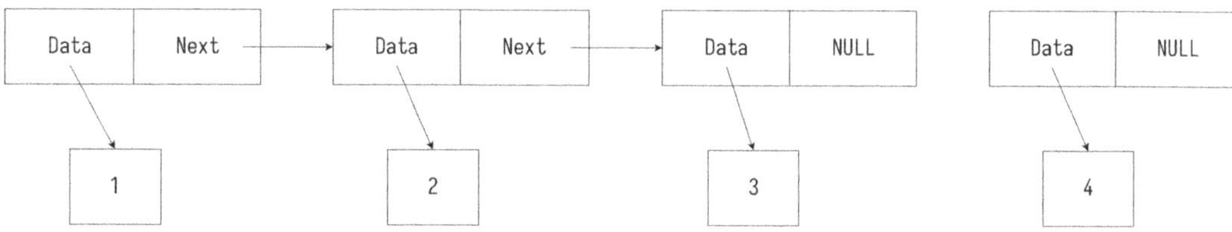

And then overwriting the final "NULL" of the original list to point at the new cell:

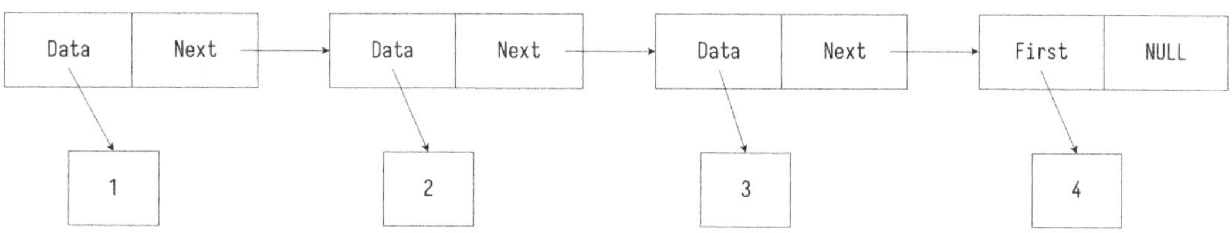

* * *

The IBM 704 had a word size of 36 bits, which were divided in four parts: two parts of 15 bits each that could be used for addressing, one part of 3 bits that could be used as an "opcode" or prefix, and one part of 3 bits that could be used for tagging the register value with extra information (See Figure 4.1).

The 3 bit prefix was used as an short opcode for frequently occurring operations, and these opcodes would interpret one of the 15 bit ranges as a memory address and the other 15 bit range as a negative offset to that address—effectively that part of the word decremented the address, so the two 15 bit parts of a memory word (called "register" at the time) were called "the address part" and "the decrement part" of the register. Using these parts for the "data" and "next" bits of a list cell was a natural decision: the IBM had special functions to efficiently operate on these parts, and the 15 bits allowed for over 32,000 words to be addressed which was the maximum memory size of the machine anyway. As the words of core memory were called "registers" and their location its "number," the expression "the contents of word register number 5" would point at whatever the 5th word of core memory was containing.

FLPL and the Road to Functional Programming

Function composition was seen as a clean way to approach the problem of working with lists, so to make FORTRAN operate on lists a small library of essential functions was created. For example, a function `cwr` ("contents of word register at memory address ...") would fetch the contents of the word in the indicated "register number" (memory location), and other functions could then access the subparts of that register (address, decrement, and the tag and opcode bits which were not otherwise used in this context so were free for things like type information). However, it turned out that it was natural, for example for list traversal, to have "fetch register at location," and then "extract this bit from that register" as a paired operation that occured frequently, so four compound functions `car` ("contents of the address part of the word at address ..."), `cdr` ("contents of the decrement part of the word at address ..."), `cpr` ("contents of the prefix ...") and `ctr` ("contents of the tag ...") got added to the FORTRAN subroutine library that combined fetching a word and getting the needed bit out of it in one step. It helped that the IBM 704 had built-in instructions to fetching the address and decrement parts from a memory location directly, greatly simplifying the implementation of these compound functions. Together, these functions could read and traverse lists and fetch their values.

To construct lists, a `cons` subroutine was proposed which would have four arguments for the four parts and combine them into a single memory word. The word location to be allocated as a new list cell would come from a special list that would hold all free words (more on that later). `cons` stands for "construct (a list cell element)," but has become a term of its own: Lisp people will talk about the list element data structure as "a cons cell" and creating one is "consing." The word "proposed" here is important: all this work was done before the IBM 704 was installed, and only later two people—Nathaniel Rochester and Herbert Gelernter—set to work to actually implement these ideas as part of a project that IBM was doing involving plane geometry project. The extensions for list processing were called "FLPL"—FORTRAN List Processing Language—which did not yet have the conditional expression and also painfully lacked recursion.

Mutable and immutable data structures

In the example above, we added the (one-element) list (4) to the list (1 2 3). If we would have a reference to that one-element list before the operation, it would still be valid after the operation. A reference here means a variable that *refers* to the list, normally by pointing at the first element. In pseudocode:

```
a = (1 2 3)
b = (4)
c = a + b
```

We have a list we refer to as `a` of three elements, a list `b` of one element, and `c` adds them together (concatenates them) so will have four elements. Now, `b` will still contain the same list, and in fact `a` and `c` share the very same memory space for that part of the list. Note, though, that list `a` has changed because of the operation as its last cons cell was changed. It started out as:

```
a -> (1 . (2 . (3 . nil))
```

and because the addition `a + b` overwrite that last cons cell `(3 . nil)`, we end up with:

```
a -> (1 . (2 . (3 . <pointer to b>)))
```

If we'd print all three variables:

```
☞ > print b
  (4)
☞ > print a
  (1 2 3 4)
☞ > print c
  (1 2 3 4)
```

Now consider what would happen if we use the same simple "edit the last cons cell of the list" trick to add `(5)` to list `b`. Probably something like this:

```
☞ > d = b + (5)
☞ > print d
  (4 5)
☞ > print b
  (4 5)
☞ > print c
  (1 2 3 4 5)
```

Not what we want, and probably not what an inexperienced programmer would expect! The field of "persistent data structures" helps us with algorithms that are efficient but still save us from such surprises, ensuring that things like list concatenation work as intended, leaving their operands unaffected. We talk of "immutable" data in this case, meaning that the values that variables refer to will never change. In the most trivial case, an immutable "list concatenation" would mean that the first operand here would be duplicated, so that the edit of the last cell happens on a copy, leaving the original in tact. So, to give a quick preview of how the Scheme implementation of Lisp does this correctly:

```
☞ > (define a '(1 2 3))
☞ > (define b '(4))
☞ > (define c (append a b))
☞ > a
  (1 2 3)
☞ > b
  (4)
☞ > c
  (1 2 3 4)
```

Everything works as intended as Scheme copied all the data that was held as a under the hood to make sure that it would not change the contents of this variable.

It is important to know how your programming language works, and it should come as no surprise that Lisp implementations, in their 70+ years of rich evolution, may support either the "mutable" or the "immutable" variants, and likely often both at the same time. As always, *Caveat Emptor* applies.

* * *

Back to our story, "off-computer innovation" came up additions that were needed:

- Real conditional expressions that could be used to write recursive functions. Recursion needs a way to end, and it is a natural thing to write recursive functions as a conditional. To go back to our earlier example of the factorial function, a concise way to write it in pseudocode is:

  ```
  n!(x) := if x = 0 then 1 else x * n!(x - 1)
  ```

This only works if we can use the `if` as a (sub)expression and not if it is a statement. The elegant one-liner above becomes this in FORTRAN:

```
C FACTORIAL FUNCTION
    READ INPUT TAPE 5, 100, IX
100 N = 1
101 IF (IX) 111, 112, 113
111 STOP 1
112 GO TO 200
113 N = N * IX
    IX = IX - 1
    GO TO 101
200 ... print answer in N on tape
```

The recursion here is implicit and spread out, and composing bits of code becomes much harder.

- Inventing what we now call "functional programming,", McCarthy proposed a `maplist` function that would apply a function (passed as argument) to every element of a list (passed as another argument). Looking at JavaScript again, the built-in `map` function does pretty much the same thing:

  ```
  > plus_one = x => x + 1
  [Function: plus_one]
  > [1, 2, 3, 4].map(plus_one)
  [2, 3, 4, 5]
  ```

  Such a function would greatly simplify things like differentiating sums. A function that takes functions as its arguments is called a "higher order function," an important concept in functional programming and the official term for what we've already seen in abundance when dealing with the Lambda Calculus, where in principle every function takes functions as arguments and is therefore a higher order function.

- For higher order functions like `maplist`, it would be beneficial to have a concise notation for functions so they could be directly specified as arguments. McCarthy had read Church's book on the Lambda calculus, and it made sense to borrow the syntax. The borrowing stopped there, though—Church went much beyond what McCarthy needed and he confessed at one point that he didn't understand much of the book to begin with. Notably, Church did not need conditionals to achieve his goals but a conditional expression was much simpler to implement on a computer than the somewhat esoteric abstract machinery that Church had invoked.

- "Erasure of list structure," the term McCarthy used for what we now call "Garbage Collection." The initial attempts with FLPL had no provision to automatically free lists or list cells that were not needed anymore, and erasing lists so the memory they used would be available again for subsequent `cons` calls had to be done by hand. This made code hard to follow, as the core logic of the geometry code had to be mingled with manual memory management, a messy and somewhat error-prone method. Some way to have the computer do this automatically would come handy, making code much more readable and with less risk of "memory leaks" caused by forgetting to reclaim cells that weren't in use anymore."

The shortcomings of FLPL were serious enough to stall the implementation of a full differentiation engine in the geometry theorem prover project, and this signalled the requirement for something that kept the good parts (lists and how they were implemented) but also added the things outlined above. Extending FORTRAN had run its useful course, and creating a new language pretty much from scratch was really the only option left on the table.

Building on the Church Foundation

Work started on that new language in the fall of 1958, when McCarthy transferred to MIT as an Assistant Professor. McCarthy found Marvin Minsky again, and together they started the MIT Artificial Intelligence Project. The project fell under the umbrella of a large defense contract that MIT's Research Laboratory of Electronics had landed and that allowed a lot of freedom in research topics. When the director of the lab, Jerome Wiesner, asked the two what they needed he not only gave them what they asked for ("a room, two programmers, a secretary, and a keypunch") but also tasked them with supervising six graduate students that were apparently yet without a project.

The task of writing a compiler was seen as too daunting, so initially, the ideas that formed the foundation of the new language were implemented on paper, and translation to something the computer could run had to be done by hand. The computer level language consisted of "symbolic expressions" that were parenthesized lists of lists and "atoms," for example as in the following two lists of three atoms each:

```
(COLOR,CAR,RED)
(WEIGHT,CAR,THOUSAND)
```

A human may interpret this as the statements "the color of the car is red" and "the weight of the car is (a) thousand (pounds)," but to the computer they're just symbols to manipulate. In Lisp, these symbols are called "atoms" as they are the most elemental building blocks. Where lists can be broken down into their elements, atoms can't, they're the end of the road.

The hand-compiled language, however, mostly avoided such symbolic expressions (which were called "s-expressions" or "s-exps") but was written in something that closer resembled FORTRAN. It was called "M-notation" (with the "M" standing for "Meta"). It looked like FORTRAN-with-recursion but used characters that were not available on the IBM keypunch, like square brackets to keep the use of parentheses exclusive to the symbolic language. An M-expression like

$$\mathrm{third}[\texttt{(A, B, C, D)}]$$

therefore contains the s-expression `(A, B, C, D)`, the rest is part of the M-notation. To keep the two languages distinct, we will typeset one as mathematical notation, and the other with the book's fixed space code font.

Apart from this convention, the M-notation had the conditional expression McCarthy so desperately needed. It was written as:

$$p_1 \rightarrow e_1; p_2 \rightarrow e_2; \ldots; p_n \rightarrow e_n$$

with the p_x elements being expressions that return a logical true or false (called "predicates") and the e_x ones the respective expressions to be evaluated when its p_x evaluates to true. The conditional is short-circuiting in that it stops evaluating on the first predicate that returns true. Again using the factorial function as an example, M-notation would define it as:

$$n! = [n = 0 \rightarrow 1; T \rightarrow n * (n - 1)!]$$

(where T is the Lisp atom `T`, representing a boolean true value).

The M-notation also included Church's lambda notation to convert "forms" into "functions." In this way, a function to retrieve the first element of a list, given as:

$$ff[x] = [atom[x] \rightarrow x; T \rightarrow ff[car[x]]]$$

could be written as a lambda function:

$$\mathtt{ff} = \lambda[[x]; [\mathtt{atom}[x] \rightarrow x; \mathsf{T} \rightarrow \mathtt{ff}[\mathtt{car}[x]]]]$$

However, this required yet another notational convenience to make the recursion legal: the ff on the right hand side cannot refer to itself, as it is not yet defined! To fix that, a *label* helper was introduced, where label α; ϵ stands for "if α is a name and ϵ is an expression that contains α, let the α stand for the whole thing inside the expression." Rewriting ff this way, we get:

$$\mathtt{label}[\mathtt{ff}; \lambda[[x]; [\mathtt{atom}[x] \rightarrow x; \mathsf{T} \rightarrow \mathtt{ff}[\mathtt{car}[x]]]]]$$

Using label, ff can refer to itself and we have a clean and correct recursive lambda-style expression for our function without the complexities of things like the Y-Combinator.

The "M notation" was convenient on paper, but the group never implemented it as a proper programming language, nor did they mean to (which is one of the reasons they were free to use all sorts of special symbols that were not available on the machine). M-notation was hand-coverted to the symbolic "S-expression" code and to machine code. Computers were about to become a full player in this game, but at this point, humans still had to do a lot of work.

* * *

For the implementation, a couple of things still needed deciding. The list structure, with FLPL's functions *cons, cwr, car, cdr, cpr* and *ctr*, got simplified to use only the data and next pointers that were minimally needed. This reduced the number of functions needed to support lists to only three, but more importantly made everything the same type (a 15 bit value) as the 6 now unused bits where not holding type information anymore. After this simplification, list operations merely needed `CONS` to construct a list cell, `CAR` to access the first part of the cell (stored in the address part of the register word), and `CDR` to access the second part of the cell (stored in the offset/decrement part of the register word). The function names *car* and *cdr* referred to specific implementation details of the IBM 704, but most Lisp implementations still use these terms for list access; figuring out what is what is somewhat akin to a rite of passage these days, with the simplest mnemonic being that "the car is pulling the whole train"—it's the first element in the whole list. Most Lisps have functions like `FIRST` and `REST` these days.

HOW TO SPEAK LISP — When talking about Lisp, you probably can figure out how to pronounce "car." "cdr" is a bit less obvious: it is not pronounced as "cee-dee-ar" as that would be too much work for something used so often; the term got shortened to something like "coud'r" (think "could") in spoken English. Some want "cahd'r" but that is fonetically too close to "car" and compound functions like "cadr" we'll encounter later. Using the International Phonetic Alphabet, /ˈkʊdər/ is the way to go.

The other open issue was how to do automatic "erasure" of unused data (or garbage collection, as we would call it today). The group considered two options:

- Reference counting could use the 6 unused bits in words to count how often a list cell was referenced (a list cell can be part of multiple data structures, this sharing makes lists and operations on them quite efficient). A list cell with a reference count of "0" would be available.
- "Real" garbage collection was a bit more involved—it would basically halt regular processing when no more free memory was available, traverse all data structures that could be reached and marking them as in use, and then sweeping everything else on to the list of available memory words.

As 6 bits for reference counting would risk overflowing the reference counter and the IBM did not have any support to combine the two 3 bit fields into a single 6 bit number to begin with, full garbage collection was seen as the more practical method and this is what the first implementation used (and most implementations still use).

These choices made the language elegant and a practical vehicle for working with functions, certainly compared with Church's and Turing's earlier attempts which may have been elegant in their own right, but were certainly not practical. And while practicality is never a primary concern for mathematicians, computer people like McCarthy's group had to actually implement their stuff on a severely limited machine, so being concise and easy to implement was a major advantage.

Still, ever the mathematician, McCarthy decided to formalize the essence of the language and publish a two-part paper on it. The first part (published in 1960 as *Recursive Functions of Symbolic Expressions and Their Computation by Machine, Part I* [52]) described the Lisp programming language. The second part would show some sample applications but was never finished or published. As it happened, function theorists pretty much ignored the paper, since it didn't give them anything novel to work with. Although the paper failed in its goal to make mathematicians pay attention to the group's work, it still serves in giving us a neat definition of this old programming language. So neat, in fact, that computer scientist Alan Kay once labeled the paper "the Maxwell equations of computer science" since it went much beyond the initial Lisp to define a basic but universal machine for evaluating code. In that sense, the article reads much like Turing's, but defines something that was actually implementable on a real-world computer and decent to work with. The next chapter will dive into that formal definition in some detail and it will hopefully help you appreciate why Kay made this analogy.

The Grad Student Who Wrote The First Lisp

As mentioned, writing a new compiler was seen as a daunting task in that time–FORTRAN was just out and that was one of the first compilers ever attempted. It is probably one of the reasons that McCarthy (trained as a mathematician, not as a computer programmer) was beating around the bush with M-expressions, S-expressions, and a lot of formal logic to define the language without actually implementing it. People wrote Lisp code with pencil and paper, and then manually translated it into executable machine code. The computer would then make short work of executing it, spit out the answer (or, probably equally likely, a mysterious error code), and back to pencil and paper the human programmer went.

TIMESHARING — These expensive machines were used in dedicated timeslots, but McCarthy thought that this was a wasteful way of interacting with computers—it would be much more logical to have people share the resources at the same time, so while one person was thinking another could do a quick run, say. He pushed hard to add timesharing facilities to the systems at his disposal; the first "modern" timesharing system, CTSS, was therefore implemented at MIT. Alas, it was a design-by-committee effort that was a far cry from what McCarthy (who by that time had moved to Stanford) envisioned.

Luckily, McCarthy had some graduate students that were too inexperienced to realize that implementing a programming language compiler was a massive task best left to seasoned professionals. One of these, Steve Russell, thought that implementing this short formal definition would be less work than all the back and forth between M-expressions, S-expressions, and IBM 704 assembly. Despite McCarthy's protestations that the code in the paper was just meant for expository purposes, never as the foundation for an actual implementation, Russell took the definitions, translated them to IBM 704 machine code, and implemented the first Lisp system.

LISP I

LISP I, described in *LISP I Programmer's Manual* [51], was a system that behaved much like the system we'll describe in the next chapter, but had not only atoms, but also numbers. It had a facility to define functions (using `DEFINE` which took a list of function names paired with their definitions as a lambda function), supported constants, and could be extended by subroutines in machine code or functions implemented as compiled Lisp functions.

The number system could handle only handle floating point (it roughly covered the range of numbers that we now call 'single precision floating point'). Arithmetic operations did not use special symbols (like + or -), instead functions like `PLUS` and `DIFFERENCE`. A quick example from the manual shows how to calculate the length of the list:

```
(LABEL LENGTH (LAMBDA (Y)
  (COND ((NULL Y) (QUOTE 0.0))
        (T        (SUM (LENGTH (CDR Y)) (QUOTE 1.0))))))
```

The meaning of `LABEL` and `LAMBDA` should be clear from the previous sections in this chapter; `COND` is the conditional expression taking a list of predicate/expression pairs just like in the M-language. Translating to English, this defines the length of a list as:

> Zero if the list is empty, else one plus the length of the `cdr` of the list.

The manual still uses a comma-separated form for writing lists; it does mention that commas got dropped "accidentally" and if you open up the LISP I manual, you will probably agree that this was a happy accident. Here's the same statement as it appears in the book without the cheating with whitespace that I used above:

```
(LABEL,LENGTH,(LAMBDA,(Y),(COND,((NULL,Y),(QUOTE,0.0)),(T,(SUM,
  (LENGTH,(CDR,Y)),(QUOTE,1.0)))))))
```

There are a lot of interesting features and implementation details to explore in LISP I, but before we do that, let's further explore the genius of Lisp by opening up its formal definition, those "Maxwell equations of software."

> SPECIAL FORMS — `QUOTE`, `COND`, `LAMBDA`, and similar functions are called "special forms", usually because their arguments must be "quoted" (hidden from interpretation, as it were). If you look at `LAMBDA` above, for example, in normal Lisp `(Y)` means "the value of the function or variable Y", but what we want here is the uninterpreted meaning "a list with one element, the atom 'Y'." Like in human speech, quoting prevents or delays interpretation:
>
> This is a sentence where I quote "this is a sentence".
>
> Try that without the quotes and it loses all meaning. The same goes for Lisp quoting. Special forms get caught early on in the compiler or interpreter and their arguments receive special treatment, often by silently quoting them. This happens a lot in the small snippet above (the lambda definition is a special form, the conditional is a special form as well), and it's often important to realize that you're working with a special form when programming Lisp because otherwise, the special treatment it receives might surprise you.

Poor Programming Style

– Richard P. Gabriel

"Show me." John held up the chalk, holding it by the top, the bottom pointed at his feet. His smile was slight but visible, visible to everyone in the lecture hall; his smile was aimed at me. Who was more scared, the students, or me—the TA? That's something no one can ever know, but there were 50 of them and one of me; if my answer is wrong, their answers would have been wrong.

Three months earlier, in my first quarter as graduate student at Stanford, in the Lab at the top of the hill, just before a volleyball game, I asked John McCarthy—*the* John McCarthy—whether I could have an office at the Lab and be supported by it. The Lab being SAIL, the Stanford AI Lab, and I having been assigned elsewhere, in that dusty summer of 1975, with the sharp fragrance of volleyball-courtside tarweed splattered on a background of eucalyptus; hot and dry. Hazy and dusty.

"Sure," if I TAed 206, the Lisp course. OK, I knew Lisp, had learned it from the blue book—the Lisp 1.5 Programmer's Manual. His book. His language.

Some call his classes "Uncle John's Mystery Hour," in which John McCarthy can and will lecture on the last thing he thought of before rushing late through the door and down the stairs to the front of the lecture hall.

But this class started out like anything but a mystery hour: John was reviewing the answers to the midterm. The first few problems were routine, but this one maybe not, and he said, "Ah, this problem was intended to show you that there are some problems that Lisp is not good for."

I can hear the worried thoughts behind me: "Er, but multiplying two polynomials seems so easy. I musta got it wrong." And I, maybe I had graded it wrong.

John: "It turns out you need to pass global information, and the control structure is not regular. Here are the six functions and two globals you need."

So now you're thinking that the problem was stated funny. Well, here it is: Let $a_0 + a_1x + a_2x^2 + \ldots + a_nx^n$ be represented by the list `(a0 a1 … an)`; write a function that multiplies two such polynomials. The solution is easy too: if `add-poly` adds two such polynomials, and `constant-multiply-poly` multiplies a polynomial by a constant, then this is just:

```
(defun multiply-poly (p1 p2)
  (cond ((null p1) nil)
        (t (add-poly
             (constant-multiply-poly (car p1) p2)
             (cons 0 (multiply-poly (cdr p1) p2))))))
```

And those two helper functions are an obvious one or two lines of code.

John finishes his complicated explanation to a wash of silence.

I, lowly first-year grad student TA, peep: "I think Lisp can do better than that." And hope I haven't blown it. "Show me," the smile begins with his eyes and spreads downward.

John's world is a world of ideas, a world in which ideas don't belong to anyone, and when an idea is wrong, just the idea—not the person—is wrong. A world in which ideas are like young birds, and we catch them and proudly show them to our friends. The bird's beauty and the hunter's are distinct.

And when John catches a bird on the way to class, we see it, and just the way he does.

So I write the few lines of code on the board, and John wonders at it: "Well, it looks like you're right, but you see, I was working on this other problem, talking to Gosper,[1] and it threw me off track on this one, ..."

Sometimes a bird flying past in a blaze of pretty song will distract a bird-catcher and maybe confuse him, too.

"That's OK John," I say, my own smile flicking, "I would have given you partial credit."

"I would expect that you'd be able to see my solution is correct and give me full credit."

"Nah. I would have taken off 5 points for poor programming style."

Some people won't show you the birds they've caught until they are sure, certain, positive that they—the birds, or themselves—are gorgeous, or rare, or remarkable. When your mind can separate yourself from your bird, you will share it sooner, and the beauty

[1] R.W. Gosper

of the bird will be sooner enjoyed. And what is a bird but for being enjoyed?

And if John's mystery hour is because he found a new bird, well, heck, let's just love him for it.

Ever since that day I've patterned myself after him, and we've had a long, strange road together—catching birds. Ha, that's it!

Chapter 5

The Maxwell Equations of Software

The best way to understand something technical is to build it, so let's emulate McCarthy and his grad students, and build the core of LISP 1.5. They managed to define the language in less than a page, but only after introducing helpers in the ten-or-so preceding pages. So, like them, we will take some time to build things up until we get to the crucial two functions: `EVAL` and `APPLY`.

These two functions are defined in terms of one another, and together realize a universal model of computation. It's a different model of computation from Turing's, but no less impactful. Alan Kay dubbed them "the Maxwell equations of software" with good reason: They are arguably the most important functions ever devised in the area of programming languages. So even though what we are about to build here will fall short of a fully useful programming language, it is important to really understand what underpins Lisp: the principles here, laid out in code, underpin every modern Lisp implementation and a lot of programming languages that on first blush have nothing in common with Lisp but did manage to borrow a lot of the ideas developed here in 1958. This chapter will let you step (a bit) in the shoes of the small team that changed programming forever.

To build Lisp 1.5, we'll proceed as we did with Church and Turing's work and do a simple translation to JavaScript. Everything that follows is based on MIT's *LISP 1.5 Programmer's Manual* [53], as that is the version that is widely available. So go grab that book and something that can run JavaScript (NodeJS is used here and is recommended) and follow along. We do need to make some preparations though, mostly because we do not want to spend a lot of time with utility functions for printing and parsing. Therefore, some NodeJS packages need to be pulled in. When using the code from the book, you can go to `code/js` and run `npm i` to install the declared packages; if you want to tag and type along with the examples, run

```
npm install lodash parsimmon
```

to use the library. If you checked out the book's code, you have a little header on `js/lisp.js`, the file that contains this chapter's code and you can run the whole file in one go. For now, we'll assume you want to type along, so fire up `node` and enter:

```
lodash = require('lodash')
util = require('util')

debug = false
log_debug = (...args) => debug && console.log(...args)
```

(Note that by setting `debug` to `true` you can get some helpful extra output here and there). With that out of the way, let's make us some LISP I.

Lisp in JavaScript: Atoms and Lists

Lisp only has a couple of syntactic elements—it is one of the things that makes the language so attractive: it is really easy to parse. Symbolic expressions are concisely defined as follows:

> An S-expression is either an atomic symbol or it is composed of these elements in the following order: a left parenthesis, an S-expression, a dot, an S-expression, and a right parenthesis.

This is a recursive definition with the recursion always ending at a symbol. Examples of S-expressions are:

```
ATOM
(A . B)
(A . (B . C))
((A1 . A2) . B)
((U . V) . (X . Y))
(((U . V) . (X . (Y . Z))))
```

It is easy to map the *(first . next)* construct to the `cons` operation or the memory structure used for implementing a list cell in Lisp—if you're unsure, go back a few pages to the diagrams and try to map the above examples to them. Ninety percent of understanding Lisp is just understanding how lists are structured. All but the first S-expression in this list of examples recursively parse down to their individual atoms. We won't implement an actual parser for the language here, but it wouldn't be hard: a much simpler core syntax definition for a programming language is hard to imagine.

After defining S-expression syntax, the book introduces a "Meta language" syntax. We will not implement the meta language and its M-expressions directly, but in a way, our "meta" language will be Javascript. First, as good programmers, we want to make sure we're on the right track. The text comes with a lot of examples which are great material for turning into tests. A couple of simple JavaScript functions will serve as a rudimentary test framework so we can exercise our code against these examples to make sure we are not making mistakes:

```
testCount = 0
function assert(a) {
  testCount++
  if (!a)
    throw new Error("Assertion failed")
}
function refute(a) {
  testCount++
  if (a)
    throw new Error("Assertion failed")
}
function assertEqual(a, b) {
  testCount++
  if (!lodash.isEqual(a, b))
    throw new Error(
        'Assertion failed, not equals: ' +
        `${util.inspect(a)} != ${util.inspect(b)}`)
}
```

And that concludes our preparation. On to the meat of the implementation!

* * *

Like McCarthy's group did for the IBM 704, we need to decide how to represent these two basic elements of a Lisp implementation: a list and an atom. If you thought of representing them as arrays and strings, respectively, we're on the same page. We will let the atom *T* be represented by the JavaScript string `'T'`, and the list *(A B)* by the JavaScript array `['A', 'B']`. The most basic function of any Lisp implementation is cons. You can't build anything without it. Let's define it:

```
cons = (a, b) => [a, b]

assertEqual(cons('A', 'B'),
            ['A', 'B'])
assertEqual(cons(cons('A', 'B'), 'C'),
            [['A', 'B'], 'C'])
```

To access the parts of the cell, we need to define car and cdr:

```
car = l =>
  Array.isArray(l)
  ? l[0]
  : undefined

assertEqual(car(['A', 'B']),
            'A')
assertEqual(car(['A', ['B1', 'B2']]),
            'A')
assertEqual(car([['A1', 'A2'], 'B']),
            ['A1', 'A2'])
assertEqual(car('A'),
            undefined)

cdr = l =>
  Array.isArray(l)
  ? l[1]
  : undefined

assertEqual(cdr(['A', 'B']),
            'B')
assertEqual(cdr(['A', ['B1', 'B2']]),
            ['B1', 'B2'])
assertEqual(cdr([['A1', 'A2'], 'B']),
            'B')
assertEqual(cdr('A'),
            undefined)
assertEqual(car(cdr(['A', ['B1', 'B2']])),
            'B1')
assertEqual(car(cdr(['A', 'B'])),
            undefined)
assertEqual(car(cons('A', 'B')),
            'A')
```

So far, so good. Note that we use JavaScript's "undefined" to stand for the concept with the same idea in Lisp, NIL.

The book defines a predicate to test whether a value is an atom, which we have to implement somewhat clumsily as:

```
atom = (a) => {
  return a === null ||
    a === true ||
    a === false ||
    (typeof(a) === 'string' &&
       /^[A-Z][A-Z0-9]*$/.test(a))
}

assert(atom('EXTRALONGSTRINGOFLETTERS'))
refute(atom(cons('U', 'V')))
assert(atom(car(['U', 'V'])))
```

The special clauses for "null,' "true,' and "false" allow us to use the natural JavaScript implementations of the equivalent Lisp concepts, which simplifies the rest of the code a bit. Another simple helper function that the book defines tests for equality, but between atoms only:

```
eq = (a, b) => {
  let retval = null
  if (!(atom(a) && atom(b)))
    retval = undefined
  else
    retval = (a == b)
  debug && log_debug("eq?", a, b, ':', retval)
  return retval
}

assert(eq('A', 'A'))
refute(eq(cons('A', 'B'), cons('A', 'B')))

assertEqual(eq('A', ['A', 'B']),
            undefined)
assertEqual(eq(['A', 'B'], ['A', 'B']),
            undefined)
```

We now have a basic language that can do some list operations, like creating lists with cons, picking them apart with car and cdr, and testing elements for "atom-ness" and equality. However, constructing lists is painful. A five-element list has to be built up manually, in the book's M-expression language that looks like:

$$\mathrm{cons}[A;\mathrm{cons}[B;\mathrm{cons}[C;\mathrm{cons}[D;\mathrm{cons}[E]]]]]$$

In a "real Lisp,' this would be written a bit shorter as s-expressions:

```
(A . (B . (C . (D . E))))
```

But this is still a bit annoying and not really intention-revealing: while it is technically correct that we have a nested list of cells here, what we *mean* is that we have a simple list of five terms. We want to be able to write something like:

```
(A, B, C, D, E)
```

The book agrees and introduces "List Notation,' in which

```
(A B C D E)
```

stands for the more primitive S-expression

```
(A . (B . (C . (D . (E . NIL)))))
```

Note the trailing `NIL`, which serves as an unequivocal terminator of the list. A nil-terminated list is normally called a "proper" list, and most functions that traverse lists will expect this terminator. Note, too, that this does not mean that `NIL` cannot be an element itself:

```
(NIL A B C)
```

expands to

```
(NIL . (A . (B . (C . NIL))))
```

This is perfectly valid and not ambiguous at all. Only when `NIL` is used as the *next* pointer it will be interpreted as the end of a list. Also, note that the simplest list is the empty list `()`, which in Lisp is exactly the same as `NIL` - the two can be used interchangeably.

For our code, let's add a utility function to construct lists using JavaScript's variable arguments feature. We're departing a bit from the book here, but the book continues mixing S-expressions and M-expressions, and we don't really want to write a parser for M-notation. So, we define:

```
list = (first, ...rest) => {
  if (rest.length == 0)
    return cons(first, null)
  else
    return cons(first, list(...rest))
```

```
}

assertEqual(list('A', 'B', 'C'),
            ['A', ['B', ['C', null]]])
assertEqual(list(list('A', 'B'), 'C'),
            [['A', ['B', null]], ['C', null]])
assertEqual(list('A', 'B', list('C', 'D')),
            ['A', ['B', [['C', ['D', null]], null]]])
assertEqual(list('A'),
            ['A', null])
assertEqual(list(list('A')),
            [['A', null], null])
assertEqual(list('A', cons('B', 'C')),
            ['A', [['B', 'C'], null]])
assertEqual(car(list('A', 'B', 'C')),
            'A')
assertEqual(cdr(list('A', 'B', 'C')),
            list('B', 'C'))
assertEqual(cons('A', list('B', 'C')),
            list('A', 'B', 'C'))
assertEqual(car(list(list('A', 'B'), 'C')),
            list('A', 'B'))
assertEqual(car(cdr(list('A', 'B', 'C'))),
            'B')
```

This allows us to be at least somewhat concise and to postpone or avoid writing a parser for S-expressions. Note what we did there: the simplest way to construct Lisp's recursive list structure is to use a recursive function.

Bootstrapping Our Way into Lisp

It is now time to get to the meat of the meta language. With the tools above (`cons`, `car`, `cdr`, `atom`, and `eq`) we almost have the tools needed to bootstrap ourselves a full Lisp implementation. All we lack is the ability to make decisions. As you may recall from TODO, conditional expressions are defined as:

$$p_1 \rightarrow e_1; p_2 \rightarrow e_2; \ldots; p_n \rightarrow e_n$$

We need to make a decision on how to represent this in JavaScript. There is no direct equivalent in JavaScript, but we can wrangle its ternary operator a bit. If you're not familiar with JavaScript, the ternary operator works as follows:

```
predicate ? true_expression : false_expression
```

JavaScript inherited this from C, and the ternary operator has had its supporters and adversaries ever since it was introduced there. Some say it is a handy shorthand, others say it is entirely unnecessary and the regular "if" does the job just fine. But do note that one is a *statement*, and the other an *expression*. In a lot of languages in the C family, `if` does not return a value, while `? :` does. Opponents usually support their point by showing terribly convoluted abuses of the ternary operator, and we are about to give them some more ammunition by translating Lisp's meta language's conditional expression directly into ternary notation:

```
p_1 ? e_1 : p_2 ? e_2 : ... p_n ? e_n : undefined
```

This works the same as the M-expression notation above, and is a fairly straightforward translation: we replace arrows by question marks, semicolons by colons, and just have to add a final clause to explicitly return "undefined" if nothing matches manually; the M-expression construct does that implicitly. If the last predicate is T:

$$p_1 \rightarrow e_1; p_2 \rightarrow e_2; \ldots; T \rightarrow e_n$$

we can shorten our translation a bit into:

```
p_1 ? e_1 : p_2 ? e_2 : … : e_n
```

But that's merely syntactic sugar. With the conditional expression in hand, we can now immediately use the conditional expression syntax for recursion to define more complex functions. Here is `ff` to return the first atomic symbol of an arbitrary s-expression:

```
ff = x =>
  atom(x)
  ? x
  : true
    ? ff(car(x))
    : undefined

assertEqual(ff(list('A', 'B', 'C')), 'A')
```

And indeed, we don't need any more primitive functions to bootstrap ourselves into a full Lisp implementation. Let's define the final helper functions, now just using our JavaScript variant of M-expressions. You can verify that all the definitions below only use our primitive functions and the conditional expression. Essentially we now have defined a small subset of JavaScript that is exactly as powerful as M-expressions.

* * *

Where eq narrowly defines equality as equality of atoms, we can define an equality function for any arbitrary s-expression:

```
equal = (x, y) =>
  atom(x)
  ? (atom(y)
     ? eq(x, y)
     : false)
  : equal(car(x), car(y))
    ? equal(cdr(x), cdr(y))
    : false

assert(equal('A', 'A'))
refute(equal('A', null))

assert(equal(list('A', 'B'),
             list('A', 'B')))
refute(equal('A',
             list('A', 'B')))
```

Then there is `subst`, to essentially search-and-replace in an S-expression:

```
subst = (x, y, z) =>
  equal(y, z)
  ? x
  : atom(z)
    ? z
    : cons(subst(x, y, car(z)),
           subst(x, y, cdr(z)))

assertEqual(
  subst(cons('X', 'A'),
        'B',
        cons(cons('A', 'B'), 'C')),
  cons(cons('A', cons('X', 'A')), 'C'))
```

We have the function `nil` to test whether its argument is `NIL` (called "null" in the original text, but that is a reserved word in JavaScript and we have to make do with the tools we have chosen):

```
nil = x => eq(x, null)

assert(nil(null))
assert(nil(cdr(list('A'))))
```

Next up, append, to mash two lists together:

```
append = (x, y) =>
  nil(x)
  ? y
  : cons(car(x),
         append(cdr(x), y))

assertEqual(
  append(list('A', 'B'),
         list('C', 'D', 'E')),
  list('A', 'B', 'C', 'D', 'E'))
```

and `member` to test whether something is an element of a list:

```
member = (x, y) =>
  nil(y)
  ? false
  : equal(x, car(y))
    ? true
    : member(x, cdr(y))

assert(member('A', list('B', 'C', 'A', 'D')))
refute(member('F', list('B', 'C', 'A', 'D')))
```

This is a flurry of code, so please pause here and check that you really understand what these functions do and how they do it. We're about to deep dive into more complex stuff, so understanding these "helper functions" will really help you keep track of what we're doing.

These functions also help us to introduce an important concept in Lisp, "association lists." One recurring job in programming is to look up stuff, and Lisp uses "association lists" for that. They're key-value lists, and the concept is so common that Lisp pepole shorten the term to "alist," and we will follow that convention. The idea is simple: construct a list of lists where each cell's `car` is the key and `cdr` is the value:

```
((A . X) (B . Y) (C . Z))
```

Now you can look for a cons cell that has "B" in its *cdr* and get "Y" from that cell's *cadr*, and one interpretation of this is to access data by name. We need two functions to support alists, one to construct them called pairlis:

```
pairlis = (x, y, a) =>
  nil(x)
  ? a
  : cons(cons(car(x), car(y)),
         pairlis(cdr(x), cdr(y), a))

assertEqual(
  pairlis(list('A', 'B', 'C'),
          list('U', 'V', 'W'),
          list(cons('D', 'X'),
               cons('E', 'Y'))),
  list(cons('A', 'U'),
       cons('B', 'V'),
       cons('C', 'W'),
       cons('D', 'X'),
       cons('E', 'Y')))
```

and one to do the lookup, called assoc:

```
caar = l => car(car(l))

assoc = (x, a) =>
  equal(caar(a), x)
  ? car(a)
  : assoc(x, cdr(a))

assertEqual(
  assoc('B', list(cons('A', list('M', 'N')),
                  cons('B', list('CAR', 'X')),
                  cons('C', list('QUOTE', 'M')),
                  cons('C', list('CDR', 'X')))),
  cons('B', list('CAR', 'X')))
```

Note how we define a shorthand function caar here to define the car of the car of a list. Lisp implementations usually come with a bunch of these shorthands that allow quick traversal of more complex list structures, and they all follow the pattern cXX...r, where the X stands for an a to take the car and a d to take the cdr at that point in the traversal. It's a convention that is often used in lower-level code and an important one to remember. A final helper sublis substitutes all elements of alist, much like subst, but now by using an association list as a lookup table for the substitions to make:

```
cdar = l => cdr(car(l))
```

```
sub2 = (a, z) =>
  nil(a)
  ? z
  : eq(caar(a), z)
    ? cdar(a)
    : sub2(cdr(a), z)

sublis = (a, y) =>
  atom(y)
  ? sub2(a, y)
  : cons(sublis(a, car(y)),
         sublis(a, cdr(y)))

assertEqual(
  sublis(list(cons('X', 'SHAKESPEARE'),
              cons('Y', list('THE', 'TEMPEST'))),
         list('X', 'WROTE', 'Y')),
  list('SHAKESPEARE', 'WROTE', list('THE', 'TEMPEST')))
```

Look how far we've come using just five helper functions, the conditional expression, and the power of recursion: We can now build arbitrarily complex data structures and do complex operations on them like substituting occurrences in one of them using the high level concept of lookup tables! Like Church and Turing, McCarthy made a lot out of a little, but with the difference that computer implementation turned out to be actually feasible and practical.

Drumrolls for evalquote

We now approach the promised grande finale, `evalquote` (dubbed "the Universal LISP Function" in the book), which is defined by two foundational functions that, as you will see, are closely intertwined. First, `apply` (which we have to name differently given the name's special status in JavaScript):

```
lisp_apply = (fn, x, a) => {
  console.log('apply >', pp(fn), pp(x), pp(a))

  let retval =
    atom(fn)
    ? (eq(fn, 'CAR') ? caar(x) :
       eq(fn, 'CDR') ? cdar(x) :
       eq(fn, 'CONS') ? cons(car(x), cadr(x)) :
       eq(fn, 'ATOM') ? atom(car(x)) :
```

```
        eq(fn, 'EQ') ? eq(car(x), cadr(x)) :
        lisp_apply(lisp_eval(fn, a), x, a)
    )
    : eq(car(fn), 'LAMBDA') ?
        lisp_eval(caddr(fn),
                  pairlis(cadr(fn), x, a)) :
      eq(car(fn), 'LABEL') ?
        lisp_apply(caddr(fn), x,
                   cons(cons(cadr(fn),
                             caddr(fn)), a)) :
    undefined

  console.log('apply <', pp(retval))
  return retval
}
```

This is our primitive application function—if it is called with an atom in its first argument that is any of our five primitive functions, we can execute that directly. If it's a different atom, we switch to `eval` instead. The second leg of `apply`, matching the case where the function argument is not an atom, checks whether it's a list that starts with `LAMBDA` or `LABEL`, the constructs that we discussed earlier to support recursion, but also used to define new functions.

`apply`'s partner is `eval` (which we also prefix here with `lisp_`, both for consistency and because `eval` also makes an appearance in JavaScript. The fact that two function names from this ancient language made it into the modern *lingua franca* of the Internet is a good indication of just how much impact Lisp has had):

```
lisp_eval = (e, a) => {
  console.log('eval =>', pp(e), pp(a))

  let retval =
    atom(e)
    ? cdr(assoc(e, a))
    : atom(car(e))
      ? (eq(car(e), 'QUOTE') ? cadr(e) :
          eq(car(e), 'COND') ? evcon(cdr(e), a) :
          lisp_apply(car(e), evlis(cdr(e), a), a)
    )
    : lisp_apply(car(e), evlis(cdr(e), a), a)

  console.log('eval <=', pp(retval))
  return retval
}
```

```
cadar = l => car(cdr(car(l)))

evcon = (c, a) => {
  console.log('evcon ==>', pp(c), pp(a))

  let retval =
    lisp_eval(caar(c), a)
    ? lisp_eval(cadar(c), a)
    : evcon(cdr(c), a)

  console.log('evcon <==', pp(retval))
  return retval
}
evlis = (m, a) => {
  console.log('evlis ==>', pp(m), pp(a))

  let retval =
    nil(m)
    ? 'NIL'
    : cons(lisp_eval(car(m), a),
           evlis(cdr(m), a))

console.log('evlis <==', pp(retval))
  return retval
}
```

This function defines two more keywords, QUOTE to "quote" a list, and COND to introduce a conditional expression. And this completes the list of 'special' words in Lisp. And now, we can finally define evalquote merely by starting apply's recursion with an empty list:

```
evalquote = (fn, x) => lisp_apply(fn, x, null)
```

Let's play a bit with this to better understand what is going on, because these two functions deserve that. First, a quick warm-up. Try to figure out how things thread through apply and eval before continuing reading after each example, it's much more fun that way.

```
☞ $ node
☞ > .load code/js/lisp.js
  ...
☞ > evalquote('CAR', [['A', ['B', null]]])
  'A'
```

We evaluate the atom CAR with a two-element list as arguments. The full Javascript code included with the book includes a quick parser function called ps (for "parse s-expression"), so we can write this as:

```
> evalquote(ps('CAR'), ps('((A B))'))
'A'
```

We'll continue that style from here on. There is also a pp function that pretty-prints the internal representation of an s-expression so we can make outputs look a bit more "lisp-y".

> REPL — With our helpers `ps` and `pp` we have four clear stages of execution: `ps` *reads* the string input and converts it into the equivalent internal representation of s-expressions; then we *evaluate* the code, which results into a new internal representation of s-expressions, which we then, using `pp`, *print*. Once that is done we can go back to the beginning; *loop* around, as it were. This concept of a read-evaluate-print loop is very common in Lisp, which all provide interactive sessions based on this principle. The shorthand for this is "REPL."

Note that when calling `evalquote`, the second argument is a *list* of arguments, so above we call `CAR` with a single argument, the list `(A B)`. This also explains why, when implementing `car` in `apply`, the `caar` function is used: we want the first element of the first argument. Apart from this little bit of trickiness, the five primitive functions in `apply` have straightforward implementations: when the function to be applied is an atom that is the name of the primitive function, then the primitive function is invoked (after properly "unwrapping" its arguments).

What about the case where we have a different function name? We see that the construct

```
lisp_apply(lisp_eval(fn, a), x, a)
```

is user—in this case, knowing that `fn` is still an atom, you'll quickly see that `lisp_eval` will end up looking up `fn` in `a`, the list of defined functions, returning its definition. That definition then gets used in a new call to `apply`, hopefully this time around at least one step closer to success.

The next two clauses of `apply` are a bit trickier. First up is `LAMBDA`, the universal function definition mechanism. Here's a simple example:

```
☞ > evalquote(ps('(LAMBDA (X Y) (CONS (CAR X) Y))'),
     ps('((A B) (C D))'))
[ 'A', [ 'C', [ 'D', null ] ] ]
```

Let's first unpack this on the Lisp level: we ask evalquote to evaluate the s-expression that is a function with two arguments (X and Y), defined as consing the first element of the first argument with the second argument. As arguments we pass in a list of two elements: one list with A and B as its elements, and one list with C and D as it elements. From the lambda function definition this should indeed return the first element of the first argument (A) together with the second argument, consed together into a list.

In the Lisp function definition, the implementation is only a bit harder to follow. First, we hit on the clause that checks whether the function argument starts with LAMBDA; if that is true, we do:

```
lisp_eval(caddr(fn), pairlis(cadr(fn), x, a))
```

caddr will take the car of the cdr of the cdr of the lambda form:

```
☞ > fn = ps('(LAMBDA (X Y) (CONS (CAR X) Y))')
☞ > pp(caddr(fn))
'(CONS (CAR X) Y)
```

This is exactly the form that the lambda function defines. The second argument that the we pass to lisp_eval is the pairlis invocation. Again, let's see what this returns and whether it makes sense:

```
☞ > pp(pairlis(cadr(fn), args, []))
'((X A B) (Y C D))'
```

The cadr of the function is the argument list, and using pairlis we pair its elements up with the actual argument values. This way, we get back an association list having the argument names for the keys and the argument values for the values. (Note that the pretty printer doesn't know what we actually mean by this—(X A B) and (X . (A B)) are the same, so ideally we would see the latter interpretation here). In short, we unwrap the lambda function to get to its forms and argument names, combine the latter with the actual arguments, and send that off to the Lisp *eval* function to execute. And that brings us to the second part of the universal Lisp function, *eval*.

Form and Function

While *apply* handles functions, *eval* handles forms. We've seen the first clause of eval, it does a variable lookup. The second clause checks whether we have QUOTE or COND (which we'll deal with a bit later) and then the else clause that... goes straight back to apply, again after peeling off a new layer:

```
lisp_apply(car(e), evlis(cdr(e), a), a)
```

Given that the whole expression in e is a form, the first element *must* be a function name. (This is an optimistic Universal Lisp Function, which assumes that the human knows what they're doing and all the Lisp code entered therefore is faultless). Its argument? Well, whatever the rest of the list evaluates to, and that's where the evlis helper comes in—it takes a list and evaluates it, recursively, until it hits NIL. The core of that function is typical of how you can recurse over lists in Lisp:

```
cons(lisp_eval(car(m), a), evlis(cdr(m), a))
```

We do the work we can do on the first element (which we interpret as a form, so we evaluate it), recurse with the rest, and cons the two together. Adding some tracing to the JavaScript code, we get:

```
☞ > e = ps('(CONS (CAR X) Y)')
☞ > a = ps('((X.(A B)) (Y.(C D)))')
☞ > pp(lisp_apply(car(e), evlis(cdr(e), a), a))
evlis ==> ((CAR X) Y) ((X A B) (Y C D))
eval => (CAR X) ((X A B) (Y C D))
evlis ==> (X) ((X A B) (Y C D))
eval => X ((X A B) (Y C D))
eval <= (A B)
evlis ==> null ((X A B) (Y C D))
evlis <== NIL
evlis <== ((A B) . NIL)
apply > CAR ((A B) . NIL) ((X A B) (Y C D))
apply < A
eval <= A
evlis ==> (Y) ((X A B) (Y C D))
eval => Y ((X A B) (Y C D))
eval <= (C D)
evlis ==> null ((X A B) (Y C D))
evlis <== NIL
evlis <== ((C D) . NIL)
evlis <== (A (C D) . NIL)
apply > CONS (A (C D) . NIL) ((X A B) (Y C D))
apply < (A C D) `(A C D)'
```

Try to match the trace with the Universal Lisp Function definition (and toy with the code some more, tracing all the way from the top, for example). One thing that is interesting here is how "variables" like `X` and `Y` are pretty much the same as functions. They get "evaluated" just the same, and—as we'll see, how variables and functions are treated does not differ to this implementation of Lisp.

> LISP-1 AND LISP-2 — These days we call Lisp versions that treat names for functions and variables the same a "Lisp-1," in contrast with later variants that are called "Lisp-2" by virtue of having two distinct namespaces, one for functions and one for variables. There are advantages and disadvantages to each choice: one risks confusion–"Am I referring to a function or a variable here?"–and the other often requires special syntax to indicate whether a function or a variable reference is intended.
> Needless to say, the pros and cons have resulted in no universal agreement on what is the better option, and modern Lisps can be either (and some can be both!). For a detailed overview, Richard Gabriel and Kent Pitman did a deep dive in their article *Technical Issues of Separation in Function Cells and Value Cells* [24]

We have a couple of clauses left, so let's quickly go through them. `LABEL` is the construct we discussed earlier that lets us define names, `COND` is the conditional expression, and `QUOTE` basically delays evaluation: instead of saying

here is a form

When we quote it:

"here is a form"

we tell the Lisp interpreter to treat the list as data (for now—we may want to evaluate it later), and not care about the contents. Note that in this example, the first sentence is not a proper form and the second one is. Quoting is an indispensable tool in Lisp.

> QUOTING — It can not be understated just how important quoting is in Lisp. It is the basis for all sorts of cool stuff that we will encounter later on. Take a pause here and ask yourself whether you understand what `QUOTE` does; if not, go back and re-read the sidebar at the end of the previous chapter as well.

Exploring Our Lisp-in-JavaScript Machine

As an example that combines LABEL, COND and QUOTE, we can go back to the simple recursive function *ff* which we so far only saw in M-notation. Let's define it and call it with tracing enabled to see exactly what happens in our LISP 1.5 machine. The example here is taken off page 10 in the LISP 1.5 manual which shows how to translate m-expressions to s-expressions, in this case the function FF to find the first atom in its argument. We take the result of that translation and test it. The output here has been massaged a bit for readability, with the last argument to number of functions (which holds all the definitions) made to stand out a bit and rendered as the alist it is.

```
☞ > ff = ps('(LABEL FF (LAMBDA (X) (COND ((ATOM X) X)
  ((QUOTE T) (FF (CAR X))))))')
☞ > args = ps('(A B C D)')
☞ > evalquote(ff, args)
  apply > (LABEL FF (LAMBDA (X) (COND ((ATOM X) X) ((QUOTE T)\
  (FF (CAR X))))))
          (A B C D)
          null
  apply > (LAMBDA (X) (COND ((ATOM X) X) ((QUOTE T) (FF (CAR X)))))
          (A B C D)
          ((FF . LAMBDA (X) (COND ((ATOM X) X) ((QUOTE T) (FF (CAR X))))))
  eval => (COND ((ATOM X) X) ((QUOTE T) (FF (CAR X))))
          ((X . A)
           (FF . LAMBDA (X) (COND ((ATOM X) X) ((QUOTE T) (FF (CAR X))))))
  evcon ==> (((ATOM X) X) ((QUOTE T) (FF (CAR X))))
            ((X . A)
             (FF . LAMBDA (X) (COND ((ATOM X) X) ((QUOTE T) (FF (CAR X))))))
  eval => (ATOM X)
          ((X . A)
           (FF . LAMBDA (X) (COND ((ATOM X) X) ((QUOTE T) (FF (CAR X))))))
  evcon ==> (((ATOM X) X) ((QUOTE T) (FF (CAR X))))
  evlis ==> (X)
            ((X . A)
             (FF . LAMBDA (X) (COND ((ATOM X) X) ((QUOTE T) (FF (CAR X))))))
  eval => X
          ((X . A)
           (FF . LAMBDA (X) (COND ((ATOM X) X) ((QUOTE T) (FF (CAR X))))))
  eval <= A
  evlis ==> null
            ((X . A)
             (FF . LAMBDA (X) (COND ((ATOM X) X) ((QUOTE T) (FF (CAR X))))))
```

```
evlis <== NIL
evlis <== (A . NIL)
apply > ATOM
        (A . NIL)
        ((X . A)
         (FF . LAMBDA (X) (COND ((ATOM X) X) ((QUOTE T) (FF (CAR X))))))
apply < true
eval <= true
eval => X
        ((X . A)
         (FF . LAMBDA (X) (COND ((ATOM X) X) ((QUOTE T) (FF (CAR X))))))
eval <= A
evcon <== A
eval <= A
apply < A
apply < A
'A'
```

We can see how `LABEL`, `COND` and `QUOTE` work here. `QUOTE` is simple: it just delays evalutation, and the implementation, `cadr(e)` just retrieves the bits after the `QUOTE` (essentially unwrapping it). `COND` is implemented in the `evcon` helper function, which itself—not entirely unexpectedly—is implemented in terms of the conditional expression:

```
lisp_eval(caar(c), a) ? lisp_eval(cadar(c), a) : evcon(cdr(c), a)
```

Again allowing for some list nesting, basically it says "if my predicate is true, evaluate my expression, else evaluate the rest of the conditional expression." Not much to see there, so we can wrap up our dissection of the Universal Lisp Function with `LABEL`. You may have thought that *label* might be tricky to implement, but nothing is further from the truth: as you can see both in the code and in the trace, all we do in the code that handles `LABEL` is to unwrap the expression and use it twice: once as a function to be evaluated, and once as a variable with the name specified by the label. When this is run through the machinery, everything becomes just as trivial as the "straight" `LAMBDA` example before.

* * *

And with that last step, congratulations! We now have a functioning Lisp machine, implemented on top of JavaScript. Well, this is only "technically correct": Yes, it's a complete universal computing machine, but I don't think you'd want to write code in it. There are still a lot of choices left in the implementation, and in the next chapter we'll dive into the sort of decisions that the team made when implementing all of this on their first (and only) computer, the IBM 704. But don't let implementation details blind you to how powerful this simple machine is (conceptually): It is the equivalent of Church's and Turing's work, but now, for the first time, made practical to implement and use.

Chapter 6

Implementing LISP I

In the previous chapter, we implemented a mostly theoretical language on top of JavaScript, both to show how general McCarthy's universal functions are and how simple they are to implement. Earlier, we mentioned that McCarthy was mostly a theoretician and never really expected the language to be implemented, let alone take off as it did; furthermore, S-expressions were merely a theoretical vehicle and M-expressions seemed to be the more interesting venue for an implementation as they were a bit closer to how other high level computer programming languages looked.

Luckily, one of McCarthy's graduate students, Stephen B. Russell, cared more about getting something running than about theory or his professor's preferences (and probably, he cared most about avoiding all the tedious manual translation work). Once he realized that the universal function could be implemented in a lower level language and that the whole thing was simple enough to let that lower level language be IBM 704 machine code, he was off and pretty much overnight implemented a first Lisp interpreter. Thus bootstrapped, subsequent work became easier and before long, a complete Lisp system was released as LISP I.

While the exact implementation details are not too important, they are instructive as they illustrate the design choices a Lisp implementer has to make on one of the simplest machines imaginable. We will therefore go into some detail, including specifics about the group's hardware gleaned from the IBM 704 Reference Manual [35]. "LISP I" here refers to the version described in *LISP I Programmer's Manual* [51]; while there is much more material on the later LISP 1.5, the idea here is to showcase the very first Lisp implementation.

Figure 6.1: Image of NASA's IBM 704 system in use

A quick rundown of the IBM 704

The IBM 704 was quite a computer for the time: it came with magnetic "core" storage, tapes, drums, a CRT terminal, had fast memory access times (12 microseconds), and a large word size of 36 bits.

Main working memory was the magnetic core memory. It was random-access and could hold 4,096 to 32,767 words (depending on storage unit size); drums and tapes could be swapped out, where drums would hold 8,912 words and tapes 33 1/3 words per inch of tape. Finally, punch cards had room for 24 words on each card. All in all, the IBM 704 had the sort of performance and storage capabilities that you would find on a small microcontroller today, but back then, it was a beast of a machine.

A machine word of 36 bits is large and can hold a lot of information. Three different main kinds of information are specified:

Numbers A word can hold integers or floating point numbers of up to 35 bits, where the left-most bit indicates the sign. Floating points are stored much like they are today, as an exponent and a mantissa part packed together in the word;

Alphanumerical data A word can hold 6 alphabetic characters of 6 bits each using the then somwhat standard "BCD" encoding. With 6 bits for each character we have room for the alphabet in upper case, numbers, and then a handful of special characters like comma, dot, space.

Instructions Two kinds of instructions, named type A and type B, exist. Type A instructions we've already visited: they contain two arguments called "address" and "decrement" taking up most of the space of the instruction (twice 15 bits, leaving just 6 bits for "prefix" at the start, and "tag" in the middle, which together define the operation). Type B instructions have 11 bits for the operation, 5 reserved bits, a three-bit tag and then a 15 bit address. Two bits in the operation field are always set to zero, probably to indicate the instruction as being of type B.

> BCD — *Binary-Coded Decimal* is a way to represent numbers in a computer. In binary, four bits are sufficient to represent the numbers 0-9, so BCD will take each digit of a regular base-10 number and use four bits to represent it. This takes a bit more space than regular binary representation, but can sometimes be simpler to work with. The 6-bit character encoding is technically not "binary-coded decimal" but still was known as "BCD."

Apart from that, the central processing unit has some buffer registers, an instruction pointer, two general arithmetic registers (the second one specialized to hold results for multiplication and division) and three index registers that can be used to offset locations for instructions. All in all, while a bit more restricted, the machine's instruction set of around 90 instructions is quite recognizable to today's programmers.

LISP I memory layout

We already have touched upon how `car` and `cdr` came about: the "address" and "decrement" fields of a type A instruction are exactly the size to hold a pointer, and the 704 has fast (2 cycle) operations to move the bits of these fields to and from index registers. As such, using the contents of the address and decrement parts of words in memory for the "data" and "next" parts of a cons cell make eminent sense; IBM, in fact, couldn't have done much better if they would have created a machine for the specific purpose of running Lisp!

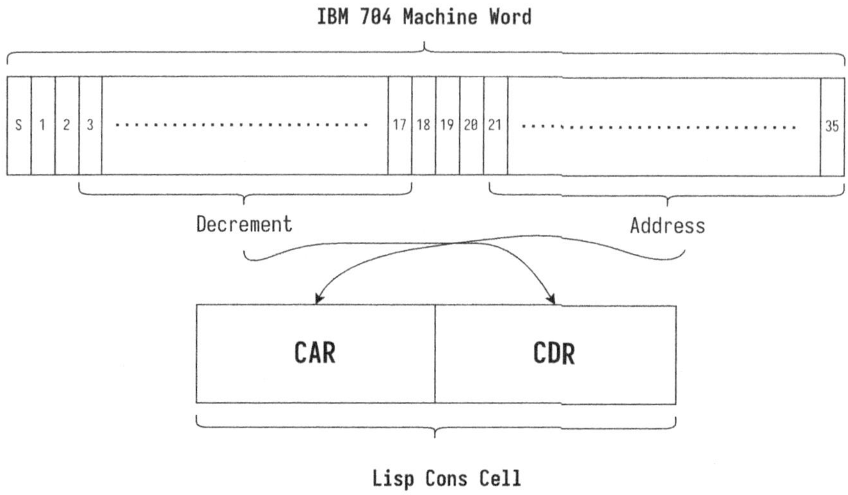

Moving one level up, we ignore the exact layout of machine words for now and consider just the cons cell it represents. To recap, a cons cell can link to another cons cell to form a linked list of cells:

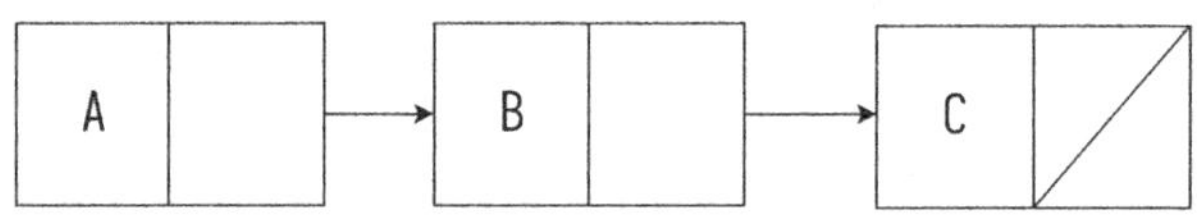

Each cons cell contains a pointer to the next cell. The final cell contains a null pointer which we designate with a slash through the cdr part of the cell. Pointers, in this context, are simply (15-bit) integers representing memory locations. The above diagram represents the list `(A B C)`, but lists can share structure as well. For example, a list `(A (B (C . A)) (C . A))`—which is a valid list, not just a *proper* list as the final cdr is not nil, can be represented in memory as:

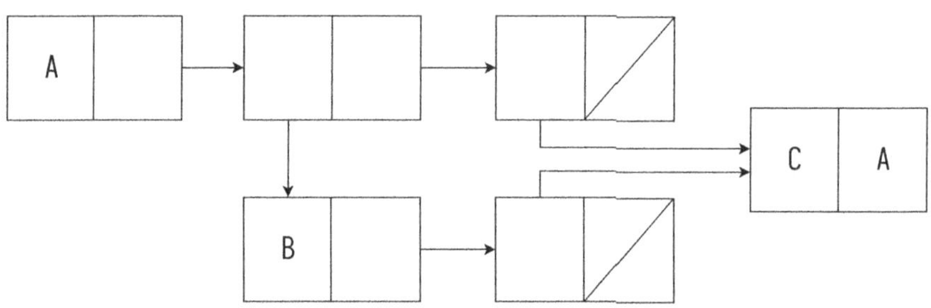

This does not say anything about the "contents of the address register"; we represented cells here as atoms, but it should be obvious that any random atom name will not fit in the 15 bits room we have there: that would limit them to two characters (of 6 bits each), and clearly we're allowed longer names. Also, the computer is not interested in the name of an atom—that is something for humans, so making the print representation of an atom leading is not really necessary. If we can make them addresses, then the computer is just happy to manipulate these numbers and only if a human needs to look at something, the name can somehow be looked up and used instead.

Furthermore, atoms can play different roles. As a symbol, it just "is", it resolves to itself. But atoms can also have meaning when they are used, for example, as a label for a function or a value; in LISP 1.5, the function can be a Lisp function or what we would now call a "native" function, one written in IBM 704 machine language directly. So atoms need a type and optionally a value.

The solution chosen in LISP I is to associate atoms with *property lists*. A property list is a special kind of list, which starts with the value `-1`, and then has pairs of properties with their values; each property has a name (which is an atom) and a value (which usually is a list). Here is the full property list for `NIL`:

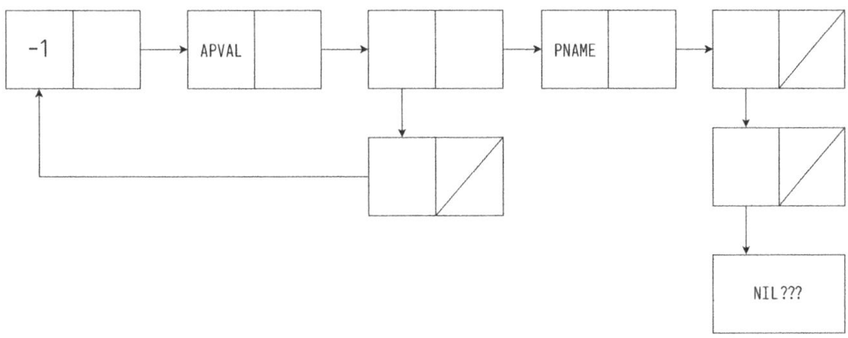

`NIL` has two properties, both pointing to a list (needed for more complex constructs as we'll see later, so they always take this form):

`APVAL` This contains atom's permanent value, and the value of an atom is itself, so the value is a list that points right back at itself.

`PNAME` The atom's printable name. This is the string "NIL", and as we saw, the IBM 704 has 6 bit characters so we can put 6 of them in a word. We only need three here, so the word is padded with the invalid character '77' in octal (which in ASCII would be the question mark, so we use that for display here).

For longer words, the name would just have a longer list, for example `EXAMPLE` would have the `PNAME` property:

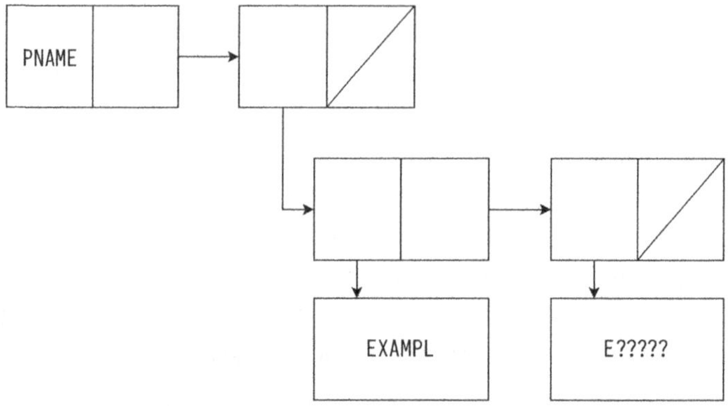

LISP 1.5 defines two other elements in the property list: EXPR indicates that the symbol is a function and points to the S-expression defining it; SUBR indicates that the symbol is a machine language subroutine, its value is a jump instruction that invokes the subroutine.

One thing to note here is how self-referential this structure is. APVAL is itself an atom represented by a property list (with for its APVAL a pointer to itself, like NIL and, indeed, every other atom). To bootstrap this, the Lisp implementation comes with a set of predefined properties (NIL, APVAL, ...) that are data statements in its assembly code. There is a list of symbols the system knows about (in other words, a list with all its elements pointing to the -1 header cell of property lists) that starts out with these predefined atoms and Lisp's predefined functions and then is expanded as new functions and atomic symbols are encountered in user code; this list can also be used to find symbols by name, simply by scanning it and looking up the PNAME for every element and comparing it to the name that is being searched. No preferential treatment is given, or indeed needed, for "built-in" functions like CONS or CAR or CDR.

In summary, all known symbols to a running LISP I system are contained in a list with pointers to property lists for its values; the property lists define name and value of the symbol. Atoms, functions (whether in Lisp or in machine code) all live in that section of memory.

Numbers

We have explained how atoms, strings (stored the same as atom names, in a linked list of 6-character blocks), and function definitions are stored but glossed over numbers as they're not that essential for a system that concentrates on symbolic computation. And that showed in the implementation: In LISP I, only floating point numbers are defined. Interestingly enough, they are defined as a kind of atom: a value pointing to a property list with `FLO` having the floating point value. Floating point numbers encountered in source code are thus stored and kept on a separate floating point value list.

Changing data

So far, everything we looked at has been "pure" functional code, that is code with no side effects. The universal Lisp machine can evaluate a single function, but once that is done, a result may be returned but nothing else has changed. This is nice from a theoretical point of view but highly impractical to work with. For starters, we can't really define new symbols—given a pointer to the start of the symbol list, we can traverse it all we want, but we cannot *change* it and that is exactly the thing we need to extend the system.

Two operations are defined to take care of this on the lowest level (in M-notation):

- rplaca[x; y] replaces the address part of a cons cell x with y, overwriting whatever was there.
- rplacd[x; y] replaces the decrement part of a cons cell x with y, also overwriting whatever was there.

We've now gone from being powerless to being in possession of a very large hammer, and the Lisp manual emphasizes:

> *These operators must be used with caution.*

Most of Lisp is defined in Lisp—`NIL`, `APVAL`, `QUOTE`, `COND`, and other "built-ins" come with the system, they are not "hardcoded" in the sense that they are specially defined; they are represented by the same kind of property lists as user defined atoms, variables, and functions and can thus be modified with `rplaca` and `rplacd` in exactly the same way. Also, while endless lists can not be directly defined, these functions have no problem editing existing lists into lists with loops and that can have serious consequences as well. As the saying goes, with great power comes great responsibility, and responsible Lisp programs probably won't see any use of these two operators. However, to do the low-level bookkeeping, they're much needed.

Overriding properties

One interesting abuse of property lists is that the search for a certain property stops at the first one found. So if you have a built-in function, you can—using `rplaca` and `rplacd`—edit its property list to insert an EXPR in front of it. Your expression will now be called instead of the built-in one, and in this way it is possible to, for example, add tracing to existing functions: create a wrapper that, say, prints its arguments, calls the original function, prints the return value, and returns that return value and you can use that code to override anything in the system.

Needless to say, this is something that is too easy to abuse, with great power come great responsibilities etc., but it does show how flexible this essentially trivial system is and how "open" it becomes by default. The special form DEFINE, to define functions, uses this writing mechanism under the hood to insert the new function definition into the list of known symbols, for example. Similarly, the functionality is used to insert a compiled-to-machine code version "in front of" the standard interpreted version for performance reasons as we'll see in a bit.

Garbage collection

Early on, it was decided that trying to model thinking using symbolic expressions (remember, this is what started it all!) did not mesh well with manual memory management. Mixing high-level symbolic manipulation with the nitty-gritty details of allocating and freeing memory is aesthetically unpleasant, error-prone, and forces users that aren't necessary primarily computer programmers to think at a level they preferably should not have to think about. Automatic memory management, therefore, was as much a requirement as the sort of language extensibility that we've seen so far.

LISP 1.5 has a elementary garbage collector that operates in two phases:

1. First, it *marks* all memory that it is in active use;
2. Second, it *sweeps* all memory that does not qualify as "in active use" onto a free list.

The free list is essentially a single list that comprises of all memory that is not in use. If a program needs a word of memory, the first item on the list is removed to be used and this continues until the first item on the list is NIL, marking the exhaustion of memory. When that happens, the garbage collector is run and hopefully that results in new items on the free list (if not, the system will crash with an out of memory error).

How does the garbage collector know what memory is in use? Well, if everything is a list then everything that is in use by lists that are in use is in use. The concept is called "reachability": when we exhaustively traverse lists and everything they reference, all the data we visit is "reachable" and everything we have not encountered, by definition, is qualified as unreachable data or "garbage." You need to start this journey somewhere, and the small list of items where you start is collectively called "garbage collection roots." In the case of LISP I, the collector starts at the list of all symbols, and it also knows about things like lists of local variables and lists of intermediate results—as the garbage collector can be invoked at any given moment, it might well be during some complex list manipulation or computation that needs extra storage space, so "what is currently going on" needs to be on the list. When it is time to do a garbage collection run, the implementation starts with these roots and then visits everything it can reach from there by traversing `car` and `cdr` pointers; each cons cell thus encountered has its otherwise unused sign bit set to 1 (note that when the marking process sees a cell that has its sign bit already set to one, it can stop there, knowing that it already visited it and its descendants previously). When that is complete, the sweep phase just needs to go through all of memory, ignore everything with a sign bit set to one, and put everything else on the new free list. Finally, all the sign bits are reset to zero. Special treatment is given to strings and numbers, which are kept in a separate section of memory—strings and numbers don't have unused bits so the trick of using the sign bit cannot be used for them. This separate section has a bitmap for free/in-use marking instead.

Mark-and-sweep garbage collection has been the go-to garbage collection method for decades, until memory sizes increased much faster than memory access times and this scheme–that loops over all of memory and writes it potentially twice–became too slow.

Compilation

So far, we have viewed Lisp as an interpreted system: S-expressions contain code, get parsed into their equivalent memory representation, and whenever invoked are executed from there. This system is flexible–new expressions can be added at any time–but not as fast as one would like to, especially not on a machine like the 704. Therefore, Lisp I comes with a compiler, but one that keeps the character of the system in place: it can be invoked at run-time and it can only compile functions that the system already knows about and are stored regularly as symbols having `EXPR` in their property list. The workflow is to first test whether a system works by using the interpreted variant so the programmer receives quick feedback, and only compile functions that prove to be bottlenecks after they are shown to work (and, likely, after they are shown to actually be bottlenecks). Compilation, therefore, is more an optimization tool than an integral part of the system.

The compiler is a regular Lisp function called `COMDEF`, for "COMpile DEFinition". A list of names to be compiled can be passed, and the compiler then proceeds in three stages:

1. First, the S-expression for the definition is looked up and converted into an intermediate form, which is machine code in list/Lisp form called "LISP-SAP" for "Lisp Symbolic Assembly Program":

   ```
   (
     (,LXD,0,4),
     (,TXI,G0007,4,-1),
     (,TRA,*+5),
     (G0008,BSS,0),
     ...
   )
   ```

   The items are small lists in *(label, instruction, args...)* format and the comma-separated syntax for Lisp I comes in handy here to "skip" the label field for instructions that don't have labels. On the 704, `L..` are load instructions, `T..` are transfer instructions (now commonly called jumps with `J..` mnemonics), and `BSS` is a pseudo-instruction for the assembler (to mark a location purely for reference but without allocating storage for it). `BSS` is an interesting instruction; it came from an earlier assembler for the 704 and stands for "Block Started By Symbol". To this day, the name survives to designate a part of memory that is "statically" initialized by code declarations that reserve memory blocks, much in the fashion as shown here.
2. Then, the list is converted to actual binary code. The details should not concern us here but the end result is the binary code corresponding to the assembly code somewhere in memory.
3. Finally, the function symbol's property list is modified to have a `SUBR` property pointing to the new code *in front of* the `EXPR` property. All subsequent invocations of the function will now hit the machine code `SUBR` first and execute it over the slower `EXPR` version.

This first compiler wasn't perfect, of course. The functions it compiled could only call already compiled Lisp functions but it did not know anything about dependencies nor could it decide to compile the targets of function invocations it "saw" during compilation on-the-fly. So you had to compile functions that did not call any other functions first, then you could compile functions that called these functions, and so on until everything you wanted to compile was compiled. It was up to the programmer to make a dependency graph of functions and order `COMDEF` invocations such that everything was compiled in the right order.

Moving on

There could be much more to discuss about Lisp I and its environment, the IBM 704. Both are fascinating in terms of their "modern" design: not so much arcane relics of an era long gone, but the first steps towards computing as we know it: a dynamic language with flexible compilation options running on a contemporary Von Neumann architecture. Sure, we added more since then, but these are mostly convenience layers: for example, we now take systems for granted that pretend that different hardware is similar, or that pretend that many users each have their own computer. Things along that direction were already brewing, but we will leave historical computers here and continue the story by diving into the first wave of AI optimism that Lisp and McCarthy helped trigger.

Part II

Fame

Chapter 7

The Golden Age of AI

While McCarthy's group was polishing LISP I into LISP 1.5, the man himself wasn't exactly twiddling thumbs. Not only did he serve on the ALGOL standardization committee (thus attaching his name to two out of the three early high level progrmming languages that became mainstream), but he was also thinking about better ways to interact with computers.

LISP was not just a system to do symbolic manipulation, but by its design was also very dynamic. Programs could be built piecemeal, tweaking and changing an existing system in a highly interactive way. Well, *theoretically*, that is.

In practice, the only way to talk to the IBM 704 was to hand an operator a stack of punched cards and wait. On a good day, wait for maybe only three hours, but if things broke it could easily be a day. Or two. And the whole LISP program had to be completely executed, restarting from scratch every time. This was not only slow, it was a waste of expensive computer time to run the whole thing over and over again.

McCarthy moves on to timesharing

McCarthy proposed a better way to do this: *time sharing*, and interacting through something more real-time like a teletype terminal. He wasn't the first one to think of the real-time sharing of computer resources, but he realized that it was not necessarily enough to make programs coexist peacefully in memory: programmers made mistakes, so errors needed to be contained to just the erroring program, leaving concurrently running programs untouched. This required a bit more than just attaching a couple of teletypes, and in a 1959 memo to MIT computation center director P.M. Morse he listed a set of requirements and hardware changes that would be needed to allow the forthcoming fully transistorized IBM 709 machine to support timesharing.

It is important to realize just how big of a deal this was, both from the perspective of the programmer as well as from the perspective of maximally using scarce computing resources. Computer runs in the old style are wasteful: not only does all context need to be setup, but programmers will go through great lengths to add lots of information to dump in case the code crashes, because the stack of paper is all you have. In the course of developing a small program, the whole thing is run from scratch maybe a dozen times, each time requiring the whole computer to load the program from slow storage, execute the thing, write results back to slow storage, and finally wait for the print-out. Remember, we're talking about a multi-million dollar machine here of which MIT had exactly one in their posession. Between repairs and runs, all that money was mostly just wasted on a very large space heater.

And then consider the programmer's perspective. Deliver a stack of cards, wait, receive a stack of paper, then back to the office to peer over the output in the hope that when (not if, of course) it crashed, it left enough information to find the bug. Adapt the program, re-punch cards, make the trek to the computer room, hope that there's uptime and availability, ad infinitum. Modern software development is big on "flow"—staying concentrated and keeping context in ones head has been found extremely helpful in keeping developers productive, and good organizations will go to great lengths to keep their coders uninterrupted. Needless to say, coding as a flow of interruptions between various steps of a convoluted process probably didn't get the best out of these early software makers.

Time-sharing solves both issues at the same time. Multiple people use the computer at the same time, keeping it occupied. Furthermore, it would work using interactive terminals instead of punch cards and print-outs, meaning that a programmer could inspect memory locations and step through code, all without the expensive task of starting the program over and over again. So not only does the addition of time-sharing makes an enormous difference for the programmer, the end result is that the computer has to do way less work and therefore can serve many more users. It's not often that such enormous gains are to be had, and even though it wasn't seen as an easy task to build a supervisory system that could let programs share memory but without them interfering with each other, the benefits were too large to ignore.

People therefore got to work, and the result of McCarthy's and others' efforts was the first public demonstration at MIT of timesharing on a general computer in 1961. It used an operating system called

Compatible Time-Sharing System, or CTSS, which was the first of a line of operating systems that would eventually result in Unix. Not only were computers now able to manipulate data and knowledge on a symbolic level, they were interactive as well so people could experiment and tinker much quicker than before. Two important foundational technologies for research on thinking and intelligence were now starting to become available.

Wrapping up LISP I with LISP 1.5

While this was going on, development of the LISP language did not exactly stop. The first version of LISP had a lot of shortcomings, ranging from the absence of numbers to the slow interpreter. Remember that LISP was a theoretical system that got accidentally actually implemented by a grad student. Basic things lacked, like support for numbers that weren't implemented as symbols, a facility to update lists by inserting and changing elements, but most importantly, a solution for what is now called "The Funarg Problem."

What happened was that one programmer, James R. Slagle, "in all innocence" (as McCarthy later recounted) created this helper function to find a pattern in an arbitrary list:

```
testr[x, p, f, u] ←
  if p[x] then f[x]
    else if atom[x] then u[]
    else testr[cdr[x], p, f, λ: testr[car[x], p, f, u]].
```

(note that this is in a sort of M-notation, S-expressions where still seen as an intermediate form not suitable for humans to work in). It didn't work, but Slagle expected it to work. Let's see what this is supposed to do:

- We look for an `x` that satisfies the proposition `p`. If we find one, we call the passed in function `f` with it (and we're done).
- If the pattern does not exist but we have an atom, we call `u`.
- Else, we call ourselves recursively with the rest of the list `x` and a new function `u`.

The tricky bit is in the recursive call with the new `u`. What we intend to do is that if the list is exhausted, then `cdr[x]` returns `nil`, we recurse, `atom[nil]` is true and so we call `u` which is that lambda expression that calls `testr` as well, but now with the first element of `x` instead of the rest.

It's not how you usually would search, but it looks valid. Except for one thing: it does not work, and that has everything to do with "what is x the moment that the lambda expression is evaluated?" A modern programmer would expect that the x in

```
λa: testr[car[x], p, f, u]
```

refers to the x that is in scope when the lambda is *defined*. In lambda terms, all four of x, p, f, and u are free variables and they need to come from some place outside the lambda—its environment. Today, we expect to be able to look at code and conclude by reading it that these four are the four values passed in, but LISP I and LISP 1.5 were not setup like that: the lookup happened at run-time, when the lambda was evaluated, and the values obtained where the values in scope at the moment the code was run. Let's make this clear with an example:

```
testr[(a b c), p, f, u]
```

Gets called and we drop through to the final bit of code, the recursive call:

```
testr[cdr[x], p, f, λa : testr[car[x], p, f, u]]] →
testr[(b c), p, f, λa : testr[car[x], p, f, u]]
```

So far, so good, and this goes on eating through the list until we call it with just (c) and get:

```
testr[cdr[x], p, f, λa : testr[car[x], p, f, u]]] →
testr[nil, p, f, λa : testr[car[x], p, f, u]]] →
```

so x now satisfies atom[x] and we call u[]—the lambda expression here. Slagle expected that car[x] in there to refer to the value when it was still (c), but this is not how LISP works. The whole expression is not evaluated until it is invoked, so the actual value is not resolved until the call to u[] happens:

```
u[] →
λa : testr[car[x], p, f, u][] →
λa : testr[car[()], p, f, u][] →
λa : testr[nil, p, f, u][] →
testr[nil, p, f, u]
```

where u is unchanged and it's not hard to see that the recursive call will again hit on the second leg of the function, never returning. This was different from the programmer's expectation, which essentially is "evaluate that car[x] in the context of the *definition* of that lambda".

In current terms, what was expected was *lexical binding* and what LISP offered was *dynamic binding*. McCarthy considered this an implementation bug, but Steve Russell (LISP's original implementor) probed deeper into this problem and concluded that LISP was *technically* correct, but this sort of binding would be very helpful. He added a special form `FUNCTION` to wrap the lambda in which got translated into a three-element list containing a special form called `FUNARG`, the lambda, and the current environment of the expression. When (later) evaluated, `FUNARG` would use that third element to evaluate the lambda in the environment that was active when it was declared—what we now call its lexical scope—in order to have the code inside resolve to what the programmer expected here.

The funarg problem was born, giving birth to lots of pondering, a handful of academic papers, and a decades-long discussion of the relative merits of dynamic and lexical scoping; for the mainstream, the latter eventually won—even though it might be more complex to implement, it is easier for programmers to reason about because what you read it what you get, you don't need to think through how things are called in order to figure out what your values are. This simplicity led to lexical scoping becoming the default in most of LISP's offspring and pretty much all other programming languages. A couple of the most commonly used versions of Lisp today, though, still have at least ways to make scoping dynamic, even when it is not the default anymore.

Apart from that little issue, LISP 1.5 matured in other ways: it had a compiler, it could work with numbers directly, lists could be mutated for performance, it got better support for imperative programming (through `PROG`, the "program feature" which basically held a list of statements to execute one-by-one) and the first steps towards macro/meta programming were made as eval was available and some budding support was added LISP 1.5's built-in functionality. More about Lisp and metaprogramming later, though.

Stanford and the founding of SAIL

McCarthy was not happy at MIT. Even though he was popular, with students affectionately calling him "uncle John", it was hard to move up through the ranks, and after a couple of years of finding himself at the bottom rungs of the academic career ladder, he started looking elsewhere. From the other end of the continent, Stanford was luring him with an offer of a full professorship and before long, McCarthy said goodby to MIT and accepted what would be his forever job, professor at Stanford.

He was appointed as a professor of Mathematics, because there was no computer science department yet. Indeed, even before Stanford had a computer science department, McCarthy started SAIP, the Stanford AI Project, the predecessor of the Stanford AI Lab, or SAIL. Working on "just" AI was never enough for him, apparently, so he continued his work on timesharing systems, creating the first interactive editor for the DEC PDP-1, and writing about how "utility computing" should be a thing (an idea whose time came more than four decades later in the form of "cloud computing").

Stanford acquired a partially finished modernistic circular building in the hills above the campus from phone company GTE, where SAIL found a home for both its staff and its first computer, a DEC PDP-6. Research in Artificial Intelligence was well underway by that time.

Initially, AI was all about replicating the human mind: neuronal networks, capturing thoughts and learning, that sort of stuff. However, it quickly became clear that the available hardware was woefully inadequate and the field quickly moved its attention to things that were thought to be more attainable, like how logic could be used to play chess. The game itself was just a model, like other scientists build models in labs; it was seen as rich enough to represent reality and simple enough to, well, build in a lab.

Lisp was the common theme in all these early efforts: to play chess, to model the real world as "seen" by various early robots that could be found at the lab, and later on to capture knowledge symbolically in the form of expert systems - rule-based repositories of facts and knowledge that quickly proved to be quite useful in applications in, well, pretty much every field where knowledge matters.

LISP 2

LISP 1.5 was a practical tool, but it was hardly perfect. Even though its origin was pure mathematics, the implementation was a string of ad-hoc choices, accidents, and hacks and that made a number of people less than happy. They saw that the ideas were sound but too much was missing to really enable symbolic computing and AI research, so they set out to define a successor, called LISP 2.

A collaboration of two early software companies—System Development Corporation and Information International, Inc.—resulted in a proposal for a language that fixed a lot of LISP 1.5's deficiencies, starting with the strange parenthesized syntax. LISP 2 had an Algol-60 inspired syntax. Indeed, "fixing" LISP's syntax was seen as a primary goal; while LISP I and LISP 1.5 had the "meta" language, the "symbolic" language was what actually was used. LISP 2 introduces a proper and first class "Source Language" which looks much like a regular language. For example, a simple random number generator:

```
REAL FUNCTION RANDOM(A, B);
  REAL A, B;
BEGIN Y <- 3125 * Y;
      Y <- Y  67108864;
      RETURN (Y / 6708864.0 * (B - A) + A)
END;
```

This code is exactly equivalent with the "Intermediate Language" version:

```
(DECLARE (Y OWN INTEGER))
  (FUNCTION (RANDOM REAL)
    ((A REAL) (B REAL))
      (BLOCK NIL
       (SET Y (TIMES 3125 Y))
       (SET Y (REMAINDER Y 67 108864))
       (RETURN (PLUS (TIMES
           (QUOTIENT Y 6.7108864000E+7)
           (DIFFERENCE B A )) A)))
```

There were a couple of ideas behind this split:

- The wealth of existing Algol algorithms could pretty much directly be translated into LISP 2 Source Language, and presumably people used to Algol would be able to get going faster in Source Language;
- At the same time, because every Source Language program was exactly represented by a single Intermediate Language program, the possibility to manipulate code as data, which was a big reason that LISP had so much power, was retained.

In essence, LISP 2 combined the best ideas of Algol (and its descendants) and LISP: it kept things like symbols and code-as-data, but married them with a syntax that was easier on people and things like type specifications to ensure that efficient code would be emitted. It was an excellent effort by a group of very smart people, and would run on an IBM military system that would be more powerful than the IBM 7040/7090 systems that powered LISP I and LISP 1.5.

Alas, the actual hardware only had 48k words which was not sufficient for such an ambitious project, and the authors started looking for alternative platforms. They decided to hedge their bets and target both the IBM 360 and DEC PDP-6 systems; Information International was acquiring the former and the other participants, SDC, but also Stanford and MIT, preferred the latest offering from Digital Equipment Corporation. This likely did not help in bringing such an ambitious and complex project to fruition, and eventually the whole project was dropped. McCarthy recalls:

> From a 1970s point of view, this was regrettable, because much more money has since been spent to develop LISPs with fewer features.

Digital Equipment Corporation

We just mentioned "DEC" in passing, but you can't really talk about AI and LISP in the 1960s without encountering the PDP computer series by Massachusetts startup Digital Equipment Corporation (DEC). IBM enthusiastically supported AI research efforts in the 1950s, but got cold feet later on: customers viewed the whole thing as scary and potentially harmful to their bottom lines, and banks paid more than universities. If commercial customers didn't like AI, IBM was more than happy not to like AI, too.

LISP got ported onto anything that resembled a computer, and DEC's hardware became an especially popular target, which is not a surprise given the company's origins. Digital Equipment Corporation was founded in 1957 by MIT "hackers" Ken Olsen and Harlan Anderson. At MIT, an Air Force project got an 18-bit computer built, the TX-0, as a prototype for a much bigger machine, the TX-2, which had so much memory capacity that TX-0's core memory got stripped to save cost. The TX-0 was much less powerful than the IBM 704, but students still lined up for computer time; Olsen and Anderson concluded that the difference laid in the fact that the TX series was interactive. It had a system console for direct interaction rather than a puched card reader and its popularity proved McCarthy right: interactivity was everything.

The pair founded Digital Equipment Corporation on this basis with as its first product the Programmed Data Processor 1, or PDP-1; the first of a venerable line of computers that would stretch into the 1980s. The PDP-1 holds a long list of firsts: it sported the first time-sharing system, the first text editor, the first word processor, the first debugger, and even the first computer game. It also launched the budding MIT hacker culture by providing an affordable, interactive computer.

Of course, LISP 1.5 ran on the PDP-1 (McCarthy himself worked on the port while he was still at MIT), but it was a somewhat limited machine; unlike the IBM, the word size was not nearly large enough to hold the two pointers needed for Lisp's main data structure, the CONS cell, so two words were needed. That made any Lisp implementation slow and memory-hungry.

This changed in 1964 with the introduction of the PDP-6. The PDP-6 was still essentially an 18 bit computer, but it now sported a 36 bit word size; this let Lisp implementors use a single word for a cons cell and widened the available theoretical memory space from 32,768 words (in the 704's 15 bit model) to a whopping 262,144 words. It was expensive, complex, unreliable (mostly because of the cutting-edge Germanium transistor technology that powered its electronics), but it was built for interaction and for Lisp. Indeed, DEC was the first manufacturer to offer a time-sharing system out of the box with a machine, and a manufacturer-supported version of Lisp ensured its importance in the Lisp world. Only 23 were sold before DEC was able to refresh the model with the PDP-10 which was essentially the same machine, but, thanks to progressing technology, cheaper and more reliable. A whopping 1500 PDP-10s found their way to customers, time-sharing system included.

Lisp leaving the lab

With LISP 2 not going anywhere, Lisp users who wanted to make improvements or just run Lisp on their own systems were essentially on their own. We should not forget that this was the 1960s, with ARPAnet still in the future and communication between researchers done with typewriters and paper mail. LISP 1.5 was adapted and ported to IBM machines, the DEC PDP machines, but also to computers by other vendors, like Sperry Rand corporation's Univac mainframes. Even though the ports often came with tweaks to the original system (either out of necessity, convenience, or simply because the implementor came up with a neat idea), they were all recognizable as LISP 1.5 systems. There were probably enough ideas floating around, but the average AI lab did not have the funding to do language research, and hacking on Lisp itself (instead of just using it as a programming language) was hard and something arcane, something that maybe one or two people in such a lab were capable of doing, if they had the time.

Maclisp

This changed when a group at MIT started tweaking their Lisp implementation on the PDP-10 to make it more suitable for what we shall call for lack of a better term "production" use cases. The focus was on making a Lisp that was stable, predictable, and understandable. Their version of Lisp would become known as Maclisp, named after the project that hosted it, the Project on Mathematics and Computation (Project MAC), the precursor to MIT's AI laboratory.

For example, Lisp 1.5 has two kinds of variables. We don't need to go into too much detail here, but there were "common" variables that could be used by interpreted and compiled functions alike, and "special" variables which could only be shared between compiled functions but were much faster to access. The new Lisp did away with that confusing distinction and had only one kind of variable.

Similarly, while LISP 1 already had support for higher level constructs to allow user to enhance the language with "special forms" like `if`, there were differences in how to write them for compiled and interpreted versions, the syntax was not especially clean, and it made a powerful feature much harder to use than necessary. Maclisp came with a new construct, `DEFMACRO`, which enabled users to extend the language in a much simpler fashion.

To understand why `DEFMACRO` was such a big thing, let's go back to LISP 1.5 and implement a special conditional, `ifbig`, that executes the "true" branch if its first argument is a large number (randomly set at 10), and will otherwise execute the "false" branch. A first attempt, coded up for LISP 1.5 on the IBM 7094:

```
      TEST  IFBIG1
define ((
  (bigp (lambda (x) (greaterp x 10)))
))

bigp (6)
bigp (12)

define ((
  (ifbig (lambda (v c1 c2) (cond
                                 ((bigp v) c1)
                                 (t c2))))
  (main (lambda ()
          (ifbig 12 (print (quote yes)) (print (quote no))))
))

main ()
```

```
STOP
          FIN        END OF LISP RUN
```

We first `DEFINE` a predicate, `BIGP`, that does the test for us (`GREATERP` is a built-in predicate in LISP 1.5). Then we define `IFBIG` to take three arguments, the value to test and two clauses to execute; implementing it is just simply passing everything to the built-in `COND`. A `MAIN` function exercises our new if statement and finally, after defining everything, we call it. (How to run the emulator is detailed in Appendix B so you can follow along if you're interested). Running this leaves us with the following output:

```
        TEST  IFBIG1

THE TIME ( 0/ 0  000.0) HAS COME, THE WALRUS SAID, TO TALK OF MANY THINGS .....   -LEWIS CARROLL-
EVALQUOTE OPERATOR AS OF 1 MARCH 1961.    INPUT LISTS NOW BEING READ.

THE TIME ( 0/ 0  000.0) HAS COME, THE WALRUS SAID, TO TALK OF MANY THINGS .....   -LEWIS CARROLL-
FUNCTION   EVALQUOTE   HAS BEEN ENTERED, ARGUMENTS..
DEFINE
 (((BIGP (LAMBDA (X) (GREATERP X 10)))))

END OF EVALQUOTE, VALUE IS ..
*TRUE*

FUNCTION   EVALQUOTE   HAS BEEN ENTERED, ARGUMENTS..
BIGP
(6)

END OF EVALQUOTE, VALUE IS ..
NIL

FUNCTION   EVALQUOTE   HAS BEEN ENTERED, ARGUMENTS..
BIGP
(12)

END OF EVALQUOTE, VALUE IS ..
*TRUE*

FUNCTION   EVALQUOTE   HAS BEEN ENTERED, ARGUMENTS..
DEFINE
(((IFBIG (LAMBDA (V C1 C2) (COND ((BIGP V) C1) (T C2)))) (MAIN (LAMBDA
NIL (IFBIG 12 (PRINT (QUOTE YES)) (PRINT (QUOTE
 NO)))))))

END OF EVALQUOTE, VALUE IS ..
*TRUE*

FUNCTION   EVALQUOTE   HAS BEEN ENTERED, ARGUMENTS..
MAIN
NIL

YES
NO
END OF EVALQUOTE, VALUE IS ..
YES
```

```
THE TIME ( 0/ 0  000.0) HAS COME, THE WALRUS SAID, TO TALK OF MANY THINGS .....   -LEWIS CARROLL-
END OF EVALQUOTE OPERATOR
       FIN      END OF LISP RUN
```

Note how the output is structured—statements are executed by feeding them to EVALQUOTE, the special variant of EVAL that we encountered on page 72 and which quotes its arguments. There is still the uncertainty around "should we use M-expressions or S-expressions?" in that how we invoke things, like BIGP(6) more resembles the regular mathematical notation for functions in the M notation, and not S-expression form (BIGP 6) we use today when interacting with a Lisp system. Finally, note the lack of interactivity: we created a batch job, fed it to the Lisp interpreter, and received its output. A far cry from the expectations of today's Lisp hackers!

In any case, back to the code: we define BIGP and test it with two values. To help you read the output, here is the output corresponding to the first test, BIGP(6):

```
  FUNCTION EVALQUOTE HAS BEEN ENTERED, ARGUMENTS..
 BIGP
 (6)


END OF EVALQUOTE, VALUE IS ..
NIL
```

It returns NIL, which is correct because that is the value LISP 1.5, and many later ones, uses for false. In the full output you can see that BIG(12) returns *TRUE* so all is well there. We then define IFBIG and MAIN and call it. Let's focus on the output there, try to understand what happens:

```
  FUNCTION EVALQUOTE HAS BEEN ENTERED, ARGUMENTS..
MAIN
NIL


YES
NO
END OF EVALQUOTE, VALUE IS ..
YES
```

What would we expect here? 12 being bigger than 10 we'd expect YES to be printed. EVALQUOTE prints the final return value, which whould also be YES because PRINT returns its (last) argument as its return value. So why is NO printed as well?

The reason is with how Lisp systems evaluate function arguments. When it executes this line:

```
(ifbig 12 (print (quote yes)) (print (quote no)))
```

The system will first do `(print (quote yes))` (which prints `YES` and then evaluates to `YES`), then `(print (quote no))` (which evaluates analogously to `NO`), then calls `IFBIG` with the arguments `12`, `YES`, and `NO`. Clearly, this eager evaluation does not work and that is why LISP 1.5 introduced "special forms". Because, come to think of it, how can `COND` work if there is no way to tell the system to not immediately evaluate function arguments?

The solution in LISP 1.5 is to use a special tag; whereas normal user-defined functions are stored with their alist having the tag `EXPR`, a special form can be tagged `FEXPR` and this will do nothing but delaying evaluation of the arguments on calls to such a special form, essentially by quoting them. We used `DEFINE` before to define functions (which implicitly tags them as `EXPR`s), but to define a special form, we need to use `DEFLIST`:

```
deflist ((
  (ifbig (lambda (args alist)
           (prog (v c1 c2)
              (setq v (car args))
              (setq c1 (cadr args))
              (setq c2 (caddr args))
              (cond ((bigp v) (eval c1))
                    (t (eval c2)))
           )))
) fexpr)
```

One of the drawbacks of FEXPR immediately becomes clear: it is verbose. Instead of getting three individual arguments, like our failed first attempt, an FEXPR always receives two arguments: the actual arguments, and an alist which essentially holds bindings from where it was invoked. We don't use these here, but we do need to pick apart the first argument to retrieve the three items we really want before we can feed them to `COND` again. Because `C1` and `C2` are now s-expressions, we need to feed them back to the Lisp interpreter by using `EVAL` on them when we want to actually execute them; in this way, `IFBIG` now controls evaluation and will, indeed, only actually execute the clause that matches the condition. Once we slot this new definition into our code, we get:

```
  FUNCTION   EVALQUOTE   HAS BEEN ENTERED, ARGUMENTS..
 MAIN
 NIL
```

```
YES
END OF EVALQUOTE, VALUE IS ..
NIL
```

Only YES is printed, as we wanted. A side-effect of the new way of calling the code seems to be that we don't get our final value back (hence the NIL return value), but for now, this is sufficient to prove the point: to implement certain functions, you need to be able to control evaluation and LISP 1.5 has FEXPR for that.

FEXPR works and is immensely powerful: we get the code as pure S-expressions and it is up to us to decide whether to evaluate it, and how to evaluate it: we could transform the code before passing it to EVAL, for example. The extra argument, which we called ALIST here, allows us to prod around in our caller's environment and do, well, really weird stuff. But it comes at a cost: we need to manually call EVAL, which also means that we cannot compile the code that we pass in—especially on early machines, where the performance difference between interpreted Lisp and compiled Lisp could be quite large, that was a huge drawback. When people started working on optimizing compilers, FEXPRs needed to be left out: they do their work at run-time and therefore compiler optimizations do not apply. All that power, these problems, for essentially just a simple moving around of evaluation time: FEXPR felt a bit like using the proverbial cannon to kill a mosquitto.

The solution that Maclisp, and indeed most of the other Lisps that followed it, came up with was as simple as ingenious: just move the evaluation shuffling to the compiler. This is easier to explain by an example, so let's plug in a PDP-10, fire up MIT's Incompatible Timesharing System, and start a Maclisp session (again, see Appendix B for details on how to accomplish this). This is what IFBIG looks like in that environment:

```
☞ :lisp
  LISP 2156
  Alloc?
☞ n
☞ (defun bigp (v) (greaterp v 10))
  BIGP
☞ (bigp 2)
  NIL
☞ (bigp 22)
  T
☞ (defmacro ifbig (v c1 c2) `(cond ((bigp ,v) ,c1) (t ,c2)))
  ;Loading BACKQ 53
  ;Loading DEFMAX 98
```

```
;Loading DEFMACRO 166
;Loading MACAID 120
;Loading CNVD 2
IFBIG
☞ (defun main () (ifbig 12 (print (quote yes)) (print (quote no))))
MAIN
☞ (main)
;Loading LET 98
YES
T
```

One big thing to note is that this is an *interactive* Lisp session. There is even `(ledit)`, which escapes the Lisp session to let you edit code in Emacs! We are conversing with the Lisp interpreter here, and as soon as we close the parenthesis to a matching level, the interpreter takes our input and evaluates it. The ITS version used here is not the earliest version of Maclisp, but in a short span of not even 15 years we have moved from feeding a mainframe batch jobs and restarting from scratch to a somewhat "modern" interactive system.

In any case, back to the code (which we kept as close to the original as possible, even where Maclisp has nicer ways to do things). We again define our predicate, which is exactly the same code but now we define it directly as a function using `DEFUN` instead of having to jump through the `LAMBDA` hoop. Then the big change: instead of FEXPR, we define what looks like an ordinary function but as `DEFMACRO`—ignoring the funny backtick and commas in there for a bit—and then we're back at our main function definition and its invocation. It's immediately clear that the code works, no extraneous outputs, just the `YES` we hoped for. And much simpler than the LISP 1.5 equivalent, too.

To be historically accurate we need to mention that Maclisp initially had a `MACRO` tag for regular functions to perform work at compile time and only later did the syntax change into the combined "defined a function and mark it as a macro" syntax explained below; similarly, the quoting and unquoting shortcuts are later additions. The way things worked were essentially the same, however, and we explain how things work using a later version of Maclisp's macro facility because it is essentially the same as modern Lisp systems.

How does `DEFMACRO` work? Essentially by making the Lisp interpreter/compiler extensible. Whereas `FEXPR` received a plain s-expression at run-time, `DEFMACRO` works with the Lisp system on a much deeper level. It tells Lisp "if you encounter this symbol when parsing code, immediately invoke the associated function". So instead of quoted lists being sent around at run-time, here at compile time, the system sees:

```
(ifbig 12 …)
```

and as it knows that IFBIG is a macro, it proceeds calling IFBIG right there and then. Now, what does this macro function do? At the face of it, it executes a COND statement but that is not how macros work. Macros return *code*, not values, and the code is essentially the macro body with the parse-time arguments spliced in. Here is where the backtick and the commas come into play.

QUOTE was, and is, used often enough in Lisp systems that a shorthand was added: the apostrophe. So, for the "main" code above, in a newer Lisp like Maclisp, the following is exactly the same:

```
(defun main () (ifbig 12 (print 'yes) (print 'no)))
```

Another new addition to support macros introduced by Maclisp is the backtick, `. It does the same as QUOTE, with one exception: if, in the quoted expression, subexpressions are "escaped" by a preceding comma, the quoting stops, as it were, and the subexpression is evaluated instead. Here is an example, still in Maclisp:

```
☞ (setq a 42)
  42
☞ (setq b 43)
  43
☞ (list a b)
  (42 43)
☞ '(list a b)
  (list a b)
☞ `(list a b)
  (list a b)
☞ `(list ,a ,b)
  (42 43)
```

If you understand this, you understand one of the trickiest bits of Lisp, because the backquote (in the "Scheme" variant of Lisp, which we will introduce in Chapter 8, also called "quasiquote"), is used in macros all the time. Here is why:

```
☞ (macroexpand '(ifbig 12 (print 'yes) (print 'no)))
  (COND ((BIGP 12) (PRINT (QUOTE YES))) (T (PRINT (QUOTE NO))))
```

MACROEXPAND is a utility to "expand" a macro, which essentially means calling it to have it return the code it "expands" to. Going back to IFBIG's definition:

```
(defmacro ifbig (v c1 c2) `(cond ((bigp ,v) ,c1) (t ,c2)))
```

If you would define this as a function, then you could do similar things by hand:

```
☞ (defun test (v c1 c2) `(cond ((bigp ,v) ,c1) (t ,c2)))
  TEST
☞ (test 1 2 3)
  (COND ((BIGP 1) 2) (T 3))
☞ (test 12 '(print 'yes) '(print 'no))
  (COND ((BIGP 12) (PRINT (QUOTE YES))) (T (PRINT (QUOTE NO))))
```

All we do is write a function that returns an s-expression which happens to be valid Lisp code. Quasiquoting is a shorthand to allow us to write the returned code in a way that reads nicely, but nothing would preclude us from building the same s-expression manually and returning it. It's just more typing work, and you're unlikely to encounter it in the wild.

* * *

So what does DEFMACRO do, at the end? Define a function that is used at *compile* time (or interpreter time—that is essentially the same) to figure out what code really should come in its place. When a construct like:

```
(defun main () (ifbig 12 (print 'yes) (print 'no)))
```

is encountered by the parser, it sees IFBIG and notices it has a macro with that name. It grabs its arguments, and, like FEXPR before, ensures they're quoted before calling the macro function:

```
(ifbig 12 `(print 'yes) (print 'no))
```

The function executes and returns code spliced with its arguments:

```
(cond ((bigp 12) (print 'yes) (print 'no))
```

And, finally, the compiler takes that s-expression and puts it in place of the macro invocation:

```
(defun main () (cond ((bigp 12) (print 'yes) (print 'no))))
```

Now we have regular Lisp code again that can be fed to the interpreter or compiler as if nothing happened. That is the essence of Lisp macros: code-writing code that extends the parser. And if you extend the parser, you extend the language. While theoretically, LISP 1.5 could do all the things that macros do (and FEXPR probably can do more), Maclisp's introduction of macros gave users a clean, simple, and performant way to morph Lisp into the language they needed for solving their problems.

InterLisp

While at MIT people were tweaking LISP into a sharply honed tool to write high-performance code, a bit further down the road in Cambridge, MA, at Bolt, Beranek and Newman, people went... well, not the opposite direction, but certainly a *different* one. Where Maclisp preferred minimalism and performance, BBN Lisp, late named Interlisp, grew a rich set of tools around it to make programming easier, and richer. It was based on Warren Teitelman's 1966 PhD thesis, describing a system called "PILOT", implemented in, of course, Lisp [78]. The new thing about PILOT was that it was a programming environment where the computer was actively assisting the programmer. PILOT could translate pseudocode into (MAC) Lisp, and could be extended this way as well, effectively engaging in a dialogue with its user to adapt itself to the user's preferences. Teitelman's work was heavily inspired by Licklider's coining of the term "man-computer symbiosis" in a 1960 paper bearing that term as its title [41]:

> Among the problems toward which man-computer symbiosis is aimed–problems that men and computers should attack in partnership–are some of great intellectual depth and intrinsic difficulty. The main problems that must be solved to bring man-computer symbiosis into being, however, appear not to be of that kind. They are not easy, but their difficulty seems due more to limitations of technology than to limitations of intelligence.

Where Maclisp focused on the nuts and bolts and plumbing of a Lisp system, InterLisp looked at how people could interact better with a Lisp system. After its inception at BBN, the project's main authors moved to Xerox PARC in 1973, the same place where computer scientist Alan Kay was already working implementing ideas around user interfaces and object orientation in a system called Smalltalk. Where Smalltalk had an emphasis on end users, Interlisp took similar approaches to support Lisp developers, and both systems ended up looking pretty similar. For example, this is how a desktop looks when starting Medley, a port of Interlisp made available for modern systems:

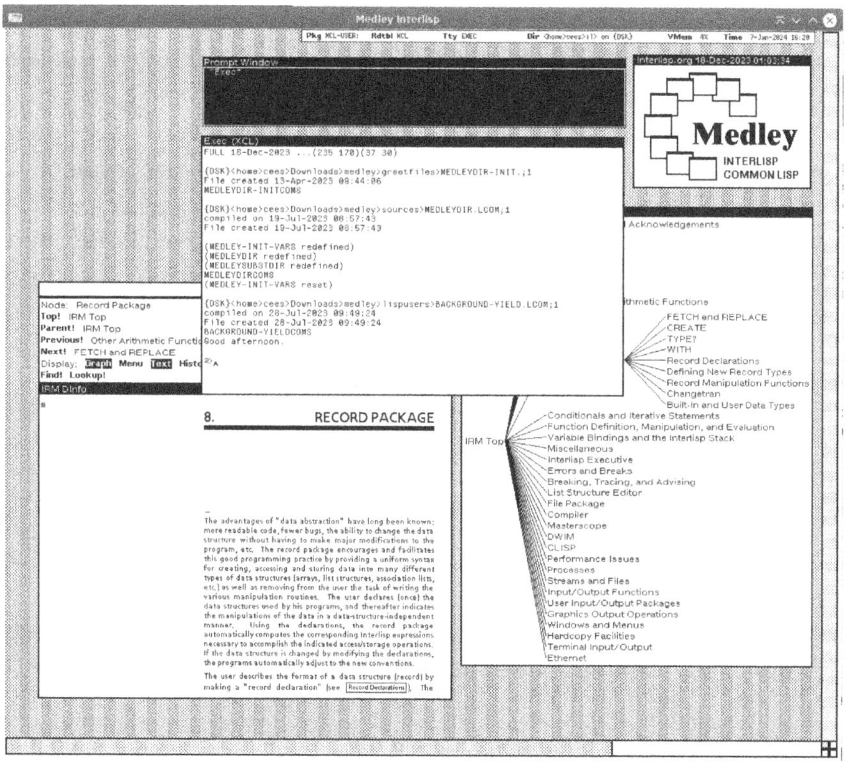

The system comes with a structure editor, debugger, and is pretty much a precursor to the modern Integrated Development Environment that today's developers have come to expect. InterLisp came with a full graphical UI, where developers could run multiple Lisp sessions, open structure editors on functions and variables, and a subsystem called DWIM ("Do What I Mean") that helped fix various mistakes in spelling, parenthesis matching, and so on.

Both Smalltalk and InterLisp were full environments: Operating System, Graphical UI, language implementation, and development tools. They were the only thing that ran on the computer, providing all the bits and pieces needed to implement the windows/icons/-mouse/pointer desktop metaphor developed by Alan Kay's group at PARC. This was unlike Maclisp, where Lisp and an editor provided an environment that integrated in its host OS (ITS in our case). Working with MacLisp is similar to working with a modern IDE like VisualCode: it runs on top of an operating system and often uses it tools. However, InterLisp and Smalltalk *were* the operating environment. This had some big ramifications, not the least the amount of freedom that it offered to users: most code for these systems was written in a single language, whether networking, windowing system, or compiler and utilities. Users would essentially start with a standard IDE but could morph this standard environment into something completely tailored to their problem space: a language workbench, an artificial life research environment, whatever the user is working on, the whole environment changed to assist the work.

Apart from kick-starting the concept of integrated development environment, a concept still used (albeit in a less extreme implementation) by most practicing developers today, InterLisp also spun off a highly successful commercial line of machines that would just boot into a graphical Lisp system and nothing more (or less) by companies like Symbolics. Because even better than a "Lisp operating system" would be a full Lisp "machine", purpose-built to run something like Interlisp from the ground up, not?

Lisp Machines

The PDP-6 and PDP-10 machines were, in essence, machines that were if not created for Lisp then at least heavily influenced by it. A 36 bit word size is ideal for Lisp, with a dotted `(CAR . CDR)` pair nicely fitting inside it making operations fast and efficient and allowing a reasonable amount of memory to be addressed.

Still, they were general-purpose machines and while becoming ever faster, not a perfect match for the workloads that Lisp presented. Garbage collection was slow, and a lot of computer power lay unused because Lisp's simplistic treatment of data types. In 1973, L. Peter Deutsch, then at Xerox PARC, proposed a specialized Lisp system, MicroLISP, that would run much closer to the hardware. It showed that such a Lisp system could benefit in multiple ways from being intertwined with "the bare metal": garbage collection could be more efficient, and type tagging could help a compiler produce much more efficient code. Efficiency gains could also translate into a smaller word size, making the hardware much cheaper to produce.

A year later, Richard Greenblatt started a project to build such a machine at MIT. The machine, dubbed "CONS", was to be cheap (for that time that meant under $70,000), stable, user-centric, would have hardware support for type checking and garbage collection, and would be Lisp from the ground up: just enough assembly to get things going, but Lisp from there. Of course, with Lisp-specialized hardware one could say that Lisp *was* a sort of machine language anyway.

The machine was built and deemed successful enough that work on a successor started. "CADR", the successor of CONS, improved on its predecessor enough that it cost under $50,000, ran on a powerful 32-bit microprocessor, and it was well liked by its users. MIT produced some 25 of these machines and even sold some of them off-campus, and before long CADR machines were the main computing vehicle used at MIT's AI lab. One of the reasons the machines were so loved was that there were hardly any annoying garbage collection pauses: the system, especially its editor, was so efficient with memory that allocations were minimized, and thus garbage was generated only very slowly. So slow, in fact, that a user could work for weeks before memory filled up. The earliest versions did without a garbage collector altogether: when memory filled up, a user dumped all data to disk, restarted the machine, which reloaded the data but in a compacted way. A reboot every couple of weeks was much preferred over continuous garbage collection pauses.

Such success almost begged for commercialization, and commercialization happened. However, there was disagreement between the project principals at MIT about exactly how to go about it. Russell Noftsker was convinced that a commercial launch, with venture capital and all, would be successful but Greenblatt wanted to keep the relaxed hacker culture of MIT. The competing ideas were presented to the MIT Lisp hackers, who sided with Noftsker; a company was started under the name of Symbolics, and most MIT Lispers got to work for it from MIT's premises (in exchange for the company's promise to allow MIT free and unlimited access to whatever Symbolics produced). Meanwhile, people from CDC and the West Coast Lisp hacker culture approached Greenblatt which ended up with CDC bankrolling a second Lisp machine company, aptly named Lisp Machine, Inc. (LMI).

Both Symbolics and LMI started by building (improved) versions of the CADR, largely by hiring MIT people—most of them joined Symbolics, a couple joined LMI, and just two stayed "independent" MIT hackers: Marvin Minsky and Richard Stallman. Apart from blaming the commercial ventures for the demise of MIT hacker culture at the tail end of the '70's, Stallman had strong feelings about how their work turned into proprietary systems and vowed to work on keeping up with the companies, replicating their results, and keeping a freely available alternative alive so that there would not be a commercial monopoly. You might recognize the name: he went on to start the Free Software Foundation and the GNU project, which currently is the larger part of the Linux version of the Unix operating system.

Both companies flourished: the AI summer was still in full swing, and there was huge demand for machines that could support the sort of advanced work that both research and application of AI required. But the machines were costly, and just a short decade later the rise of the Personal Computer would kill the idea for good: general purpose computers got cheap, fast and ubiquitous and the only reason that Symbolics survived longer was because they eventually caved in and ported their Lisp operating system, Genera, to standard systems. Eventually, though, the "Maclisp" style won: general purpose hardware, general purpose operating systems, and then editors and compilers on top of that to write code. Language-specific operating systems were a beautiful idea, but whether we will ever revisit the concept remains to be seen.

The Early Successes

We can't talk about "the Golden Age of AI" and just lay out a timeline of Lisp development, so let's pause and highlight a couple of actual projects. This list is inconclusive, and each project mentioned deserves more attention, but the constraints and pace of a book are relentless—if you come away with a taste for more and follow the various links, I think we can all call it a success.

Playing Chess

Emulating how people think in a computer is a vast topic. Even though early AI researchers were relentlessly optimistic ("we will have a general artificial intelligence in five years" was probably said a couple of times too many in the early ages), they did acknowledge the limitations of current computers and looked for bite-sized problems they could work on (presumably abiding their time while the hardware people did the real work of scaling up their tools).

Games were a good microcosm, and Chess, the king of all games, was being targeted even before computers really existed. Turing wrote probably the first chess program but without a computer, it never really ran; it did probably help him devise the "Turing Test", a test to see whether an artificial intelligent machine was truly intelligent. If you would play chess against it, you should, for starters, not be able to distinguish its moves from a human.

Other great minds worked on the problem: Claude Shannon, the father of Information Theory, published the first article on how to program a computer to play chess, and even the people at Los Alamos National Laboratory, normally occupied with much more grave things, gave coding a chess program a spin.

A breakthrough was when the "Alpha-Beta" pruning strategy was developed by three scientists at Carnegie-Mellon University (McCarthy suggested such a strategy as early as 1956, but they probably were the ones to first create a working example). Allen Newell, John Shaw, and Herbert Simon worked on the problem how to decide which moves to pursue and what not. Chess is a combinatorial explosion when you start thinking ahead: "If I move my pawn D2-D4, then black can move its pawn E7-E5, and then I need to defend my pawn; or it can also move its Knight, ..."—the list *literally* goes on and on. How to decide which of the variations to pursue? Alpha-beta pruning essentially says that when the search for the best move finds a move with a potentially worse outcome than what's already known, the search can stop there. It is a simple approach and the heuristic is used to this day.

Alan Kotok took all this and other work for his B.S. thesis at MIT, and wrote the first (documented) chess program that played a credible game in 1962. The program ran on an IBM 7090 and could evaluate over a thousand positions per second. It received some serious critique by actual chess players, as its pruning algorithm implementation probably was overly conservative and it tossed out pathways to strong series of moves. Richard Greenblatt, also at MIT, contributed an other early implementation, called Mac Hack, for the PDP-6. This was the first program that played in competitions and tournaments and received a rating.

Even though predictions were, at the time, that latest by 1970 computer chess would be good enough to beat grandmasters, we now know that it took until 1977 for a blitz game (Michael Stean bearing that "honor") and until 1988 until DEEP THOUGHT defeated grandmaster Arnold Denker in a regular game. Finally, in 1997 computers settled the score in their favor when Deep Blue for the first time beat a reigning world champion, Gary Kasparov. Currently, there are two rating scales for chess players: the classical ELO rating for humans, and a seperate one for computers which are by now much stronger than human players.

Moving about in a micro world

Apart from implementing games, a lot of effort in "shrinking the problem" revolved around the concept of micro worlds, an idea introduced by Seymour Papert and Marvin Minsky. By having an artificially (and arbitrarily small) context for a computer, it became easier to explore a computer's understanding of natural language just in that context. There was less vocabulary to deal with, less room for interpretation, and therefore (encouraging) results could be obtained quicker.

The most famous of all these efforts was by researcher Terry Winograd, a program called "SHRDLU" (after "etaoin shrdlu", an approximation of the most frequently occurring letters in English text used by early typesetters). Its fame probably stems large from it be-

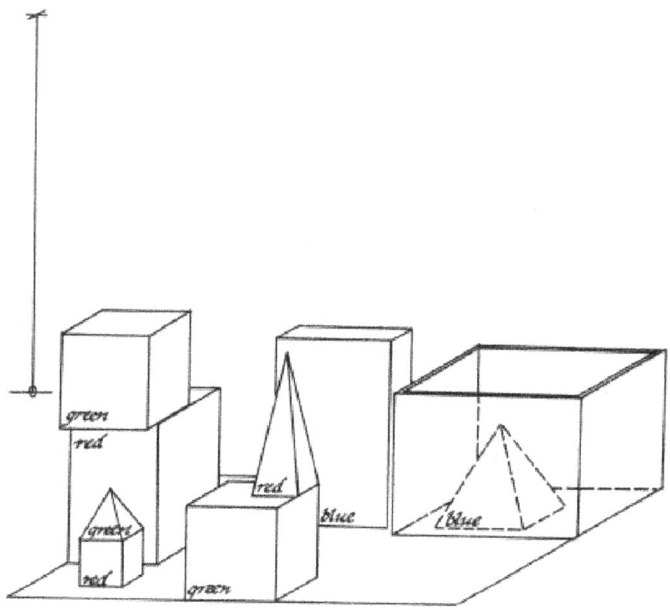

Figure 7.1: SHRDLU's "world"

ing highly visual and therefore easy to demonstrate. From Terry's PhD thesis [89], we see the full world the program operates in Figure 7.1.

As you can see, it is a restricted world: some blocks with different shapes and colors, and a "robot arm" that can pick them up and move them about (a later iteration replicated this imaginary world with physical objects, even more increasing the demoability of SHRDLU). Interaction was in English, and what you could do was truly impressive:

```
> pick up a big red block.
OK.
```

(Note that the big red block is underneath a green block—the program will move it out of the way before continuing)

```
> grasp the pyramid.
I DON'T UNDERSTAND WHICH PYRAMID YOU MEAN.
> find a block which is taller than the one you are holding
  and put it into the box.
OK.
> what does the box contain?
THE BLUE PYRAMID AND THE BLUE BLOCK.
> what is the pyramid supported by?
```

```
THE BOX.
> how many blocks are not in the box?
FOUR OF THEM.
> is at least one of them narrower than the one which I told
  you to pick up?
YES, THE RED CUBE.
> is it supported?
YES, BY THE TABLE.
```

And so forth. Following the dialogue in the thesis shows that the program has an impressive mastery of English, knowing how to work with references to earlier sentences, and of course some knowledge about physics as well. It would refuse to stack a block on top of a pyramid, knowing that it'd fall off.

The source code is available through Stanford's archives [90], and a quick line count shows that we are "talking" to just twenty-two thousands lines of Maclisp, running on a computer that is probably less powerful than your home's thermostat.

Going to the shrink

Another impressive display of how "easy" mastering English is was the program ELIZA, first created by Joseph Weizenbaum in 1964 at MIT. It was a simple system to parse English and try to make conversation, and it is widely recognized as the world's first chatbot. ELIZA could be fed with "scripts" to make it act differently, and its most widely known script was "DOCTOR", which would make it act like a psychiatrist or therapist at an intake, trying to be non-judgmental and non-directive, teasing information out of the patient to direct future treatment.

To this date, ELIZA can be found as a standard part of every Emacs distribution, so if you have access to one, you're just one "`M-x doctor`" away from your own personal therapist. If not, let's play a sample session:

I am the psychotherapist. Please, describe your problems. Each time you are finished talking, type RET twice.
> I don't feel well
Why do you say you do not feel well?
> Because I'm down
Is it because you are down that you came to me?
> Yes
I see... Well, what makes you believe this is so?
> Why I am down?
What do you think?

> I am trying to finish a book about Lisp and I keep missing deadlines

Earlier you said you are down?

> Yes, because of the deadlines

Are you sure that is the real reason?

As you can see, there's some simple parsing of what you share with the computer, and some attempts to bring conversations "back on track". In its current incarnation in Emacs, ELIZA is small: just a bit of 1600 lines of Lisp code, and remember that this program worked, pretty much in the same way, on a 1964 computer.

With early wins like SHRDLU and ELIZA, it was no wonder that people thought that they were well underway to crack the problem of computer language processing and generation. Just some new hardware, some more complex programs, done. However, Winograd, Weizenbaum, and everybody else quickly discovered that their systems refused to escape outside their microcosm: making it more general invariably ended up in failure, and during the '70s, this path of research was all but abandoned.

Playing the expert

One thing that did see some initial success (as far as "industry adoption" is the measure here) is the concept of Expert Systems. The idea is simple: talk to some experts in a certain field, write down all their knowledge in a computer accessible form, add some software to look things up, and everybody can now use The Computer to be An Expert.

While creating a knowledge base as part of AI research was done all the way back to the earliest days, it was computer scientist Edward Feigenbaum who first formally described them while working Stanford at a project called the "Heuristic Programming Project". Before, informal expert systems existed but the focus was more on reasoning, logic, and less on just amassing data to operate on. While prior research focused on general problem solving in micro worlds, the focus of expert systems were on specific problem solving in specific areas of expertise, like diagnosing infectious diseases. You could tell the computer the symptoms a patient has and the results of lab tests, and the expert system—which has a database full of knowledge about infectious diseases, and only that—spits out potential diseases that may ail the patient.

Prolog

Let's make a quick sidestep to another language that made it big in those days in the field of AI and especially for Expert Systems. In the US, most development around expert systems started in Lisp, and then progressed to expert system "shells", generic software that could be turned into a specific expert by feeding it knowledge and rules and heuristics. But you can't talk about expert systems without mentioning the Prolog programming language, which was the tool of choice for most European researchers. In a nutshell, Prolog is a declarative programming language: you tell the computer the rules, and the computer sorts out what needs to be done. This can feel like nothing short of magic, for example when trying to solve the Towers of Hanoi.

In case you have never heard of it: The Towers of Hanoi is a puzzle usually presented as an allegory about Vietnamese Monks that spend their time moving differently sized disks from one stack to another one. All disks started, aeons ago, nicely stacked by size with the largest one on the bottom and the smallest one on top. The rules the monks need to follow are simple: they can never put a larger disk on a smaller one, they can use a third stack for temporary storage, and once all sixty-four disks have been moved, the world will end. Minus the world-ending bit, the code looks like this in Prolog:

```
move(1,X,Y,_) :-
   write('Move top disk from '),
   write(X),
   write(' to '),
   write(Y),
   nl.
move(N,X,Y,Z) :-
   N>1,
   M is N-1,
   move(M,X,Z,Y),
   move(1,X,Y,_),
   move(M,Z,Y,X).
```

All we do here is lay out the rules. The disks are numbered 1..N from top to bottom, and `X`, `Y`, `Z` are the towers. The first clause says that to move the top disk, we can simply move it and we do that by printing the move. To move another disk, we move the disk above it (indicated by `N - 1`) to the auxiliary stack, then our target disk is the top disk so we can simply move it, then we move the disk above it back. Of course, if we want to move a disk that has more than one disk above it, the whole program recurses. To move the third disk, you move the second disk first, which requires moving the top disk, etc. In GNU Prolog:

```
☞ $ gprolog hanoi.prolog
GNU Prolog 1.5.0 (64 bits)
Compiled Jul  8 2021, 09:35:47 with gcc
Copyright (C) 1999-2024 Daniel Diaz

☞ | ?-  [hanoi].
compiling hanoi.prolog for byte code...
hanoi.prolog compiled, 8 lines read - 1427 bytes written, 5 ms

☞ | ?-  move(4,first,second,aux).
Move top disk from first to aux
Move top disk from first to second
Move top disk from aux to second
Move top disk from first to aux
Move top disk from second to first
Move top disk from second to aux
Move top disk from first to aux
Move top disk from first to second
Move top disk from aux to second
Move top disk from aux to first
Move top disk from second to first
Move top disk from aux to second
Move top disk from first to aux
Move top disk from first to second
Move top disk from aux to second
```

Trace the steps if you want, it's a correct solution. Writing down the rules and just letting the computer figure out how to achieve a goal seems nothing short of magic and you'd wonder why we don't all use Prolog all the time. As usual, there are shortcomings that turn Prolog from a silver bullet into just a handy tool for specific problems: the system can often be led into the woods, backtracking from wrong choices through enormous amounts of data which turns the thing into, essentially, a slow memory tester. Early Prologs were very prone to this behaviour, and while modern ones are smarter, they aren't smart enough to avoid issues like these all the time. However, in the 1980s, it served as an excellent tool for expert systems: write down the knowledge and the rules, and let the computer figure it all out using the formal system of logic that Prolog is based on.

Whether implemented in Lisp or Prolog, expert systems were a success and got deployed in many fields: medicine, law, engineering; everywhere where there was a somewhat formal body of knowledge these systems could be employed to capture that knowledge and let either experts have their work checked or serve as a tool to empower people with less expertise to use some of the experts' knowledge.

Connectionism wins the day.

Expert systems, for all their power, also were the last successful "computationalist" form of AI. Since the earliest days, AI research went roughly along two paths: the computationalist path, where logic and capturing knowledge and understanding human reasoning were directly captured in software, and the connectionist path, where the focus was on emulating the hardware of the brain and, well, hoping that it would end up emulating human thinking. Roughly speaking, the computationalist worked from the top down, and the connectionist from the bottom up.

Capturing knowledge and applying logic to it, as done in expert systems, is a computationalist approach; as are the other examples we've visited. This form of AI is very approachable, and—as we have seen—can generate good results on even limited hardware. Connectionists, however, quickly found out that both their methods and their tools fell short of what was needed, and they had to wait until the 1980s before the technique of "backpropagation" made training multi-layered neural networks possible; at the same time, Moore's law ensured that processors had progressed to the point where interesting things could be accomplished, and research on topics like image and speech recognition and self-driving cars quickly took off.

Presently, connectionism has won so thoroughly that, for better or for worse, the term "AI" is synonymous with "neural networks", "large language models", or "deep learning". Most of the research and development efforts seem to be in that area, except for some hold-outs that maintain that computationalist approaches help us better in understanding the human mind and are the only way to achieve computer models that we can explain.

The win of connectionism, which requires pure computational power, also dealt a death blow to Lisp as the main tool for AI. Most neural network software revolves around feeding lots of numerical data to processors that can do things like matrix operations extremely fast, which is more the domain of Lisp's sole predecessor in the world of high-level programming languages, Fortran. The language has had quite a career in numerical computing, and even when it is currently hidden under layers of libraries and Python code, it's quite likely that a lot of "modern" AI code involves running some Fortran somewhere.

While AI has been all but a dead end for Lisp, there is still a whole world of computer problems where symbolic manipulation and languages that can morph into problem-specific languages is very valuable, and we'll see plenty of that in the next chapters.

The Fog Starts Down

– Richard P. Gabriel

Awash in CRT green his white hair and beard and his hinged black glasses were all that was visible—almost dark an hour after sunset: 9:11pm Sunday August 6, 1978. I was doing my routine walkabout around the AI Lab, coming to the front part from the Annex out back where my office was. I had come back in to work on some program or other on a Sunday night when not many would be on the machine we all shared: a PDP-10. Dozens would use it during the day, so night was the work day for some of us.

The Lab is near Felt Lake off Arastradero Road in the foothills behind the bulk of Stanford Campus. At the top of a small rise, the Lab was a semicircle with an asphalt volleyball court at it center. John's office was off to the right from the main entrance; out its many floor-to-ceiling windows you could see a stand of eucalyptus and behind them the textured green foothills separating the Lab from the Pacific. I wanted to see who was in. John's office looked dark from up the corridor, but my route always went past it down to Elaine's office and then Moravec's lair. About to pass by I looked in and I saw him behind his CRT screen, looking at it intently. He often played a solitaire game called "Spider" or read the AP news feed or the BBoard message posting file where threads of discussions, announcements, flames, and screeds were posted, one per page in the page-oriented text editor we all favored. John posted there a lot.

I walked in and stood—John had an informality that made gestures like this OK where others preferred to invite you in. Some time passed while I watched the darkening sky behind him, the view out his windows familiar from my many stops by to chat. He said to me without preface "she's not coming back."

He didn't look up from his screen; I was certain he knew I had walked in. The papers and books on his oak desk and the books and papers piled up everywhere were just as they always were. He was two years younger than my father, and there were other coincidences: John's father's name was John P., like my father; John's mother was Lithuanian like my father's parents; and both John and my father were born in Boston.

My path to Stanford was neither the prodigy's nor the talented's —I was whiteballed, which means that someone on the inside pulled my application aside and said "this one." When I got to Stanford in 1975 I had been assigned to Ed Feigenbaum's group but I wanted the AI Lab. I went up to the Lab one day, rather boldy, and asked Les Earnest—the Lab's administrator—about joining the Lab; he said "ask McCarthy," so I did. "Can I live up here" I asked and he said "what do you mean by 'live'?" Puzzled I said "have an office"—not realizing yet that some actually lived at the Lab in its unused parts. That's another story, though. Over the four years in between, I had transformed the Lab from a Stanford Lisp 1.6 house to a MacLisp one. This meant faster and more modern programs. I think—or I think I think—this earned me some respect from John. I was in effect SAIL's Lisp wizard.

After a minute or several he continued, probably because my silence. "Vera. I just took her to the airport, and she's not strong enough. I'm a better hiker than she is right now. We went just the other week to the Sierras and she couldn't keep up with me. She isn't coming back." I sat down across his desk from him, facing the oncoming night.

Vera Watson was John's Wife #2. Wife #1 had the exuberant name "Martha Coyote"—I never met her that I recall, probably because they divorced before I got to Stanford; but it's possible I did even though Lab spouses were a rare sight. Vera was a programmer at IBM Research in San Jose. As a mountaineer she was accomplished: in 1974 she made the first woman's solo climb of Aconcagua in Argentina; she climbed Mount Robson in Canada and made several first ascents in the Kenai Range in Alaska. But she was foremost a rock climber. I believe I met her once or twice.

Vera had been asked to join the team attempting the first ascent on Annapurna I by an all-woman team: the American Women's Himalayan Expedition led by Arlene Blum. Annapurna is in Nepal and is considered one of the most dangerous eight- thousand meter mountains. Vera did much of the fundraising but on the expedition she had no major area of responsibility.

I sat there with John for about an hour quietly while he stared at his screen—every now and then he typed a few keys. Behind him fog started down after reaching the top of the Coastal Range; coyotes made their racket. He and I were both lousy at personal matters, and I knew he knew nothing more needed to be said. I believed he was crying because above his beard his face was red and shined in the screen's light.

McCarthy was frequently right. Sadly so. Vera did not come back. Not her, not her body—it is still in the crevasse the sherpas saw her in, still roped to Alison.

On October 17 Vera Watson fell to her death on Annapurna I. She and Alison Chadwick-Onyszkiewicz were climbing roped together on a steep, icy slope near Camp V when they fell. Both were killed. Earlier that day they had left Camp IV toward the last camp. From there they had hoped to reach the summit of Annapurna Central. They had no sherpa support.

Arlene Blum wrote a book about the expedition, Annapurna: A Woman's Place. When I read it I thought I saw hints: "I shouldn't be eating these, I'm so fat"; Vera was a slow climber the higher up she went; the sherpas called her "Mummie"; Vera was disappointed in her role; Alison was also discontented and wanted to try the more technical, more aesthetic rock-climb route which played to Alison's and Vera's strengths—it would be a better accomplishment than the main objective where the climbers used oxygen and had sherpa help.

But that night all this was unknown, nothing had played out; Vera was on a plane to Asia; I had work to do; John was bereft but I was inept. I got up and went back to the Annex.

Three months later when we knew, I recall walking just before twilight up the short slope toward Felt Lake and watching—for a while—the fog return.

Chapter 8

Sussman and Steele make Scheme

The proliferation of Lisp systems was waiting for a reaction. Much like the relative austerity of neoclassicism followed the overload of frills from the baroque period, the never-ending addition of features to Lisp almost begged for someone to stomp their foot down and yell "enough is enough!"

Now, that did not *literally* happen, of course, but what did happen was the development of a new Lisp that would radically simplify and clean up the last decade-and-a-half worth of Lisp work. This is the Scheme language, created by MIT hackers Gerald Jay Sussman and Guy L. Steele.

Scheme started as a small Lisp interpreter to, among others, help understand the finer details of actor systems as described by Carl Hewitt in his paper introducing the concept [31]. Actors, in Hewitt's paper, are a highly precise concept but we can make do with a basic definition here: think of them as self-contained computations that are part of a bigger whole, run independently, and communicate through the exchange of messages. A bunch of tiny computers talking to each other. If you think that this is a bit like objects, you're right on the money but that's a story for another time.

In Sussman and Steele's 1975 paper, *SCHEME: An Interpreter For Extended Lambda Calculus* [77], they introduce the system as:

> Inspired by ACTORS, we have implemented an interpreter for a LISP-like language, SCHEME, based on the lambda calculus, but extended for side effects, multiprocessing, and process synchronization. The purpose of this implementation is tutorial.

They go on to list some points that are important to them, which mostly revolve around clarifying existing LISP constructs and simplifying these concepts to land at a language that was exceptionally well-suited for experimentation with programming semantics and style. Their first version of the language was called "Schemer" but ITS had a six character limit, so "Scheme" was the name that stuck.

This first version of Scheme was written in Maclisp in around 700 lines of code for the basic interpreter. This small bit of code contains enough to implement a multiprocessing system, including critical sections (`EVALUATE|UNINTERRUPTIBLY`), all hacked together on top of a Maclisp function, `ALARMCLOCK` that can send timed interrupts to Lisp programms on ITS and Multics. We should be fine using the term "hack" here—in the 1970s it did not have the pejorative meaning that it carries today; rather, it was a badge of honor.

Closures, actors: all the same thing

When Sussman and Steele implemented Scheme, actors were front-of-mind and Scheme contained a little actor system on top of the machinery they built in Maclisp to support all that. One of the things they added, to make things nice and transparent, was a function called `ALPHA` that looked the same as `LAMBDA` but returned an anonymous actor instead of an anonymous function or "closure". Then, "invoking" this thing would just send the passed in arguments as a message to the actor, which would return a message that was the return value. A neat idea to make the step from "function-oriented" programming to "actor-oriented" programming simpler.

Much to their surprise, when implementing `ALPHA`, they found that the code was identical to `APPLY` in every sense, except for the lower-level primitive it used! They stumbled upon somewhat of a discovery that implicated that closures and actors are actually the same thing. Not only proved this helpful in further understanding actors, but it also validated their hypothesis that a small, lexically scoped language like Scheme would make for a very powerful programming language and computing research platform.

Tail recursion

However neat the multiprocessing, the first Scheme presentation focuses on computation, and specifically on *recursive* computation. It uses our friend the factorial function, which has a simple definition in scheme:

```
(define fact (lambda (n)
  (if (= n 0)
```

```
    1
    (* n (fact (- n 1))))))
```

Even without an introduction to Scheme, this should be pretty clear. Now, if we run this manually, tracing the execution steps, we'd get an ever-larger expansion, as it were. Quoting from the paper:

☞
```
> (fact 3)
(if (= 3 0) 1 (* 3 (fact (- 3 1))))
```

Essentially, what we're doing here is treating the function as a function in Church's lambda calculus, and we simply expand by substitution. Next, executing the conditional, the multiplication, and the subtraction gives:

```
(* 3 (fact (- 3 1)))
(* 3 (fact 2))
```

Let's continue to see where this lambda-calculus-like expansion leads us:

```
(* 3 (if (= 2 0 1 (* 2 (fact (- 2 1))))))
(* 3 (* 2 (fact (- 2 1))))
(* 3 (* 2 (fact 1)))
(* 3 (* 2 (if (= 1 0) 1 (* 1 fact (- 1 1)))))
(* 3 (* 2 (* 1 (fact (- 1 1)))))
(* 3 (* 2 (* 1 (fact 0))))
(* 3 (* 2 (* 1 (if = 0 0) 1 (* 0 (fact - 0 1)))))
(* 3 (* 2 (* 1 (* 1 1))))
(* 3 (* 2 (* 1 1)))
(* 3 (* 2 1))
(* 3 2)
6
```

Just simple substitution gave us the correct answer. Technically, we could have done the same substitution process for + and *, but this example is long enough. Note, though, that the expression gets longer and longer before we got rid of all the `FACT` function calls that kept appearing and we finally could start on a path towards simplification. However a computer calculates this recursion, it needs to do the same. It must keep all that state around, and that can be prohibitively expensive. Sussman and Steele came up with an alternative that iterates instead; however, it looks like just a more complex recursive function! Here it is:

```
(define fact
  (lambda (n)
```

```
(labels ((fact1
  (lambda (m ans)
    (if (= m 0)
      ans
      (fact1 (- m 1) (* m ans))))))
(fact1 n 1))))
```

LABELS defines a local function, pretty much the plural form of the LABEL function we already encountered. So let's go at it again, and just do expansions to see where it leads us. First, we essentially "jump" into the inner function:

☞
```
> (fact 3)
(fact1 3 1)
```

As you can see from the function definition, we now just proceed with calls to the inner FACT1 local function. Let's do a couple of steps:

```
(if (= 3 0) 1 (fact1 (- 3 1) (* 3 1)))
(fact1 (- 3 1) (* 3 1))
(fact1 2 3)
```

Interesting—we're back where we started, just with different arguments to the local function. Again:

```
(if (= 2 0) 3 (fact1 (- 2 1) (* 2 3)))
(fact1 (- 2 1) (* 2 3))
(fact1 1 6)
```

Still, nothing of the "growing and shrinking" behaviour we saw before. And indeed, if we keep doing this, we finish with what might be called a "flat profile":

```
(if (= 1 0) 6 (fact1 (- 1 1) (* 1 6)))
(fact1 (- 1 1) (* 1 6))
(fact1 0 6)
(if (= 0 0) 6 (fact1 (- 0 1) (* 0 6)))
6
```

Note that we did not do anything special—in "lambda calculus" style, we just substituted expressions in a loose following of Church's original rules. Somehow, the second factorial function is setup so that the state of the computation is not kept in an every-widening and then shrinking expression, but in the two variables.

The biggest difference between the two versions is in how and where they call themselves. The first one calls itself with this:

```
(* n (fact (- n 1)))
```

and the second one with this:

```
(fact1 (- m 1) (* m ans))
```

Can you spot the difference? If you worked with recursion before, the answer is simple: in the second version, the call-to-self is the *last* thing to happen; in the first one, we call ourselves but then have to take the answer and do a multiplication with it. It turns out that this mechanical substitution process turns into iteration if the recursion happens as the very last thing, and the term for this is *tail recursion*.

The beauty of this all: tail recursion can be detected by a smart parser and turned from recursion into iteration because we don't need to keep intermediate results. The process is called *tail call optimization* and was part of Scheme from day one. That you can arrive at such a result by just doggedly going through the steps of, essentially, the rules of applying the lambda calculus is nothing short of wonderful. Adding an accumulator to store intermediate results instead of relying on, in most cases, the computer's stack to do the same is a "trick" that can turn many recursive functions into properly tail-recursive ones so that they can be run iteratively, using less space.

Lexical scope

Another innovation was the elimination of dynamic scoping in favour of lexical scoping. In the section on LISP 1.5 we saw how the dynamic scoping of variables could lead to confusion; confusion that was dubbed "the FUNARG problem" and led to a lot of discussion in academic circles. To recap, Lisp's default way of looking up variables is to search in the execution environment. A quick example in a modern Lisp that uses dynamic variables (Common Lisp in this case, which uses dynamic binding by default for global variables defined with DEFVAR):

```
☞ > (defvar x 99)
X
☞ > (defun getx () x)
GETX
☞ > (getx)
99
☞ > (let ((x 1)) (getx))
1
☞ > (getx)
99
```

The LET binding "overwrites" the value of the variable *X* before calling GETX, so during the invocation inside the LET binding the variable is assigned that value; after it, the old value pops back up.

Note that you can only figure out what will happen from the source code by tracing through it, like a sort of human single-stepping debugger. The GETX code itself does not give any indication where X could be set, it can happen all over the place. This is a trivial example, but this gets messy quick. It has some powerful uses, but its counterpart, lexical binding, is overall simpler to follow. To demonstrate:

```
☞ > (defvar bumpit nil)
BUMPIT
☞ > (defvar getit nil)
GETIT
☞ > (let ((y 1))
      (setq bumpit (lambda () (setq y (+ y 1))))
      (setq getit (lambda () y)))
<FUNCTION (LAMBDA ()) {1003B53f3B}>
☞ > (funcall bumpit)
2
☞ > (funcall bumpit)
3
☞ > (funcall getit)
3
☞ > y
The variable Y is unbound.
```

The code is a bit more complex here, but essentially we store two lambda functions in BUMPIT and GETIT inside the LET binding. LET has a lexically scoped (local) variable Y, which these functions both access. Using FUNCALL, we invoke the two Lambda functions a couple of times seeing the value of Y change (why we need FUNCALL here is something we'll get to). Finally, we try to access Y and get an error—Y only exists inside the LET, not outside it. It is now trivial to figure out how Y can be changed: reading that little bit of code in the LET is all you need to do, anything else cannot possible access or, worse, change the value. The term "lexical" comes from greek *lexikos*, "pertaining to words". With lexical scoping, the words in the code tell you the scope of a variable and you can safely contain what happens to it. This is exactly the sort of thing you want when implementing actors, which are supposed to encapsulate their state much like objects do.

Shared namespace

Consider the Lisp code above, where we used `FUNCALL` to invoke a Lambda expression stored in a variable. Why is that? This was an example in Common Lisp, which has, like LISP 1.5 and most Lisps that followed it, different storage for functions and variables. In LISP 1.5, variable values are stored as APVALs on a single association list and functions as EXPRs. The system had some rules for where to look things up—depending on how a symbol was used, etcetera, but later systems like Common Lisp made this separation explicit: values are values and functions are functions, and they are treated separately. So, in Common Lisp:

```
> (setq a 42)
42
> a
42
> (setq b (lambda () 42))
<FUNCTION (LAMBDA ()) {53735B4B}>
> b
<FUNCTION (LAMBDA ()) {53735B4B}>
> (b)
debugger invoked on a UNDEFINED-FUNCTION....
> (defun b () 42)
B
> (b)
42
```

As you can see, we can't just assign `B` a lambda expression and then execute it as a function; conversely, we can use the same name `B` as a function and execute it. If we want to cross the realm from data to function, as it were, we can do that but need to make that explicit; this is where `FUNCALL` comes in:

```
> (setq c (lambda () 42))
<FUNCTION (LAMBDA ()) {53735E6B}>
> (funcall c)
42
```

There are tons of technical arguments around the pros and cons of separate namespaces, and Gabriel and Pitman did a quite technical review of the topic [24]; here, it suffices to say that Scheme took the simplest option, there is only one namespace and functions and variables share it:

```
> (define a 42)
```

```
   a 42
☞ > (define (a) 42)
   a
   <procedure a ()>
☞ > (a)
   42
```

Hygienic macros

We saw before that Maclisp introduced `DEFMACRO` to help users write high-level code. Essentially, macros allow you to splice code into templates of sorts, and that comes with problems if the splicer and the splicee use the same names. Consider this code:

```
(defmacro my-or (a b)
  `(let ((tmp ,a))
    (cond
      (tmp tmp)
      (t ,b))))
```

This macro returns `A` if it is true, otherwise `B`. Because either clause can have side effects, it evaluates `A` once and keeps it in a local temporary variable. This way, `A` and `B` are both evaluated not more than once, which is what a caller would expect, and indeed, things work nicely:

```
☞ > (my-or (progn (print "A") t) (print "B"))
   "A"
   T
```

All good, nothing to see, you say? Well… what about this:

```
☞ > (let ((tmp "B"))
        (my-or (progn (print "A") nil) (print tmp)))
   "A"
   NIL
   NIL
```

Now, that wasn't expected! The first clause returns false (`nil`), so the second clause should print "B", not `NIL`. But it's not hard to spot the error when we ask `MACROEXPAND` to tell us what is going on:

```
☞ > (macroexpand '(my-or (progn (print ``A'') nil) (print tmp)))
   (LET ((TMP (PROGN (PRINT ``A'') NIL)))
     (COND (TMP TMP) (T (PRINT TMP))))
```

This code gets spliced into our (let ((tmp "B")) ...) resulting in the complete expansion:

```
(LET ((TMP ``B''))
  (LET ((TMP (PROGN (PRINT ``A'') NIL)))
    (COND (TMP TMP) (T (PRINT TMP)))))
```

We used the same variable name as the macro and now it's getting all mixed up. Old Lispers probably called this code dirty and the name that stuck was "unhygienic macros". The problem of splicing code in code and getting names mixed up is as old as Lisp itself, and LISP 1.5 already had a solution for this: a function named GENSYM which generates a special symbol that can not be defined otherwise and returns a unique symbol every time it gets called. This way, macro writers can generate unique variable names and thus wash them clean and return them to proper hygience. For example:

```
(defmacro my-or (a b)
  (let ((tmp (gensym)))
    `(let ((,tmp ,a))
      (cond (,tmp ,tmp) (t ,b)))))
```

This works much better:

```
☞ > (let ((tmp "B")) (my-or (progn (print "A") nil) (print tmp)))
"A"
"B"
"B"
```

(Note that the second "B" is the return value of the print function which becomes the return value of the whole expression, it is still executed only once). This is what we want and MACROEXPAND shows us that with this version, there is no risk of confusion:

```
☞ > (macroexpand '(my-or (progn (print ``A'') nil) (print tmp)))
(LET ((#:G194 (PROGN (PRINT ``A'') NIL)))
  (COND (#:G194 #:G194) (T (PRINT TMP))))
```

The macro uses the generated symbol, in this case #:G194, and our calling code's TMP is left alone. All is good. However, if you followed along closely you can see that while Lisp changed in how it allows us to do this sort of programming, nasty surprises keep lurking around the corner and it is never completely safe or clean. You need to pay attention to these little gotchas.

* * *

Scheme emphasizes safety and cleanliness, as you can't do language research when the foundation is messy. While Sussman and Steele use plenty of Maclisp macros to implement their language, the language itself and the paper presenting it is silent on the subject. Scheme did not come with macros. Probably, people asked about this because in 1978, in the Revised Report on Scheme [38], macros are introduced. The revised report is also more normative than the original paper and starts talking about mandatory and optional parts of the language—clearly, Scheme was spreading its wings. Macros are introduced with a lot of optionality:

> A SCHEME implementation should have one or more ways for the user to extend the inventory of magic words. The methods provided will vary from implementation to implementation.

The revised version of Scheme comes with two macros: `SCHMAC` is system-dependent for the Maclisp implementation of Scheme on the PDP-10—while ostensibly a Scheme facility, the body of a `SCHMAC` macro is in Maclisp. This makes sense, probably, as Maclisp has access to a lot of (system-dependent) things that Scheme doesn't have, so Scheme can be extended in system-specific ways that are not in scope of a specification. The authors observe, though:

> It so happens, however, that SCHEME is a good meta-language for SCHEME, and so introducing meta-circularity provides no serious problems.

when introducing the Scheme macro definition `MACRO`. Both special forms are just introduced with their syntax and some syntax for quoting and quasiquoting, but no word about the issues above. For that, we need to step forward in time, again, to the Revised Revised Report on Scheme [1], now by a whopping 16 authors–it looks like Scheme was gaining more and more traction. We're in 1985 now, and we read:

> Scheme does not have any standard facility for defining new special forms.

The document goes on to list problems with macros, like the variable capture problem above, and recommends Scheme implementers to "continue to experiment with different solutions". A year later, the third revision is published, but the Revised^3 Report on Scheme [2] does not change its stance on macros. The experimentation continues until, finally, in 1991, the Revised^4 Report on the Algorithmic Language Scheme [3] comes with an appendix on Macros.

> With the appendix to this report Scheme becomes the first programming language to support hygienic macros, which permit the syntax of a block-structured language to be extended reliably.

Finally: hygienic macros. This fourth revision (colloquially abbreviated to R4RS) introduces a way to extend the language in a macro-like way while avoiding its pitfalls, by introducing a new set of special forms `define-syntax`, `let-syntax` and `letrec-syntax` to essentially be the macro versions of `define`, `let` and `letrec`. All of them invoke a pattern matching language called `syntax-rules` that matches up the code to be expanded with expansions. Even though it's a trivial example, let's go back to `my-or`. Here's how it looks like:

```
(define-syntax my-or
  (syntax-rules ()
    ((my-or c1 c2)
      (let ((tmp c1))
        (cond (tmp tmp) (t c2))))))
```

Essentially, what this says is that there's a new rule for the intepreter, and whenever a *pattern* like `(my-or c1 c2)` is encountered, it needs to be replaced with the `(let ....)` below it. That's all, and it works:

```
☞ > (let ((tmp "B"))
      (my-or (begin (display "A") #f) (display tmp)))
  A
  B
```

The body of `syntax-rules` looks a bit like Scheme, but isn't, and that is a good part of the reason why this works and the equivalent Lisp version doesn't. Syntax rules just pattern match and do a lexical expansion, with a little twist: anything created new, like `tmp` in our let binding, is a newly created unique object; in effect, a mechanism like Lisp's `GENSYM` is working under the hood to ensure that the various `tmp` variables in the example don't clash. However, unlike `GENSYM`, things don't get replaced with on-the-fly generated symbol names. If we expand our code using the mechanism that Scheme provides, something that should not work comes out:

```
☞ > (syntax->datum (expand
☞      '(let ((tmp "B")) (my-or
☞         (begin (display "A") #f) (display tmp)))))
  '(let-values (((tmp) '"B"))
     (let-values (((tmp) (begin (#%app display '"A") '#f)))
       (if tmp (let-values () tmp)
```

```
            (if '#t (let-values ()
                      (#%app display tmp)) (#%app void)))))
```

There's some internals of the scheme implementation peeking through, but the most surprising thing is that all the `tmp` variables print as just `tmp`—for the reader, there is no way to keep them apart. But underneath, each `tmp` lives in its own scope and they are completely different, as the fact that the example works shows.

There's a lot going on around the "simple" pattern matching of Scheme's syntax rules; you can have multiple patterns, declare fixed elements in your syntax, have variable argument lists, etcetera. While not completely as powerful as regular Lisps' macro facilities, it is almost as powerful and usually powerful enough; the trade-off of a little bit of lost expressive power for a ton of safety and a clean macro model that doesn't rely on mixes of quoting, quasiquoting and unquoting is probably a good one for Scheme's purposes of simplicity and clarity.

Scheme in use

Scheme found widespread use in teaching and research, which was pretty much the stated goal of its creation. Reports with revisions have been coming out at a regular pace, and at the time of writing the 7th revision [25] is current—this revision is called "the small edition" as it trimmed a lot of bloat that the language accrued over the years; a "large edition" is in the works. On top of R7RS there is an extensive list of Scheme Requests for Implementation or SRFIs [73]. Scheme implementations will often implement a base standard and then a list of SRFIs.

Structure and Interpretation of Computer Programs

Probably still the most widely-known use of Scheme was MIT course 6.001. an introductory course for undergraduates into the structure and interpretation of computer programs that was taught for over twenty years. The course book, Structure and Interpretation of Computer Programs [4] shows on many more bookshelves than just MIT CompSci alumni—many professional developers who take a deep interest in their craft get the book and work through it.

To say that "SICP" and 6.001 are a fast-paced course is understating it. In the time of just one quick semester, students were taken from "`(+ 137 349)` equals `486`" to implementing a compiler for register machines. Even for software developers with a decade or more of professional experience under their belts, the book is fast, deep, and more often than not, hard. But on top of all that shines elegance, where simple concepts like lexical closures are put to work. It's worth showing a little bit of the elegance that "SICP" teaches.

* * *

Most programming books start with mutating state. Let's say the aspiring coder picked up a BASIC book, there's a good chance that early on, something like this will happen:

```
10 FOR I = 1 TO 10
20 PRINT "Hello, World!"
30 NEXT I
```

The loop counter variable `I` here is assigned over and over again. It doesn't show immediately, but `FOR` is shorthand for:

```
10 LET I = 1
20 PRINT "Hello, World!"
30 I = I + 1
40 IF I <= 10 THEN GOTO 20
```

Remember how we "proved" that tail-recursion was iterative by simply applying substitution? That will not work here. Changing the value of a variable breaks the model of computation-by-substitution, it comes as it were with Dante's warning in his Inferno, "all hope abandon ye who enter here". A much more complex model of computation is needed, and SICP therefore does not treat the whole concept (packaged neatly in Scheme's `set!` function) until the reader is ready for somewhat advanced topics well into chapter 3 (out of the book's 5 chapters). By that time, the student has enhanced Scheme with a simple type system and implemented dispatching on types, then added a flexible way of computing with complex and rational numbers using such a system. All using functions that are *referentially transparent*, or, in other words, work with the substitution model.

Even then, the authors are careful to build something elegant and reusable. If you know BASIC, try to envision this example from the book in such a completely imperative language:

```
(define (make-withdraw balance)
  (lambda (amount)
    (if (>= balance amount)
        (begin (set! balance (- balance amount))
               balance)
        "Insufficient funds")))
```

to show that it works, we fire up the Guile implementation of Scheme:

```
☞ > (define acct1 (make-withdraw 50))
☞ > (acct1 10)
  $5 = 40
☞ > (acct1 10)
  $6 = 30
☞ > (acct1 50)
  $7 = "Insufficient funds"
```

The mutated state here, of course, is the original `balance` argument to `make-withdraw`, and it remains visible as the closure of the returned lambda for the latter's lifetime. There is assignment involved, but it is encapsulated in a nicely wrapped package instead of being out in the open; the big benefit, of course, is that we can have as many accounts as we want:

```
☞ > (define acct2 (make-withdraw 100))
☞ > (define acct3 (make-withdraw 50))
☞ > (acct3 40)
  $8 = 10
☞ > (acct2 40)
  $9 = 60
☞ > (acct3 20)
  $10 = "Insufficient funds"
☞ > (acct2 20)
  $11 = 40
```

By turning something as, well, "basic" as mutable variables into an advanced problem that requires a newer, more complex model of computation (also explained in the book), the authors make sure that even seasoned developers think twice about such dangerous stuff.

Racket

Scheme is like a scalpel, and Racket hones that scalpel to be a precise tool for language research, Scheme's original focus. Scheme, as a language, got something of a following in educational circles, and one of the implementations was PLT Inc.'s implementation that purely focused on producing pedagogical materials using Scheme as a teaching language. As the focus was on the materials, not the actual engine, PLT Scheme was essentially an environment built out of a collection of open source parts, like an existing Scheme library, the WX Widget library to add a graphical environment, and so on.

The engine was called "DrScheme" and the flavour of Scheme it implemented was called PLT Scheme. In 2010, the language was renamed "Racket" and the engine "DrRacket" and that is what we're talking about today. DrRacket is available for pretty much every platform under the sun, and gives an excellent and very user friendly integrated development environment for writing Lisp, both for educational purposes as well as general purpose programming. It is freely available from the Racket website [66], and you are encouraged to install it and follow along.

Scheme, like any Lisp, easily morphs into other things, so quickly new languages were added to support the pedagogical mission; for example, five levels of Scheme starting with a small Scheme for beginners building up all the way to advanced topics like "mutable state". On top of this, tools were added to help students understand what was happening, like an algebraic stepper that lets you, patiently like only a computer can do, step one by one through code showing exactly what is going on. Say, for example, we have a simple program:

```
(define (f a b) (+ a b)) (f (f 1 (+ 2 3)) 4)
```

If we load this in the "Beginning Student" language and run it, we get "10". That's not extremely interesting, but the stepper allows us to see exactly how the answer is obtained, and that's a fun and useful thing to show:

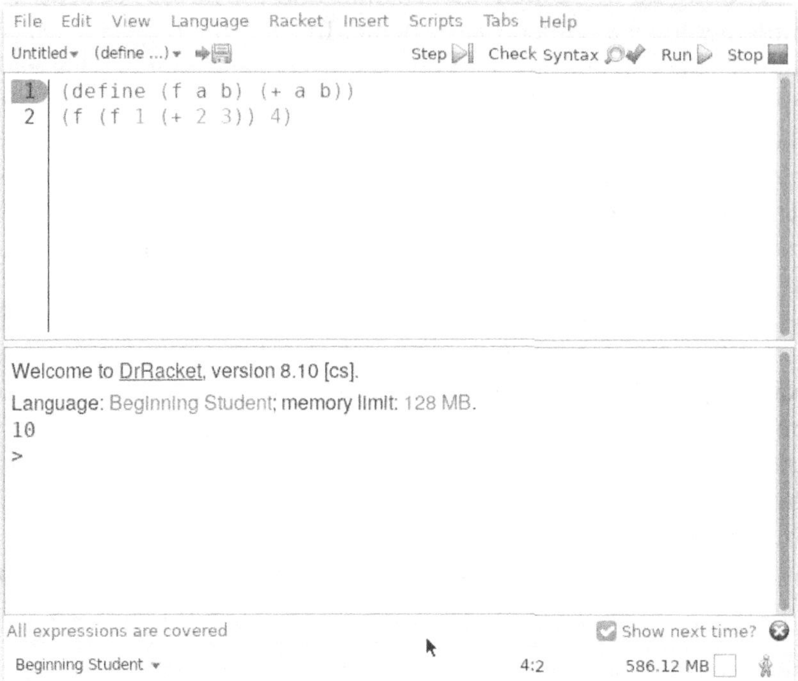

As you can see, we have the program entered, we ran it, we got 10, but now we hit the "Step" button in the toolbar:

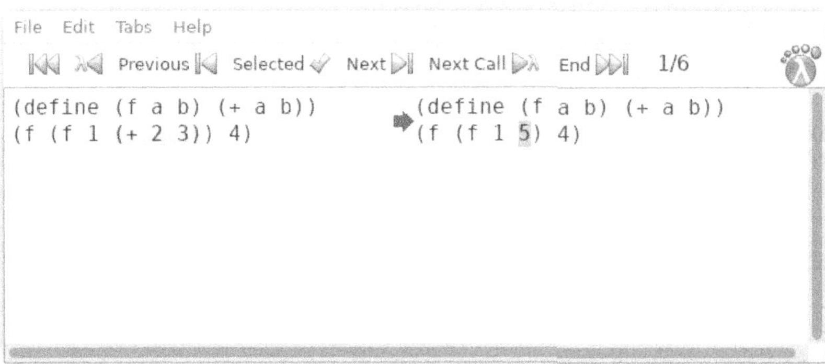

DrRacket opens up a new window and shows us that it started by evaluating `(+ 2 3)`, highlighted in green, and replaced that with `5`, the result of that expression. We hit "Next", and get:

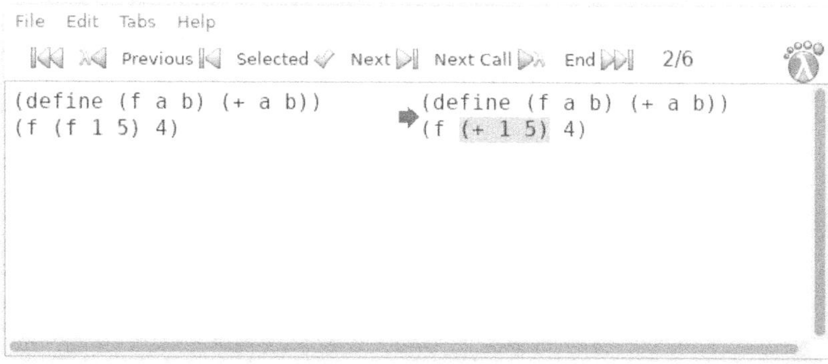

As you can see, Racket now expands the function definition—it replaces `(f 1 5)` with `(+ 1 5)`, which is the sort of mechanical replacement action we read about when discussing lambda calculus. Hitting "Next" again shows the expected replacement of that code with `6`:

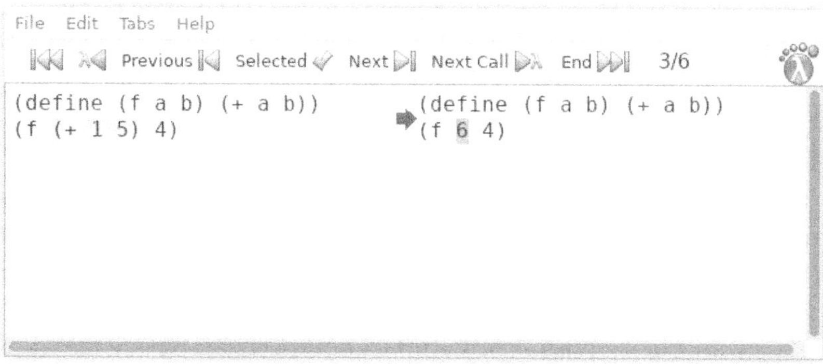

Which leaves us with just `(f 6 4)`, which another "Next" expands to the body of our little function:

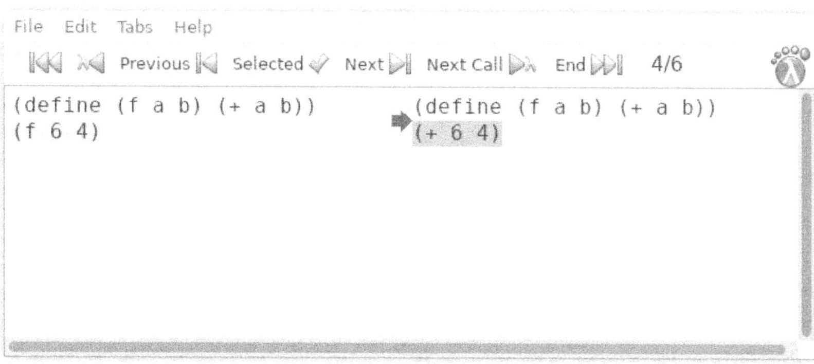

And finally, we take the step to arrive at the expected answer, 10:

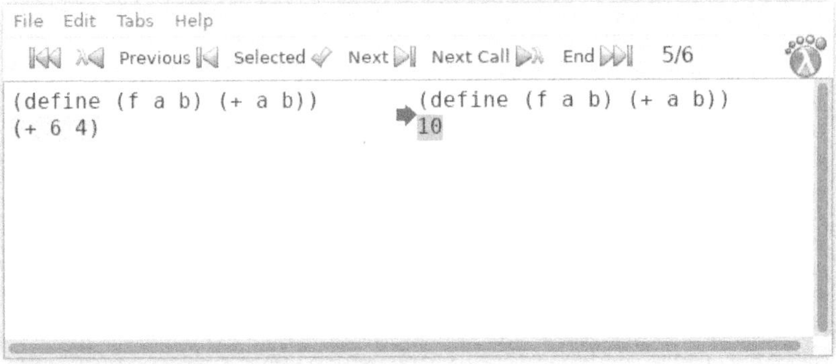

Racket's power is twofold: at every corner, it tries to be your guide. It comes with built-in debugging tools like the stepper, but also normally has much nicer error messages than most Lisps out there and comes with a development environment that does not require a PhD in computer science to operate. Next, it is not just a Scheme implementation but more of a language platform: not only can it run a whole list of variations on the Scheme theme, but it even comes with an Algol 60 implementation and domain-specific languages like "Video", for programmatically manipulating movies. It really epitomizes Lisp's core philosophy of "if you have a problem, first create a language to solve the problem, then solve the problem."

Where Scheme and its implementations like Racket are usually targeted at Lisp-in-the-small (although Racket, for example, comes with its own powerful module system to allow for building larger systems) and specific like a scalpel, some people want to build in the large and like Swiss Army knives better. The Swiss Army knife of Lisp is the system we'll look at next, Common Lisp.

Chapter 9

The Push for a Common Lisp

With the proliferation of Lisps, compatibility issues started to arise. Especially in research and academia, sharing is caring but lack of compatibility between Lisp implementations made working together harder than needed. More important, ARPA, the US Department of Defense's research agency, started to make noise about funding Lisp work—with all the fragmentation, funding would be fragmented as well and the big sort of leaps that ARPA would like to see would be impossible.

It would be that agency, ARPA, that ended up getting the Lisp community together. In 1981, it called a "Lisp Community Meeting" to specifically discuss the unification of Lisp. With the Lisp machine players still in early startup phase (and, being MIT based, largely following Maclisp anyway), the presentations fell into either the Interlisp or the Maclisp camp. Both knew what the meeting was going to be about, both groups—of course—judged "their" Lisp better, so both prepared well. Computer scientist Richard Gabriel, however, did not think in terms of winners and losers and started working on a solution that could serve as a middle ground of sorts to make both groups happy. He approached various people on both sides and pulled them together to define a new version of Lisp that borrowed from both Maclisp and Interlisp.

The new Lisp would be modern: lexical scoping, separate namespaces for functions and variables, support for packages, and an important piece of magic that was first added to Maclisp's main descendant, Lisp Machine Lisp: `SETF`. This function borrowed from Smalltalk's idea of getters and setters; while you may have encountered these in modern languages with names like `getSomeProperty` and `setSomeProperty`, Smalltalk had (and still has) a much simpler convention. Getting a property from an object in Smalltalk is written as:

```
foo someProperty
```

and setting a new value becomes:

```
foo someProperty: 42
```

The fact that there is an argument is sufficient to distinguish between one form and the other. Inspired by this, SETF was first added to the CONS machine. It makes things easy for users. If you have an expression to obtain a value, say:

```
(foo bar baz)
```

then setting that value, where it makes sense, simply becomes:

```
(setf (foo bar baz) 42)
```

This, of course, looks simple on the surface but the SETF macro does a lot of work behind the scenes to figure out exactly what "place" the user meant to set. It is extensible, too, meaning that custom data structures can define custom places that are "setf-able"

As it turned out, sketching out what the language would *be* was almost easier than what it would be *called*. This shared super Lisp needed a name to match its projected stature, but a lot of reasonable names, like "Standard Lisp", were already in use. Given that it was to be a commonly shared version of Lisp the term "Common Lisp" was coined but immediately rejected as, well, not standing out enough. Nothing better came up, though, and references in emails—for lack of a better term—kept referring to "this common Lisp" so eventually the name stuck. Common Lisp it was.

Gabriel started a tour of shuttle diplomacy, probably heartened by the fact that this first sketch was created by an already diverse group. He toured the Lisp machine manufacturers, academic groups on both coasts of the US and in between, and with various levels of success extracted promises to attend further meetings to define a Common Lisp.

ARPA provided some much-needed infrastructure by giving access to its ARPAnet system of networked computers, a system that would grow into what is now the Internet. With all participants having access to ARPAnet services, standardization efforts could commence through email which not only made things much more convenient but also resulted in an automatic archive of the full proceedings of the standardization process. More visits and talks, especially with the Lisp machine vendors, resulted in a group of 33 people from across industry and academia that committed to a serious effort to make Common Lisp a thing.

A few years later decisions had been made, a reference manual was created, and *Common Lisp, the Language* (or "CLtL" as it gets usually referred to) was published. The main implementation was in Spice Lisp, a Lisp that was started before the standardization efforts and while the standardization was ongoing it morphed both implementation and manual to be closer to Common Lisp; CLtL heavily borrowed from Spice and other Lisps, and its implementation served as the starting point for many Common Lisp implementations in the early days. The first specification was published in 1984, and a major update came out six years later (followed by an updated ANSI standard another four years after that—committees don't work quick, and that 1994 standard is still the currently valid standard for ANSI Common Lisp). It is known as "CLtL2" and is freely available on the Internet [37].

Characteristics

Common Lisp is a powerful and large Lisp, certainly if you look at computer capacity in those days. Whereas a dialect like Scheme was laser focused on a small set of problems (exploration of ideas like actor systems and developments in language semantics), Common Lisp was meant to serve as a platform for a wide array of applications throughout industry and academia. Lisp was at the forefront of computing, used in areas as diverse as artificial intelligence research and early computer graphics, and Common Lisp was to be at the forefront of Lisp.

Where Scheme is a scalpel, Common Lisp is a Swiss Army knife. Common Lisp was large, more so when an initially optional object system, Common Lisp Object System (CLOS), got folded into the second version of the language and the subsequent ANSI standard.

ISO and ANSI standards typically are not available to the public for free, so here we will focus on "CLtL2" rather than "ANSI INCITS 226-1994 (S2018, formerly X3.226-1994 (R1999))" as Common Lisp is officially known. The index references almost a thousand functions and variables that are all part of the base language; the book itself is over a thousand pages. In modern times, CLtL2 does not feel *that* big, but for comparison, a random language toolkit from that time that the author used, DeSmet C88, comes in at less than half the page count, for smaller pages, *and* it includes details on all the system-specific bits, tooling, and even details on the assembly language used as an intermediate format; the library and language themselves are maybe half that—say less than a quarter of Common Lisp's size.

One of the reasons CLtL2 is so large is that it simply refuses to make choices on behalf of the user. Well, of course *some* choices were made: Common Lisp is a Lisp-2, for example. But choices like these are necessary—you can't have a language and not define how essential concepts like names behave. But apart from that, it's mostly "if you are able to think of it, you are able to implement it". Where Scheme clearly pushes users into a direction (of what we today call "functional programming"), Common Lisp will just as happily let you organize your code as a full object-oriented system, or as a fully functional system, or as an actor system, or any combination or anything new you can come up with. The macro system allows you to write hygienic macros as well as "dirty" ones, and if you stick with built-in functions for things like I/O your code should run just fine on both a PDP-11 and a modern Macbook.

In essence, Common Lisp is a toolmaker's language, a bit like a lathe is a toolmaker's tool. Once you have a lathe, you can build pretty much every machine under the sun, and once you master Common Lisp, you can build every system under the sun. It doesn't guide you in a direction, that's all in the hands of the user, and sometimes, that's daunting. Sometimes, you don't want to build a tool to implement a solution, you just want to go out and buy one. But if you need to tool up, Common Lisp is there for you.

Common Lisp Object System

To a large extent, this flexibility comes out of CLOS. Even when you think you're not using "objects" when coding in Common Lisp, CLOS is pretty much always there lurking under the surface because a lot of the standard library is built with the help of CLOS. In that sense, Common Lisp is natively an object-oriented language; it's just quite skilled at hiding that fact. So regardless of what direction you take your Common Lisp code into, it is worth to look at CLOS for a bit.

Method dispatch

Object-oriented programming partially started with a wish to have more structure in code. Small programs can just be a collection of functions and probably some top level code that gets invoked by the operating system to start the whole machine (like C's `main` function), but as systems grew people got lost in ever larger code bases. One of the proposed solutions came out of the observation that data that the code operates on and the functions that operate specifically on that data are often closely related, and it made sense to organize code "by data". Abstracting the data away from its physical storage (on disk, or tape, or punchcards) then resulted in a logical grouping of code and data: you define the data, the code that operates on the data, add special functions for "outsiders" to call so you can hide the details of the data and the operations, and you have a nicely encapsulated package of code with a clean interface for other pieces of the system. Such a package of code is then called "a class" (first in Simula, in 1967, then popularized in Smalltalk which was released in 1980 after 8 years of iterations), and classes operate on "objects" and object-oriented programming is born. The idea was that these classes would plug together in some loosely coupled fashion to form systems of arbitrary complexity.

In the abstract, the concept seems simple enough, but there is an enormous amount of details to defined. If you made it to this point in the book you hopefully agree that even a contrived example says more than a lot of words, so let's make up an OO language. We'll fill in the details as we go, and we start by defining a class for two-dimensional points:

```
class Point(x: integer, y: integer) do
  Translate(a, b) := new Point(x + a, y + b).
end.

origin := new Point(0, 0).
origin.Translate(1, 1). # -> Point(1, 1)
```

We just lifted our language from being able to work only with integers ("primitive types") to Points. Nice. And you probably can guess what is next: move to a full two dimensions: we need a Rectangle!

```
class Rectangle(bl: Point, tr: Point).
```

And a Triangle and a Circle, of course.

```
class Triangle(bl: Point, br: Point, t: Point).
class Circle(center: Point, radius: integer).
```

All simple enough, but now we want to be able to draw them. Say we have an existing graphics package that can deal with these primitives so all we need to do is call that library, let's call it `gl`.

```
Rectangle.Draw() := gl.drawRectangle(self.bl.x, self.bl.y,
                                     self.tr.x, self.tr.y).
Triangle.Draw() := gl.drawTriangle(self.bl.x, self.bl.y,
```

```
                                     self.br.x, self.br.y,
                                     self.t.x, self.t.y).
Circle.Draw() := gl.drawCircle(self.center.x, self.center.y,
                                  self.radius).
```

Note that there's already one problem here: we're "digging into" the Point class, breaking encapsulation to get at the primitive values; we also needed some concept of "self", as in "the object we're currently operating on" and in our language, it popped into existence out of nowhere. Another option would have been to pass it in explicitly, but that's a lot of extra typing:

```
Rectangle.Draw(self) := gl.drawRectangle....
```

We've barely started and we're already smelling a whiff of trouble. Now, assume that variables can hold any class, so we can do:

```
shape_one := new Rectangle(new Point(2, 2), new Point(4, 4)).
shape_two := new Circle(new Point(2, 2), 5).

shapes := [shape_one, shape_two].

for shape <- shapes do
  shape.Draw().
end.
```

How does `shape.Draw()` know which specific implementation to call? Clearly, we need to carry that along somewhere—`new Rectangle` should return something that not only contains the two `Point` objects, but also some extra information, like its class. Conceptually, you get `{class: Rectangle, bl: Point, tr: Point}` and then the system knows which version of `draw` to call. When is this decision made? There are two choices here:

1. The *compiler* can trace the type of the shapes through the code, and emit the call to the correct type when the code is compiled;
2. The compiler can just emit the type of the shape in memory, leaving it to the *run time* to dispatch to the correct type.

Making the decision at compile time or at run time has trade-offs. If you can make the decision at compile time, you don't need to decide at run time where to dispatch to making code potentially faster. But your compiler will be more complex, often much more so, and probably will need some hand-holding by the programmer in the form of "type declarations". Object-oriented languages sometimes support both, where you have class that may contain a mix; methods where the decision is made dynamically are then called "virtual" methods.

Our toy language is not that advanced so let us ignore this detail for now and move on.

If you have used OO languages before, you will note that we have not added inheritance. Inheritance denotes "is a kind of", in that a Square is a kind of Rectangle:

```
class Square(bl: Point, size: integer).
```

It is a kind of rectangle, but we can define it a bit more precisely by specifying one point and its size. This way, we can ensure that all Squares are, indeed, square, something that would be harder to do when sticking with Rectangle's "two corners" approach. So, yes, it is a kind of Rectangle, but takes a different form in our system. How do we implement `Draw` here?

```
class Square(bl: Point, size: integer):
   Rectangle(new Point(bl.x, bl.y),
             new Point(bl.x + size, bl.y + size)).
```

This is one option, maybe there is some magic where we `shape.Draw()` won't call the method on `Square` but the one on `Rectangle` instead? More direct:

```
class Square(bl: Point, size: integer) do
  Draw := gl.drawRectangle(....).
end.
```

But that feels like duplicate work. It'd be simple to fill pages and pages with the decisions that designers of object systems need to make, and we haven't even touched on things like multiple inheritance, abstract base classes, and whatnot here. Here's a fun one: in our little hypothetical shapes system, allow polar coordinates (distance from the origin and rotation, instead of x and y) as well as carthesian ones.

Every time you decide what the system must do as a system implementor, you take away a degree of freedom from the system's user. CLOS tries to avoid that in following the spirit of Common Lisp: maximum power to the user. It therefore feels a bit different from other systems; for starters, it decouples class and method definitions because if you *really* think about what is going on in an object system, methods don't really "belong" in "classes". Here's an example: we need to draw shapes using a plasma cutter as well as on screen. Alas, the `gl` library does not support plasma cutters, but the vendor has supplied us with their `pc` library.

```
Rectangle.Draw() := pc.drawRectangle(self.bl.x, ...).
```

and so on. But what if we want to do both? We could pass in an argument:

```
Rectangle.Draw(library) := library.drawRectangle(...).
```

but that only works if the names are the same. For sake of argument, we break that assumption. The plasma cutter library actually has `cutRectangle`. What you really want is:

```
Draw(shape: Rectangle, library = gl) := gl.drawRectangle(...).
Draw(shape: Rectangle, library = pc) := pc.cutRectangle(...).
```

So instead of dispatching on just one thing—the shape—we dispatch on both the shape and the library. Fill out the matrix of methods, and then you can say `Draw(shape, library)`. Most languages currently in use don't allow it, they only dispatch on the object's type. CLOS recognized this issue and decided to address it, allowing this form of "multiple dispatch". And multiple dispatch is why CLOS does not associate "methods" directly with "objects". Instead, you can define a generic method:

```
(defgeneric draw (s l))
```

and then write methods that dispatch on all arguments:

```
(defmethod draw ((s rectangle) (l plasma-cutter-library))
  (l cut-rectangle ....)
)
```

or on just one argument:

```
(defmethod draw ((s shape) l)
  (error "Not implemented for library" l)
)
```

Unlike other systems, there is also no preferential treatment of *where* in the code these methods appear. In languages like Java and C++, classes are typically *closed*—any given class is defined "in one go", often in one file, and if you use a class from a library and try to add your own methods to it in your own source code file, the compiler will have a stern word with you. Smalltalk pioneered a style of extensible classes, and CLOS runs with it: it does not care at all how you specify the types in your `defmethod` calls, whether the types are system types, standard library types, come from a third party library, or are your own: as long as it *knows* about them, it's all fine. Your methods can dispatch on any combination, and if you do the "single dispatch" style that is the only thing that most OO languages know about, it feels the same as if you'd extend a "base class". Remember the remark that CLOS underpins everything? `integer`, `real`, ...—all the types in Common Lisp are CLOS types and you can dispatch on them.

```
(defmethod foo ((x integer))
  ....
)
```

Essentially translates to other languages as "define a method `foo` on the `integer` class", but most other OO languages won't allow you to do that!

If that is not enough, the above only specifies `primary` dispatch. You can also have `:before`, `:after`, and `:around` methods, injecting your own code in your own or the system's or third-party code before or after the actual function call happens. And you can specify whether just the most specific method needs to be called or *all* of them. In a nutshell, "which method do I call" is more akin to a database query then the "I need to find a single pointer" way that most other OO languages do it.

Inheritance

In the dummy language example above, we had a sort of implicit concept of a shape. We did add inheritance, so it is easy enough to make that concept formal:

```
class Shape.
class Rectangle(...): Shape.
class Square(...): Rectangle(...).
class Triangle(...): Shape.
class Circle(...): Shape.
```

Maybe we want to inject "ConicSection" and "Polygon" in there somewhere as well. But if you ever tried to sort CDs or books, you know that categorizing things is a hard problem. How do you order, or categorize, a classical music CD? By orchestra? Conductor? Composer? The soprano you love so much? It is clear why "by cover color" is often the answer. Let's say that we need to have an inventory of things in our system—Shapes or otherwise, but we're only interested in inventorying things that aren't "round":

```
class InventoryItem.

class Rectangle(...): Shape, InventoryItem.
...
class Circle(...): Shape.
```

Where Rectangle was a single "kind of thing", it's now "two kinds of things". A lot of object-oriented languages, including the grandfather of them all, Smalltalk, do not allow for this. You *have* to make a choice. A rectangle is a shape *or* an inventory item. Pick one. The reason for this is often given as "the diamond problem": Say that both Shape and InventoryItem themselves inherit from a class, Printable, which is used for logging and similar things:

```
class Printable do
  ToString := "Printable!".
end
class InventoryItem: Printable do
  ToString := "InventoryItem!".
end
class Shape: Printable do
  ToString := "Shape!".
end
class Rectangle(...): Shape, InventoryItem.

shape := new Rectangle(...).
shape.ToString().
```

What's the output here? There are plenty of options: the compiler could throw an error, or we could invoke a random method out of the two options, or the first one declared, or the last one, or maybe both? One could make an argument for any of these solutions, and that is what makes multiple inheritance such a tricky thing.

There are essentially three categories of OO languages:

1. Those that say "this problem is not worth solving" and only allow single inheritance;

2. Those that say "we need it, but here is the special rules/constructs/... we added to the language to work around some problems";

3. A very small minority, including CLOS: "sure, go ahead, here's the tools to control order of evaluation so you figure it out."

`defgeneric` and `defmethod` put all the power of dispatch into the user's hands; most users will *elect*, if they "go object-oriented" at all in Common Lisp, to have simple classes, simple dispatch, and probably mostly single inheritance because it is easier to reason about but the times that the extra power is needed, it is there.

Classes

Classes are not a required element of an "object-oriented" systems; "objects" can stand by themselves, and as Smalltalk inventor Alan Kay has stressed multiple times, the dynamic dispatch of "messages" is a more important part of the whole idea than the ontology of objects and classes. One of the most widely used languages of our time, JavaScript, revolves completely about objects but has no concept of classes at all!

In that sense, `defmethod` and `defgeneric`, which control dispatch, are probalby more important than `defclass`—and they work fine without a single "official CLOS class" in sight, but to complete our quick tour, we will make a stop in the land where CLOS classes live.

```
(defclass point () (x y))
```

This is a minimal class definition. The empty list signifies that there are no superclasses, and as Common Lisp is a dynamically typed language, we don't typically need to tell the compiler the type of the arguments in advance. It should not surprise you by now that there's not much you get for free, like protected access to instance variables or even a way to create an object, usually called a constructor. CLOS has a single method to make new instances of a class, and that's what you have to use:

```
(defvar p1 (make-instance 'point))
```

Not much else we can do right now with `p1`. We need to use `SETF` to pass data to the class:

```
☞ CL-USER: (slot-value p1 'x)
unbound slot error
☞ CL-USER: (setf (slot-value p1 'x) 10.0)
10.0
☞ CL-USER: (slot-value p1 'x) 10.0
```

A bit cumbersome and not much fun, so there are helpers in `defclass` to make things nice, but these are the bare essentials: a class is just a thing with slots. Remember that we don't have—strictly speaking—"instance" or "class" methods, so the shape of the data is pretty much all there is.

```
☞ CL-USER: (defclass point ()
☞     ((x
☞        :accessor point-x
☞        :initarg :x
☞        :initform 0.0)
```

```
☞     (y
☞       :accessor point-y
☞       :initarg :y
☞       :initform 0.0)))
☞ CL-USER: (defvar p2 (make-instance 'point :x 10.0 :y 15.0))
  P2
☞ CL-USER: (point-x p2)
  10.0
☞ CL-USER: (setf (point-y p2) 22.0)
  22.0
```

We now have "constructor arguments" so we can create an object and set the value of some slots in one go, default values (:initform), and finally accessor methods (point-x and point-y) (and note that SETF can deal with these just fine to use them as "places" for setting values). It is clear here that functions and classes are somewhat orthogonal, there's no real sense of functions "belonging" to classes; having accessors named with the pattern <class-name>-<slot-name> keeps track of what's what, then.

Inheritance is simply a matter of filling out the list of superclasses:

```
(defclass shape () ())
(defclass rectangle (shape) (left-top right-bottom))
(defclass circle (shape) (center radius))
```

and so on. It should come as no surprise that CLOS allows multiple inheritance:

```
(defclass printable () ())
(defclass inventory-item (printable) (...))
(defclass shape (printable) (...))
(defclass rectangle (shape inventory-item) (...))
```

Is perfectly cromulent CLOS. The solution that CLOS takes for inheritance is straightforward and user-controllable: every class has a *precedence list* of superclasses. When querying for a matching method, the first hit is used.

Above, rectangle would have the list:

```
rectangle -> (shape -> printable), (inventory-item -> printable)
   -> standard-object -> t
```

So say we have a generic print method like the one in the previous section, with implementations for printable, inventory-item, and shape, then the search would check rectangle first, but no implementation for that, then shape and it would get a hit. This means that

```
(defclass rectangle (inventory-item shape) (...))
```

behaves differently: the implementation side for `inventory-item` would be searched first. But these are defaults, all can be overridden and if you want to change the lookup order or make it maybe depend on the kind of arguments passed in, it's all there.

The (Art of the) Meta-Object Protocol.

CLOS has a helper, which did not make it in the standard, but is available for pretty much every modern implementation: the Meta-Object Protocol. The MOP is so powerful, it has its own book [40], which contains both an explanation of the ideas behind it and a reference to the MOP-as-we-know-it. It has a cover in medieval style, evoking the idea of a book of magic; and it comes as close to being just that as any book in computer science ever has been. It's worth a read, but we'll just do a quick tour here.

The idea is simple: what is a class? What *is* `point`? It's a thing that, well, describes how to instantiate points? It is pretty much the same sort of thing as `printable`, or `rectangle`: specifications for things—instances—to be created. They have a common set of attributes (a list of superclasses and slots) and behaviours, so they're objects themselves. They are instances of a class of classes, a *metaclass*. The class of a class contains the behaviour of that class, which is essentially "what happens when you create a new instance"—data types get defined, methods are generated, and so on.

If you can control that, you can do all sorts of things: you can inject behaviour (counting the number of instances created, say, or writing to an audit log whenever a new instance is created), change behaviour (assume that Common Lisp allocates your basic slot-names-and-values as an alist, but you know that all you will store is four 32-bit integers so you can map storage to a small binary blob of memory and hugely speed up access), and so on. And the most important thing is that you can do this *orthogonally to "user" code*—you may just declare "the point class is an instance of my slots-in-assembler metaclass" and then use points just like above; all the optimized magic happens under the hood.

Lisp, and especially Common Lisp, is more of a toolkit to create a domain-specific language to suit your problem than a complete "here's how you do it" programming language. It should come as no surprise that CLOS is more of a toolkit to create a domain-specific object system to suit your problem than a complete "here's how you do it" object-oriented extension on a programming language.

CLOS comes with quite some meta-object facilities, but the full power of MOP usually comes as a separate library; consult your favorite CL implementation's documentation for details. Even if you will hardly ever use it, it is good to know it exists and the extent of what it can do. The day will come that you will remember "ah, maybe the MOP can help me here!"

Typing and optimization

Lisp has the stigma of being slow and bloated; something it inherited from the AI winter when only the most powerful hardware could run a decent Lisp system, and even there with some working around limitations (like: "don't ever run garbage collection please, I'll save and reload when I run out of memory"). For some reason, Common Lisp still carries the stigma of being a slow and bloated implementation of Lisp. That is an interesting observation about a system that was completed decades ago and ran on hardware that is currently available for probably the same amount of money as a nice cup of latte at your favorite coffee shop. It is also wrong.

We already observed that Common Lisp isn't much "larger" than modern languages. Let's see what we have to make it "fast" (it is "fast enough" for most practical purposes, and, if anything, less "bloated" than every other language today. But let's see where we can push it). We'll open the hood a bit here, using Intel/AMD assembly code to see what is *really* going on (the following examples were obtained using the SBCL implementation of Common Lisp. Your implementation may emit different things).

```
☞ CL-USER: (defun plus (a b) (+ a b))
PLUS
☞ CL-USER: (disassemble 'plus)
; disassembly for PLUS
; Size: 34 bytes. Origin: #x53734E4A             ; PLUS
; 4A:       498B4D10         MOV RCX, [R13+16]   ; thread.binding-stack-pointer
; 4E:       48894DF8         MOV [RBP-8], RCX
; 52:       488BD6           MOV RDX, RSI
; 55:       488BF8           MOV RDI, RAX
; 58:       FF142548060050   CALL [#x50000648]   ; #x52A00F10: GENERIC-+
; 5F:       488B45E8         MOV RAX, [RBP-24]
; 63:       488B75F0         MOV RSI, [RBP-16]
; 67:       C9               LEAVE
; 68:       F8               CLC
; 69:       C3               RET
; 6A:       CC10             INT3 16             ; Invalid argument count trap
NIL
```

This in itself might come as a surprise: most systems that employ automatic memory management and garbage collection come with "virtual machines", where you essentially run on top of an abstract machine that sits between the programmer and the actual processor and makes all the decisions. Implementations like SBCL, though, emit native code straight away. That's probably one argument for "Common Lisp is bloated" out of the way.

We don't need to dive into the details of this assembly listing too deeply: the `plus` function does some basic housekeeping around making a function call, prepares the arguments, calls `GENERIC-+`, and handles return values and stack cleanup. Essentially we have a thin wrapper around a call to something called `GENERIC-+`, and it should not come as a great surprise that this is a function that can deal with summing all sorts of stuff: lists, complex numbers, floating points, and so on. The "generic" in the name gives a hint that it is likely to be a generic function, meaning that a lookup for argument types will follow to figure out exactly what implementation of + we need to call. As Lisp is a dynamically typed system, our `a` and `b` can have everything—including values that you cannot reasonably sum—so this needs to happen at run-time. In other words: our function is pretty lightweight, but it calls something that most likely is not. We're going to skip ahead a couple of steps and turn the volume up to 11:

```
☞ CL-USER: (defun fast-plus (a b)
☞              (declare (optimize (speed 3) (safety 0))
☞                       (type (unsigned-byte 32) a b))
☞              (+ a b))
FAST-PLUS
☞ CL-USER: (disassemble 'fast-plus)
; disassembly for FAST-PLUS
; Size: 6 bytes. Origin: #x53735176                     ; FAST-PLUS
; 6:       4801FA           ADD RDX, RDI
; 9:       C9               LEAVE
; A:       F8               CLC
; B:       C3               RET
NIL
```

Regardless of whether you know anything about machine languages, assembly code, or specifically Intel assembly at all, you can't help but notice that this is much shorter. All that is left is `ADD` the two values and then some magic to return the result. Short of inlining `ADD RDX, RDI`, this is as concise as you can get assembly code, and it's as fast as you will get. What happened here?

- We told Lisp that it could drop safety checks with `(optimize (safety 0))`; this removes checks for wrong argument counts and wrong argument types. Essentially, "seat belts off".

- We told Lisp to optimize for speed. By default, Lisp will normally optimize for debuggability: not inlining code makes stack traces much more readable, for example.
- Finally, and probably most importantly, we told Lisp to assume that `a` and `b` would always be unsigned 32 bit values.

Armed with that guidance, SBCL knew that it did not need the runtime lookup that `GENERIC-+` provides, it could jump straight to the 32-bit optimized version. Furthermore, as we told the compiler that speed was paramount, it moved that 32-bit implementation of + inline, and then it further optimized things by realizing that the arguments would already be in the right place so it could go straight to the meat of the function, `ADD`. The other 3 bytes are just there to clean up and could be skipped as well by declaring the function inline—that would result in any mention of `fast-plus` to be simply replaced by the single machine instruction, something that you'd usually do but an empty listing is not much fun in a book.

Common Lisp is as fast or as slow as you make it. You can stay safely high level and code like it is, say, a powerful version of Java. Or you can decide to remove the safety belts and code like it is Assembler. All in the same language, and sometimes without changing too much code. In fact, you can make the argument that implementations of Common Lisp like SBCL make for the ultimate assembly experimentation machine, and [71] is a fun read if you're into that sort of stuff or just want to be surprised about just how far the elasticity of Common Lisp stretches.

Scaling up

Packaging code and sharing it, reusing it—internally within an instutition or shared on the ARPAnet: that's a mighty large topic. Coupled to that is the wish to have some sort of scoping for names—that class `point` is carving a large conceptual chunk out of a global space of class names. You have points as addressable pixels on a screen, as mathematical abstractions, even as engineering specifications for sewing needles.

Code reuse also goes into the domain of (packages of) files; in the 1980s, there was not nearly the level of standardization around organizing files that we have today, so what the designers of Common Lisp came up with had to be abstract enough to be implementable on an enormous diversity of machines but practical enough to be usable. Let's wrap up our quick tour of Common Lisp with a look at packaging.

Namespaces and packages

First, we need to get `point` where it belongs. It looks like we were talking about mathematical shapes all the time. Let's start over, now with a proper package.

```
(defpackage :maths (:use :cl))
(in-package :maths)
(defclass point () (x y))
```

That last line should return `#<STANDARD-CLASS MATHS::POINT>`, and it should be clear immediately that this means that our new `point` class lives in the `maths` package. If you restart your Lisp session and just do the `defclass`, it will return `#<STANDARD-CLASS COMMON-LISP-USER::POINT>`, so we were in a package all the time! By default, a Common Lisp REPL session will throw you into a package `common-lisp-user`, aliased to `cl-user`, which saves you from overwriting important names as everything you define is safely stashed away in its own package.

One important thing to note is the `(:use :cl)`. We say that this package uses the `cl` package—an alias for the `common-lisp` package which contains pretty much all of the standard Common Lisp symbols. Without it, your REPL would be way less fun: none of the standard functions will work, because they don't exist in the `maths` package and there is no easy way to access them. There is no set of "default imports" like in other languages. This is yet another customization point: nobody forces you to use the `COMMON-LISP` package and there are plenty of examples in the wild where it makes sense to forego the built-in library.

Let's use this point from the default namespace:

```
☞ MATHS: (in-package :cl-user)
#<PACKAGE "COMMON-LISP-USER"
☞ CL-USER: (defvar p1 (make-instance 'maths::point))
#<MATHS::POINT 100340D473>
```

We have a `POINT` instance, let's set a slot:

```
☞ CL-USER: (setf (slot-value p1 'x) 10.0)
; Debugger entered ...
When attempting to set the slot's value to 10.0 (SETF of SLOT-
VALUE), the
  slot X is is missing from the object #<MATHS::POINT 100340D473>.
It has a slot MATHS::X, while COMMON-LISP-USER::X is requested.
```

What just happened? `X` is a symbol, and namespacing applies to *all* symbols. Even slot names.

```
☞ CL-USER> (setf (slot-value p1 'maths::x) 10.0)
10.0
```

Standard facilities like USE-PACKAGE have options to wholesale import and export symbols, and usually things are setup so that this is transparent and just X will do the right thing, but—again—Common Lisp offers a choice. Note that it is possible for an object to have multiple slots named X this way: one in the MATHS package, one in the GRAPHICS package, one in the LASERCUTTER package, and so on. Again, there are few boundaries on how to organize your code, common sense should guide you into making things not too complex but if you need them, the tools are there and waiting for you to pick them up.

Systems and ASDF, Quicklisp

Packages are not the only abstraction that Common Lisp offers: one level up is the idea of "systems", which are abstract collections of code. Loading code touches the file system, and that was deemed too system-specific for Common Lisp, so this is something left entirely up to the implementation. While early implementations of code to define and load these systems circulated, the community converged in the early 2000s on an implementation called "Another System Definition Facility", or ASDF. The package comes with a library, UIOP, that abstracts away the I/O primitives that ASDF needs, and which can be implemented simply for each targeted implementation of Common Lisp. ASDF is the de-facto standard system definition facility and all that it separates from an official status is the fact that, since 1994, Common Lisp has seen no updates to the standard.

A system is usually a collection of packages in files accompanied by the system definition, conventially stored in the package as an .asd file. Let's stick with the math example and define a system for it:

```
(defsystem "maths"
  :version "0.1.0"
  :author "Cees de Groot"
  :license "Affero GPL"
  :depends-on (:my-complex-numbers-math)
  :components ((:module "src"
                :serial t
                :components
                ((:file "package")
                 (:file "main"))))
```

```
  :description "My first math package")
```

Note that all we do here is describe the system. There's nothing about "packages" or "namespaces" (and the `depends-on` defines to a *system* that our system depends on, not on a package). Just the system, some metadata, and what files comprise it. What goes in a system is up to the implementor, but there are—of course—some conventions. For example, a `package.lisp` usually contains the actual package definition—most simple systems just have a single package:

```
(defpackage maths
  (:use :cl :my-complex-numbers-math))
```

Note that while the *system* `maths` depends on the *system* `my-complex-numbers-math`, the *package* `maths` imports `my-complex-numbers-math` and these are two completely orthogonal and independent things. By convention, though, systems you depend on will provide packages you want to import and, again, by convention, these systems and packages will be named the same (or at least similarly). A single collection of source code (like a Git repository or a .tar file) may contain multiple systems. Sometimes, this will help users to only depend on a subset they need (say, a graphics library that provides systems for X11, Mac, Windows, and generic Embedded GL devices—you can just depend on `graphics-egl`, say, to pull in just what you need). Often, a separate test system is defined:

```
(defsystem "maths/tests"
  :author "Cees de Groot"
  :license "Affero GPL"
  :depends-on ("maths"
               "rove")
  :components ((:module "tests"
                :components
                ((:file "main"))))
  :description "Test system for maths"
  :perform (test-op (op c) (symbol-call :rove :run c)))
```

The two together form a modern basic library, defining two systems, one for testing and one for actual use, so that when you just want to use the functionality, you don't need to pull in testing dependencies like `rove` (one of the many packages that lend a hand with writing automated tests). With ASDF, there is a standard way to define systems and this makes it easy to share code. But ASDF itself only works locally, and we are used to the Internet providing these sorts of "things," so there is still a piece missing...

Quicklisp

Perl, with the Comprehensive Perl Archive Network [15], was probably the first programming language that made it absolutely trivial to pull in other people's code, thanks to the powers of the Internet. It defined a standard for packaging and allowed authors to declare their own namespace and upload their code for reuse. To use a library, all that was needed was to declare it and the CPAN client module, part of most Perl installations before long, did all the work of downloading and unpacking the code and installing it in some shared spot on the local disk. These days, it is table stakes for a new programming language to have such a distribution system; in fact, without it, chances are slim that your new language will gain any traction. But in the '90s, this was mind blowing. Before CPAN, the process was essentially to roll your own unless things really got complex to the point that it was worth adding a dependency: you had to scour Usenet newsgroups and bulletin boards for locations and versions, be able to connect to the correct FTP server, pull down a compressed tarball, then unpack it to see what was in it and how you could use it. With a bit of luck, that only took a couple of days' worth of work (probably more if it was a C library dependency), and more often than not you ended up copying the code into your own source repository in the hope you could track newer versions. CPAN replaced all that with a one-liner. It's probably not too much praise to state that CPAN changed the way the world developed software.

It took a while for this idea to take hold in the Common Lisp world, but in the early 2010s a system became available called Quicklisp [65]. Technically, it is (at the time of this writing) still in beta, but it does offer the "full CPAN experience" that developers have to come to expect these days. Quicklisp builds on ASDF, so that at the end you can just do:

```
(ql:quickload "maths/tests")
```

And have your packages, plus their dependencies, all available to work with. Quicklisp is—how could it be any different—open ended, so other repositories have emerged with different inclusion policies. By now, pretty much every Lisp package you'd like to use is available in one of these repositories, and thanks to ASDF's agnostic stance on where libraries come from, it is easy enough to provide for the missing ones otherwise.

Final words

As said, in the modern sense, Common Lisp is not a large system, but every part of this Swiss army knife comes with awesome power. There is a lot we haven't touched on, with things like the `LOOP` macro for example providing enough material to fill a chapter.

The most daunting thing about starting with Common Lisp is that it just sits there and waits for you, the programmer, to make up their mind not only about what kind of problem is being solved, but about the shape of the language needed to best solve that problem. You're as much a tool maker as a tool user when working in Common Lisp, and that is definitely not for everybody. Once you "grok" it, though, Common Lisp's power is probably second to none and that usually shows both in terms of code quality as well in terms of productivity. It is certainly worth giving it a spin.

But there's more to visit in the world of Lisp, so we need to get on and shift our focus again. The next stop is the grandfather of all Integrated Development Environments, arguably the most powerful editor in the world, and certainly the most wide-spread Lisp application that currently exists.

Chapter 10

Stallman Extends the Editor

In the days of McCarthy, talking to computers happened through punched cards. Code would be written by hand, transferred to cards on a keypunch, the stack would run through the computer and a print-out would show the result. The advent of timesharing changed a lot, but there was still a long road to go to the highly interactive environments of today.

Paper tape was one of the input and storage methods—essentially a long, stretched out punch card. While fixing an error on a punch card was "simple"—just swap the card with the error with a card with the fix—a paper tape was one single very long card. Probably to help fix mistakes, MIT student Dan Murphy created a Tape Editor and Corrector proram for the PDP-1: a simple interpreter that could read a program to apply edits to a character file on tape. With the advent of more interactive modes of operation, most notably through hooking up video screens to computers, Tape became Text but the name TECO remained. Initially, even on a video terminal, TECO was line oriented and would greet the user with a simple prompt:

```
*
```

where the user was expected to enter their programs instructing TECO what to do. The "programming language" was essentially a stream of single characters that, in an imperative style, told TECO to do things to the text.

```
* 5DIHello<ESC><ESC>
```

would delete five characters then insert "Hello". Escape characters terminated commands, and TECO would simply use the first character read to jump to a routine, and the routine would consume more characters as its arguments. Numbers could prefix commands, a system that survives today in the popular Vim editor on Unix-like systems.

For all its primitiveness, TECO came with basic control structures to repeat commands or conditionally execute them, and quite complex programs, called "macros", could be written this way. These programs were extremely hard to read and lots of jokes about just how hard it was to write TECO programs made the rounds, but the language was powerful and therefore popular despite its lack of user-friendliness.

The birth of Emacs

TECO was ported from PDP-1 to the PDP-6 and then the PDP-10, where it received a big overhaul. Among others, it received the possibility to bind keys to macros and a mode where the screen was updated every time the user made a change (normally, you'd instruct TECO explicitly to display some text after edits were made). MIT student Richard Stallman, in the mid '70s, visited Stanford's AI Lab where he saw their "E" editor, which was a full-screen editor that would allow to edit in "WYSIWYG" mode, directly on the screen. Upon his return, he took TECO's display improvements and refined them into a full, E-editor-like WYSIWYG mode that could work on the whole file at once as a single buffer (TECO had explicit commands to load pieces of files before that).

Interactive TECO, still with the obtuse-but-powerful macro language on board, quickly became popular at MIT and caused large collections of macros, or "MACS", to be created. Guy Steele, who we've met in the Scheme chapter, teamed up with Stallman to create a standard set of macros, and they called the result "Editor Macros", or "EMACS".

Even though technically, EMACS was just a collection of TECO macros, in practice it behaved differently enough to feel like a different thing and apart from quickly replacing TECO as the most popular editor at MIT, it also got ported to other systems under names like "EINE" (Eine is not Emacs, on the Lisp Machine), "Multics Emacs" (for, you guessed it, the Multics operating system), and so on. A lot of these "Emacsen" were written in Lisp, as that was more often that not the most powerful programming language at hand.

One of these versions, created in 1981, was written by Canadian computer scientist James Gosling, later known for the Java programming language. While his version was not written in Lisp it came with a primitive version of Lisp, or, rather, a Lisp-like language to extend the system. This language was called MockLisp but as it could not even cons, it probably should not be considered a proper Lisp. Gosling Emacs was available for various Unix platforms and Digital Equipment's latest operating system, VMS, but at a cost—it was commercial software and came with a hefty price tag.

Richard Stallman has always held very strong beliefs around software and its availability, deeply rooted in the hacker culture of 1960s and 1970s MIT where sharing was the default. He did not like the idea of a commercial version at all so he set out to write a version of the Emacs editor that would be freely available. While he started out based on Gosling Emacs, he quickly decided that it should come with a proper Lisp implementation and that decision caused him to replace all but some core code that contained tricky optimized display routines.

The choice to use a full Lisp turned out to be the right one: apart from a small core in C, most of Emacs was written in its own "extension language", Emacs Lisp, making it portable and extremely versatile. Stallman released his "GNU Emacs" in 1985 and it quickly displaced Gosling Emacs as the editor-of-choice on the systems it targeted. Not only because the free software philosophy behind it, but also because it simply was better in the sense that the full Lisp made Emacs endlessly adaptable.

> EMACS VERSION NUMBERS — Emacs was initially released as version 15.34, which is an odd version number for a new project. It makes sense when you know that Stallman started with regular "major.minor.patch" numbering and read it as 1.15.34. However, he soon realized that major versions would likely never change on this project and dropped the leading 1. So, technically, after a couple of decades, we're still on version 1 with GNU Emacs.

Emacs was so adaptable, in fact, that it started to look like an operating system in itself. The graphical version for the X Window System got an icon depicting a kitchen sink, as Emacs was jokingly referred to as "everything but the kitchen sink". With the icon, that could be shortened to "everything". Contributions poured in and in just a copule of years, Emacs came with a terminal emulator, email reader, news reader, FTP client, special editing modes for all sorts of programming languages, a built-in debugger, document processing support for the $\TeX$ typesetting system, and even an embedded therapist in the form of an implementation of the ELIZA program we've seen before.

Emacs survives to this day and is widely regarded as a somewhat weird, but powerful development environment.

Emacs Lisp

But we're here to talk about Lisp, not editors, so let's take a look at how this all works under the hood.

In a nutshell, Emacs Lisp ("elisp") is a classical Lisp-1 with dynamic variable scoping. As you may recall, a Lisp-1 has a shared namespaces for symbols depicting variables and symbols depicting functions, while a Lisp-2 has two such namespaces; Scheme is a Lisp-1, and Common Lisp a Lisp-2. The debate on which one is better will likely never be settled, so it was probably either a coin-toss for Stallman or simpy a matter of expediency, if he thought a Lisp-1 would be simpler to implement.

The situation around dynamic scoping was different, however. By the 1980s, the idea had been thoroughly discredited. Even if it were simpler to implement, this was a controversial design decision. However, it turns out that it is a design decision that works well for the nature of the problem—an extensible text editor.

There is something innately hierarchical in a text editor, especially with the way that Emacs is setup. Everything is flexible and context-dependent, so while there is, for example, a global default editing mode, upon opening some C or Lisp code Emacs "specializes" into a C or Lisp editor, with knowledge of the structure of the code so it can perform simple tasks like indentation but also more complex ones like "comment out this `for` loop". Typically, this extra functionality comes as code that specializes the basic editor.

Emacs works with "buffers", which are open files. At the same time, it can have multiple buffers open that have different kinds of files in them, and therefore also behave differently; but at the same time, everything operates in the same namespace and even memory space—there is just a single, single-threaded Lisp engine running underneath it all, and while it makes an impressive show, once the curtain is pulled away that is pretty much all that is left.

Now, these buffers all behave differently. One may have some Common Lisp code open, another displays a news reader. A third buffer shows an Emacs Lisp debugging session. They all share the same code for processing keyboard input and displaying data, but depending on the "mode" a buffer is in, there is a set of parameters controlling its behavior.

With lexical scoping, calling code in a manner that allows changing its behavior is only possible by passing function arguments. So you have a parameter "A" that you want to use to influence how some core code behaves, you have to pass it around as arguments, no matter how deeply nested:

```
function:
  A = 42
  call subfunction(A)

subfunction(A):
  ...
  call subsubfunction(A)

subsubfunction(A):
  ...
```

and so on. Now, consider that an editor's behavior is not just a single number: it's keyboard mapping, syntax highlighting, things to display on the "mode line", so you'd be passing a whole list of arguments around, up and down, through layers of code that have nothing to do with, say, syntax highlighting. It'd be a bit of a mess.

```
function:
  A = 42
  B = "Hello",
  C = 42.1
  D = [1, 2, 3]
  ...
  call subfunction(A, B, C, D)

subfunction(A, B, C, D):
  ...
  E = 52
  call subsubfunction(A, B, C, D, E)

subsubfunction(A, B, C, D, E):
  ... do something with the arguments ...
```

Dynamic scoping has a well-deserved reputation for being tricky to reason about, but as always, there's a trade-off. For most code, the "cost" of making reasoning about things hard is too high, but for an extensible editing platform like Emacs, it was the right decision. Here's a contrived example:

```
function:
  A = 42
  B = "Hello",
  C = 42.1
  D = [1, 2, 3]
  ...
```

```
  call subfunction()

subfunction():
  ...
  E = 52
  call subsubfunction(E)

subsubfunction(E):
  ... A, B, C, D are in dynamic scope, E is a relevant argument ...
```

Moreover, if we have a new function in the chain, so one that provides for a temporary editing mode that is a little bit tweaked, and would introduce a new parameter/setting, named "F", it's an easy change to make:

```
function:
  A = 42
  B = "Hello",
  C = 42.1
  D = [1, 2, 3]
  ...
  call tweakme()

tweakme():
  F = 18
  B = "Bye"
  call subfunction()

subfunction():
  ...
  E = 52
  call subsubfunction(E)

subsubfunction(E):
  ... A, B, C, D are in dynamic scope, E is a relevant argument ...
```

Initially, Emacs came with only dynamic binding. As the code base around it grew, the problems with dynamically scoped variables grew as well; certain programming patterns, like passing lexical closures around, did not translate well even though "fake closures" were added pretty early. Therefore, in version 24, Emacs got optional lexical binding as well. This made closures first-class citizens and also made it possible to build a Common Lisp compatibility package, which is, at the time of this writing, in use by around a third of the Emacs Lisp code distributed with the editor sources. Over the years, Emacs Lisp has morphed from a quick hack to achieve a very limited goal into a full-fledged programming language that can be used to tackle all sorts of coding problems.

Lucid Emacs and X Emacs

Emacs was one of the first projects of the GNU project. Stallman took issue with commercial companies spawning off the products of the MIT AI Lab (like Gosling Emacs, but also the various Lisp machine companies) and the commercialization of the Unix operating system; on top of that he also had ran into the limitations of proprietary software that restricted what users could do with hardware they owned, so he set out to change that by creating software that would guarantee its users maximum freedom to do as they please.

The GNU project—the acronym is a recursive one: "GNU's Not Unix"—aimed to build a complete operating system from scratch and Emacs was a core component. It's hard to create an OS if you don't have an editor. The experience with Gosling Emacs—it was sold to a commercial software distribution house which then told Stallman to stop using "their" source code in GNU Emacs—firmed his resolve to never let that happen with his code and the concept of "copyleft" was born. Emacs came with a license that allowed everybody to use the code for any purpose, as long as they shared changes back.

This "free" (where advocates stress that it is more about "free as in speech" rather than "free as in beer") aspect made GNU Emacs a prime candidate for budding software company Lucid, Inc.

Lucid was founded on the premise that the whole idea of Lisp Machines would be short-lived as microprocessors made general computers so cheap that you could combine an off-the-shelf operating system and a good "regular" Lisp development environment and have something much cheaper and pretty much just as good. The company came out of Stanford, nearby Lawrence Livermore National Library, and culturally very much out of "Silicon Valley." Founded by, among others, Common Lisp godfather Richard Gabriel, it planned to use the hardware of a young Stanford spin-off, Sun Microsystems, Inc.

Sun got its name from the Stanford University Network project where some of Sun's early hardware was conceived: a graphical workstation based on the Motorola 68000 processor, running the Unix operating system and optimized for use as a CAD workstation. Three Stanford graduates took their ideas and founded Sun Microsystems, and shortly after that launched a line of workstations on based on their own processor, the SPARC processor. Both the 68k and the SPARC machines that followed later ran the Berkeley Software Distribution variant of Unix, which was widely seen by then as a huge improvement over AT&T's own offering of the operating system.

So, Lucid's plan was to do Common Lisp "the easy way": take stock hardware, stock (Unix) development tools, add a really good version of Common Lisp, and sell that as a development environment rather than the "build everything from scratch" philospphy that the Lisp machine vendors had adopted. Sun Microsystems was an early supporter, but before long most other computer vendors signed up to partner. The company's version of Common Lisp indeed came close in performance to the leading competitor's implementation, Lisp Machines. Coupled to the lower cost and higher flexibility of the hardware, this proved the hypothesis that you did not need specialized machine.

Even IBM signed up and asked the budding company to do a version for their upcoming workstation line, the IBM RT PC, a RISC-based "Personal Computer". Small companies don't say no to Big Blue when it comes along with a cheque book pulled out, and before long, a good part of Lucid's staff was involved in a secretive project to, well, essentially recreate most of the Lisp Machines environment on this new hardware. Things were going swell, except for the fact that the whole AI market was tanking. All sorts of projects over-promising and under-delivering had led to a string of disappointments, and the industry soured on the ideas of Artificial Intelligence, and, by extension, its leading implementation language, Common Lisp. Before long, the whole idea that there would be a market for Common Lisp that would not only support Lucid's employees but also give its investors a return for their investment turned out to be an idea that was past its prime.

One problem of catering to innovators is that you sell to companies that are flexible and can adopt to change. Just as fast as they came running to AI and Lisp they ran away when the promised upside did not pan out, and just as quickly they embraced the next Big New Thing. That Big New Thing was a language that stlll promised very good development experiences, but at blazing speeds: called "C++," it was developed by AT&T's Bjarne Stroustrup as the logical next step for Bell Labs' "C" language, and–partially thanks to it generous licensing terms–took the world by storm after its release in 1985. C++ was hip, new, had all the right fad words, and came with the promise that existing "C" developers would have no trouble at all switching. It was pretty much the death blow for Common Lisp as a general programming language.

Lucid was likely to fold or had try something new, so they chose the second option: pivot to C++, with the idea that Lisp experience might translate to C++ tooling. C++ was in dire need of tooling: 1970s tools like `make` and `vi` were all that was available, and what worked for a relatively straightforward language like C did not work well for the complexity of dealing with class inheritance graphs which caused frequent and long recompiles in C++. If Lucid could use their existing knowledge to fill this gap, they could have a product addressing a big problem in a massive market. A local C++ compiler vendor was acquired, and Emacs was of course the logical choice for any company with deep Lisp roots to form the basis of the interactive parts.

The idea was to build the developer front-end of the C++ system in GNU Emacs. It was in Lisp, it was extensible, and moreover, people that were interested in advanced development environments would already have it on their system, saving an (often long and arduous) installation step. GNU Emacs, however, needed work, especially in the area of the graphical user interface. The upcoming Emacs version promised full GUI support but it kept being delayed so Lucid stepped in to help out by freeing up some people to work on getting that release out. However, differences of opinion between people at the Free Software Foundation (the "owner" of GNU Emacs) and Lucid cause Lucid to end that collaboration and go their own way, effectively (and probably for the first time on a large and arguably important project) "forking" GNU Emacs into their own version, "Lucid Emacs". They needed to get the C++ product done, and unlike the FSF people they were under time pressure, so skipping the debates and waiting turned out to be the only way to move fast enough.

Lucid Emacs was in many aspects a much more polished version than the original: it had a nice GUI, some architectural improvements that made Emacs play better with graphics systems like the X Windows System that Sun's version of BSD used, and most importantly it met Lucid's goals of being a good basis for their product work. Lucid kept up-to-date with improvements to GNU Emacs by pulling in updates from the project, but the reverse did not happen; for Lucid, this was probably fine as their attention lied elsewhere; Emacs was a means, not an end, in the quest for an integrated C++ environment.

The C++ environment was brilliant: Emacs on the front-end, lots of ideas from the Lisp and Smalltalk worlds like a class browser and interactive development, deep integration between a stateful backend that analyzed the code and the compiler and debugger so things could be quickly incrementally compiled instead of having to sit through full recompiles of projects, and so on. It was a hit with the technical crowds but, alas, commercially fell short of what was needed to rescue Lucid, Inc. There are many reasons for that commercial failure but here it suffices to say that the company did not survive this second product failure.

The forked code base, though, had an enthusiastic following so a group of people outside Lucid adopted it and gave it a new name, "XEmacs". This is the way of Open Source code, of course: it lives forever, regardless of what happens to the organizations that created it. XEmacs kept its roots in the sense that it made the GUI aspects the focus; not only on Unix versions, where the X Window System ruled (and rules) supreme, but also with targeted GUIs for Windows and Mac computers. It was also an early adopter of another effort that spawned from GNU Emacs, called "MULE", for "Multilingual Enhancements to Emacs". MULE initially started as a fork to support multi-byte Japanese character sets, but it quickly grew to a fully internationalized version of Emacs. The project got integrated into XEmacs in the late 1990's, but GNU Emacs hadn't exactly being twiddling thumbs during all this and adopted (or recreated) most of XEMacs' improvements.

XEmacs is still around, but—at the time of writing this—has not seen much action during the last 15 years or so. Still, most Emacs users today should recognize the contributions that Lucid Emacs and XEmacs made to the project, however indirectly.

Emacs today

The kitchensink idea is still valid today, especially because of extensions that allow Emacs to run things like web browsers right inside editor windows. There is even a plug-in that allows users to run Emacs as their window manager in the X Windows System environment.

All during the 1990's and early 2000's, users of Unix fell into two camps: either you used the Unix standard editor ("vi", which still shows its lineage back to editors in the age of TECO) or Emacs. Some more pragmatic souls decided to marry the two and created the "Extensible VI Layer for Emacs", or Evil—so deep was the chasm between the two camps that any bridge building to help people cross had to come with a term like that; if there was to be a marriage, it was to be perceived as an unholy one. Evil essentially lets vi users switch over to Emacs without thinking, fully implementing all the interaction that vi users are accustomed to. Vi users could now tap into the wealth of functionality that Emacs brought to the table, and the extension has proved successful in that it is the basis for what are arguably the two most successful "Emacs distributions" today, Spacemacs and Doom Emacs: they both start in Vi mode by default and have excessive interaction customizations around this editor mode.

Emacs has also benefited from the phenomenon that "the Internet solved software distribution". Where Perl has CPAN, and Common Lisp has QuickLisp, Emacs has ELPA ("Emacs Lisp Package Archive"), the official distribution of additional packages, but also forks like MELPA ("Milkyman's ELPA") and extensive tooling to bypass package archives completely and build straight from source code repositories like GitHub. MELPA alone sports close to 6,000 packages for Emacs which cover everything from support for obscure programming languages, editor-wide themes, to tooling to manage modern cloud infrastructure right from your editor.

And it sports unmatched extensibilty—C code only makes up for 25% of the distribution, the rest is Lisp, and for any given "package-enriched" installation, C probably is not more than a low single digit percentage of total lines of code with everything else in Emacs Lisp. All the Lisp code is dynamic, so you can change that 95%, say, of editor behavior *in the editor while you're running it*, and that means that it is quite simple to adapt to your needs. People who move to Emacs and get over the initial hump tend to stick with it for that reason; they make it theirs by a personal configuration file of small and large tweaks, and get accustomed to making their coding/mail reading/news reading/note taking/... environment do things the way they want it. Even half a century after its conception, that makes it a popular editor today.

It still doesn't come with an *actual* kitchensink, though...

Chapter 11

AI Winter

In the 1950s and 1960s, optimism about what computers could do was at its peak. Isaac Asimov wrotes stories about post-scarcity societies managed by a computer, serious scientists were speculating on the number of years it would take to fully emulate a human brain using neuronal computing, and progress was swift and impressive: computers learned to beat humans at checkers, the first programs that we now call "chatbots" appeared, and expert systems turned out to be a great boon to, well, experts. The sky was the limit.

By the 1970s, though, reality sunk in. Project successes were smaller and happened at larger intervals, and while great strides were made in the tools (like hardware and Lisp), the problems that were tackled turned out to be more and more intractable.

It was a combination of lack of knowledge, lack of tooling, and lack of understanding of the sheer complexity of the sort of things that were attempted: universal translators, speech recognition, spatial reasoning. All things that looked doable and within reach with the incredible advances in especially computer power of the 1960s and 1970s but where the solutions invariably remained out of researchers' grasps.

The Perceptron

One of the big research pushes was to emulate the brain directly. While other approaches in AI focused on basic statistical learning or manually coded rulesets, "the Perceptron" would directly emulate the human brain. Perceptrons where what we now call single-layer neural networks and saw, as everywhere in the field of AI, some early successes that were enough to keep neural network research alive in spite of the much larger successes in symbolic computing, its largest "competitor". In the land of the blind, the one-eyed man is king.

Psychologist and AI researcher Frank Rosenblatt is said to have kept his concept of perceptrons alive well past its best-before date by staying optimistic about its possibilities and especially by his capacity for selling ideas. However, Minsky and Papert ended that dream in 1969 by publishing a book that firmly outlined the limitations of single layer neural networks [58]; limitations that everybody already "sort of" knew about but which Rosenblatt always managed to talk himself out of. The book, however, was less easy to ignore and funding for perceptrons, or indeed *any* neural network research, dried up.

The issue with perceptrons was that they were a single layer neural network: you have a list of artificial neurons that each receive inputs from the same source, "fire" or not, and emit an output. Tweaking the firing rules during training would eventually allow such a list of neurons to learn, make decisions, and—the holy grail of machine understanding of human endeavors—translate between languages. The single layer model was chosen purely out of practical reasons, starting with the simple fact that nobody had an idea how to train a multi-layered neural network. The technique needed for that, called "backpropagation", was years away and when it arrived, it was too little too late to save AI. Even with all the tools in hand, the next hurdle was the 1980s lack of computing power. The idea of neural networks would slumber for another twenty-odd years, only taking center stage again in the 2010's when the ubiquitous availability of advanced vector processors in the form of computer graphics cards turned out to be just the thing that the everybody been waiting for all these years.

Vector Processing

As an aside, the concept of backpropagation over a whole network of artificial neurons roughly boils down to a series of mathematical operations that can be implemented by operating on matrices. Matrix operations are very repetitive: to multiply two matrices, for example, you perform a whole series of steps where you multiply the scalar values in matching cells in both matrices and then add them up. This is an operation that performs in cubic time relative to the size of the matrices involved, so it gets very slow very quickly as the inputs grow.

It turns out that you can build a special kind of computer processor that consists of tiny simple units that all run the same code but on different parts of the problem, and because they run all in parallel they can make short work of very long and boring computations like multiplying matrices and vectors. This was known for a long time and specialized and expensive "supercomputers" employed this architecture exclusively until video gaming happened.

A lot of problems in rendering large amounts of pixels on a screen from a 3D scene description are also of the kind that can be cast in terms of matrices and vectors and operations on them, and before long the supercomputer "vector processors" made it onto commodity PC "graphics cards". The popularity of computer gaming triggered a race to make better graphics cards, and they quickly became fast enough to not only render extremely accurate scenes in games, but also to do general matrix computing on a scale that finally cracked the problem of doing backpropagation training on very large neural networks.

Funding cuts

Both in the UK and the US, the 1970s saw a marked change in the attitude of (government) funding sources towards AI. It is probably safe to say that researchers were well aware of the fact that some of the problems were somewhat larger than computing power even for the foreseeable future could tackle, but academic funding being what it is it always helps to be somewhat optimistic about the potential outcomes for your projects towards those holding the bags with money.

Patience and suspended disbelief have an expiry date, though, and in the 1970s on both sides of the ocean the conclusion was that the spending had been on intractable projects. In the UK, a report was commissioned by Parliament on the state of AI research that turned out disastrous in the sense that all funding on AI research ended. In the US, Congress directed the Defence Advanced Research Projects Agency, one of the most important sources of AI research funding a the time, to be more focused on "goal-oriented" research and less on basic, undirected research. The UK report and DARPA's own investigations in the potential outcomes of AI led towards the organization redirecting funds to projects with more down-to-earth goals and more predictable outcomes like the development of battle management systems. Attention turned to concepts like expert systems instead, as we already noticed on page 122.

The euphoria about expert systems did not last long: large knowledge bases were nigh impossible to maintain, and expert systems turned out have little expertise at all. They would make bad recommendations when confronted with inputs just outside the norm, and on top of that were costly to run: rulebases needed to be enormous to be useful, machines were not that fast, and Lisp itself was not as heavily optimized as it is today.

Impact on Lisp

Lisp was AI and AI was Lisp. It was not the only language used in the field, but in the mindset of most, the two were heavily intertwined. While Lisp made—and still makes—for an excellent general programming language, investing in Lisp was seen as investing primarily in AI and by the late 1980s, investing in AI was simply not done.

Lisp had other advantages like its powerful Object System, but it was somehow never seen as a predominantly object-oriented language. The late 1980s and 1990s saw a surge of interest in object orientation, prompted by the release of Smalltalk-80 by Xerox PARC and almost mythical stories of its powers, but Lisp failed to capture mindshare. That mindshare went to Smalltalk until languages like C++ and, later, Java arrived at the scene. Neither C++ nor Java were as powerful as Smalltalk, but by the time these "mediocre alternatives" arrived Smalltalk vendors had so thoroughly alienated their customers that anything else that had "OO" in the name would do: if it just was more affordable and came with less onerous licensing conditions.

Lisp development did not stop in the 1990s. New implementations were created and the surge of popularity of "Free/Open Source Software" triggered by software like the freely available Linux operating system and the infrastructure provided by the Internet helped communities get together and work on freely available alternatives for the two main commercial Common Lisp vendors. It helped somewhat, oddly enough, that research institutions that abandoned Lisp were sometimes happy to release their work into the wild as Open Source Software. A good example is Carnegie Mellon University, which dropped Lisp in favor of the new Dylan language. Their "CMU Common Lisp" was taken over by a group of volunteers and a later variant of that implementation, Steel Bank Common Lisp, is currently seen as the leading free implementation of Common Lisp, fully able to compete with its commercial counterparts.

Lisp is still used, here and there. Well-known examples were startup Viaweb, an early e-commerce provider, and ITA Software, an airline search and pricing system. Both were developed in Common Lisp and both were examples of what a small, dedicated team of developers can do in that language. Viaweb's story is well publicized and shows how just a couple of people in Common Lisp could outcompete Internet behemoth Yahoo! to the point that the latter company saw no solution but to acquire the mini company. ITA operated successfully in the highly complex world of airlines and booking systems and was acquired by Google. Rumours are that the codebase is still in use and still in Common Lisp.

The AI winter has ended by now, but its end did not come with a resurgence of Lisp: all work focuses on neural networking and deep learning, where the important differentiator is not the programming language used, but raw compute power and the ability to control it; the careful craftsmanship of symbolic computing has been replaced by a brute force approach that tries to directly model the lower levels of the human brain. Whether that is the right approach or we are headed for another winter remains to be seen, but the heydays of Lisp are well and truly behind us, for better or for worse.

Of course, that statement is only true if you define Lisp quite narrowly, as we will see later. Its ideas are thriving, and some players are making headway using more direct implementations of Lisp's syntax; a popular one will be highlighted in the next part of this book.

The Bravery of German Grad Students

– Richard P. Gabriel

Summer 1983 was the first time I went to Europe, doing an excursion that started in Switzerland and eventually took me to Karlsruhe Germany and IJCAI 1983—the International Joint Conference on Artificial Intelligence. My wife and I met up with John there, and we all stayed in the same hotel. The first morning of the conference, John and I went over to pick up our registration materials: a badge, the proceedings, a festive commemorative bag, and some tchotchkes.

John McCarthy was always a little absent minded, and he relied on his admin to take care of arrangements for his travel, including conferences, but this time she didn't register him for IJCAI—and he didn't know that. He and I walked up to the registration table; it was manned by four or five grad students at the university where the conference was held. One of the students asked his name, and John said "McCarthy." The student looked at the badges and a list of names and said "I'm sorry, no one by that name is registered—did you pre-register?" John said he didn't know because his admin always did that, so he added "can I just register now?" "No, I'm sorry, registration is full." John turned and started to walk away back the way we came. No protest, no argument—this was his nature.

Sometimes I do things that I don't notice I've thought about before doing them; this was such a time. I walked up to the student who had just said no and said "wow, I really admire you, the bravery to bluntly turn away John McCarthy—the father of artificial intelligence and the inventor of Lisp—from an AI conference; you must have had some remarkable training, or maybe all German grad students have strong spines; I know I would never have the nerve to do that."

Two of the grad students bolted from behind the table and sprinted after John, one saying "Professor McCarthy, please forgive me, I did not recognize you at first; of course you can register, at no cost; please forgive me and my colleagues."

After, John told me he thought that worked pretty well. IJCAI had a special banquet the next-to-last evening of the conference, and naturally he was not registered for that, either. We decided to try the same trick.

It worked.

Part III

Present

Chapter 12

Lisp Today

You find Lisp implementations in unexpected places. Some in the plain, some hiding but still present. We'll quickly tour a couple of the more widely used or well-known ones. This chapter is very incomplete and inclusion of projects is somewhat arbitrary, if you're interested there are lists circulating of companies that use Lisp [9], libraries for (Common) Lisp [8], and more can be found by visiting your favorite search engine.

AutoCAD

Let's begin with a commercial implementation of Lisp in an application where you may not expected: Computer Aided Design.

Designing and building machinery was historically the domain of a number of people: you needed people who could think up the machine, then people who could translate the idea into drawings for the people who could build the parts that would form the machine to get to work. These skills could, of course, overlap in more artisanal settings but the industrial revolution and the introduction of things like Ford's assembly line firmly pushed them onto the path of specialization.

When computers started being able to drive plotters and show (vector) graphics on cathode ray tubes, it did not take long for people to realize that they could potentially remove one step from this process: that of the draftsperson, the skilled worker who created meticulous designs using age-old techniques around similarly age-old tools like the t-square and the compass. And for that final "build it" step, Jacquard had shown how to automate manufacturing by his punch-card driven loom—the step to letting computers punch the cards did not take too much of a leap of the imagination, so by the 1960s, developments in Computer Aided Design and Computer Aided Manufacturing were well in swing and by the late 1970s CAD/CAM was a relatively commonplace concept.

There was just one little drawback: thinking in three dimensions took a lot of computing power, and CAD/CAM was accessible only by the large companies that could afford mainframes: aerospace, large-scale civil engineering, that sort of stuff. Just the graphics "terminal" (in itself a hefty computer) cost more than what most small companies could afford.

The rise of the microcomputer would change all that. Machines like the Apple II and the early computers by Tandy were accessible to even the smallest business and their wide reach spawned a sprawling market of small software companies.

One of them was a startup called Autodesk, a company that released CAD software for the widely popular CP/M-80 system in 1982. CP/M was an early microcomputer operating system that, by that time, ran on pretty much everything that had an Intel 8080 or a Zilog Z80 microprocessor, which was the vast majority of microcomputers in the early '80s (until IBM introduced the IBM/PC based on a successor chip by Intel and a very CP/M like operating system by another startup called Microsoft).

Suddenly, the concept of CAD became accessible by every size of company that wanted to use computers to streamline physical design processes; the price of entry went from expensive graphics terminals attached to mainframe computers to a microcomputer you could buy at your local Radio Shack store, a plotter, and maybe a digitizer.

Throughout the 1980s and into the present, Autodesk kept working on AutoCAD and improving it, and by 1986 it was widely recognized as the industry leader in computer aided design. That was also the year that Autodesk added automation to AutoCAD, in the form of AutoLISP.

The need for a programming/automation facility is not hard to see. If you wonder why, take your favorite drawing program (or better, pencil and paper) and draw two gears, one with 24 teeth, the other with 40. Draw it down to the last detail with all the curves required for a gear with the right type and modulus—look it up, it's not just a simple "tooth." This is extremely repetitive work, error prone, and typically the sort of thing where you want to be able to tell the computer: "here is a gear tooth; place it along the wheel 24 times".

Why Lisp, though? History is silent on that, but it's not that hard to imagine why the language got picked. Lisp was popular, and ran on everything built since the late 1950s that vaguely resembled a computer. It might just be that a Lisp implementation, called XLISP, was available and it was the most convenient thing to start an extension language based on that. But it also makes sense if you look at the gear example: gears have various shapes (convolute, cycloid) and gear teeth vary infinitely based on their size, their function, what other gears they interact with, and so on. What you want is not to write a program to create a gear wheel, you want a program that can create programs to create all possible gear wheels. On top of that, the fluidity between code and data also helps Lisp in this area: CAD programs typically come with libraries of standard parts, and these can be expressed in Lisp (and operated upon) just as simply as the program that places gear teeth along a wheel.

AutoLISP was a resounding success. Not only in AutoCAD, but it became popular enough that other CAD vendors felt compelled to support it. There was even at some point a third-party enhanced version of AutoLISP that came with IDE, debugger, compiler and an enhanced object model to make interaction with AutoCAD easier. Autodesk acquired it and after a while integrated it back into AutoCAD; the result, "Visual LISP", is to this day a major way to extend AutoCAD and the code will readily move to other CAD vendors.

Autodesk has done its best to follow the trends of the time by adding other extension mechanisms, most notably by first supporting Microsoft's VBA platform and later .NET; during that time, development on Lisp has all but halted and Visual LISP today is pretty much the same as Visual LISP around the turn of the century. The suite of tools, utilities, and enhancements written in Lisp is so large, though, that its popularity is hardly waning and it is probably correct to say that Autodesk's Visual LISP is to this date by far the most popular commercial Lisp engine in use.

Guile and Guix

If we go back a couple of chapters, we saw that Scheme does not "like" mutability because it complicates things. But programming languages are not the only place where mutating state makes things harder. Take computer systems, for example: two clean installs of a random operating system, let's say some Unix variant, on the same hardware should be identical. Assume that the installation procedure starts at the same nanosecond, that we set the same hostname, network address, and so on. After the installation, you take the hard drives and compare them. Are they bit-for-bit identical?

Chances are that you will answer "no, of course not!" and you'd be right. What is written when is timing sensitive, things may run a nanosecond faster or slower and timestamps will differ, the order of execution is likely to differ, and this will influence what is written to disk. And that is just during installation: once you start *using* the systems, adding software, removing it, installing a security patch, all bets are off. Your Unix system is not *reprodicible* (and neither is your Mac or Windows system, of course).

This is a problem for a number of reasons. For example, you encounter a bug. You try it on a different system, the bug does not appear. Why? What is the difference between the systems? If it is a subtle bug, anything may influence it. And is it a bug or a security issue? Are all executables exactly the same as when we installed them, and if they are changed, is there a way to follow these changes so we know they are legitimate?

It would be much nicer if your system was reproducible. If you install it twice, you get bit-identical results. Updates, fixes, and upgrades are done in a way that doesn not break that propery. If there's a bug on one system, you can bring it over and be guaranteed that the system itself is identical, so that factor has been removed.

Work on such systems has been going on for a while and first was released to the general public as the Nix Operating System, a Linux distribution that builds from sources, but in a perfectly reproducible way. Each time a source package is compiled, the exact same binaries are produced, bit for bit. Patches will lead to new binaries, but every time you patch the same source with the same patch faile, it will compile into the same binaries. From this starting point, Nix built an edifice that is a complete Linux distribution that is, in essence, purely functional: state is immutable, and packages only know about their own environment, they are in effect "side-effect free."

Nix uses one language to define its low level components (C++) and a different, specialized, language (called Nix) to describe builds, packaging, and so on. Neither language is really suitable for quick experimentation, and especially Nix is somewhat limited. For starters, it heavily relies on a third language (the Bash shell scripting language) to get actual work done. In order to work on Nix, you need to be fluent in three completely different programming languages.

One user decided to clean this up using the GNU project's Scheme implementation, Guile, to help him to extend the system. Guile is a version of Scheme that is specifically meant as a system integration and extension language, and is therefore easily embeddable in other programs. This user, Ludovic Courtès, liked Nix and liked Guile and bridged the two; initially with some simple additions onto Nix, but eventually replacing most of the parts of Nix by a unified system, called Guix, collapsing Nix's three languages into a single one, Scheme. It quickly grew from one person's hack into a group effort, and finally was adopted by the GNU project as their official Linux distribution.

Guix is a Scheme-driven operating system. The core daemon that manages software builds is written in Scheme (with some remnants of C++ inherited from Nix remaining), the files that describe how packages are built are in Scheme, the files that describe how the operating system starts and what programs to run at boot time are in Scheme, and the system description that users use to tell Guix what they want installed and how they want it configured is in Scheme as well.

There is another way how Guix leverages Scheme's simplicity, and that starts with the question of trust. Nix and Guix ensure—and verify—that certain source code will always produce certain binary code while building packages, but they have to start somewhere: C++, Scheme, these are languages that need interpreters and compilers, and these won't work before they are compiled themselves. These are written in… well, sometimes C (which needs a compiler), but often times partially or completely in Scheme or C++. As you can see, there is no way out of this: we need to start installing a system with binaries that come from *somewhere else* and that somewhere else is a place we need to trust.

In 1984, computer scientist and father of C Ken Thompson showed in his Turing Award lecture "Reflections on Trusting Trust" [82] that if you could place a backdoor in a C compiler, the C compiler could then transport that backdoor through binaries into new versions it compiled of itself without having to touch the source code. You can look at the source code, run it through the "infected" C compiler, and be not sure that the resulting binary is to be trusted. It's hard, but not impossible, to inspect all source code of a system but it *is* impossible to ensure that binaries are valid and free of backdoors.

The only solution is to build a complete system from just source code. But that is ridiculous, because, well, computers don't know what to do with source code. So you need to start with *some* binary code, but if you make it a really small binary, then you can disassemble the binary and inspect it and make sure that it does not contain a backdoor. At the time of writing, the Guix people got a binary bootstrap down to 357 bytes—from there, the system bounces back and forth between ever more complex versions of C and Scheme, utilizing the fact that both languages are so simple, something minimal and easy to inspect can compile them, and finally being enough powerful to have a full Guile and C compiler to compile the tens of thousands of packages that Guix contains, all traceable back through just source code to this simple binary [59].

Nothing is impossible, and this feat probably could have been accomplished for Nix using C++ as well, but if the main language you need to bootstrap is rooted in a single page of code that describes `EVAL` and `APPLY`, your life is probably going to be a lot easier.

Commercial Common Lisps

The 1980s saw the big boom of Lisp, and with big booms come the appetite for big money, starting companies, and trying to get a slice of the proverbial pie. We've already seen Lisp machine vendors spinning out of MIT, but a similar thing happened with pure software companies. We will cover the two big players that survived since then.

Franz Lisp and Allegro

Let's start on the West coast of the US, in Berkeley. At the University of California's campus faculty and students worked on a spin-off of Maclisp they called Franz Lisp, the name being a clear pun on composer Franz Liszt. Its primary purpose was to support a computer algebra system called Macsyma, which struggled to run on the PDP-10. Franz Lisp was more portable than Maclisp and helped Macsyma run on other machines, including the newly spawned Lisp machines.

A company, called Franz Inc., was formed to further develop Franz Lisp but by that time it was clear that Common Lisp was there to stay and the efforts to keep Franz Lisp alive withered, with the company focusing on their new Common Lisp implementation, Allegro Common Lisp. It was introduced in 1986 to the public as a fully compatible implementation of Common Lisp and has been developed by Franz ever since.

Allegro Common Lisp comes with an interactive development environment, a full ANSI-compliant Common Lisp, support for CLOS, graphics, Unicode, and comes with a built-in object database and an implementation of Prolog. It is available as a restricted free ("gratis") version and as commercial editions that come with support and access to most of the source code. To this date, Franz is focused on supporting and developing Allegro Common Lisp.

LispWorks

Lisp development did not only happen in the US, however, and the other example of a commercial Common Lisp that survives to this day was born on the British Isles in 1989 as a straight-up competitor to the likes of Lisp Machines, Lucid, and Franz.

Founded in 1987 in Cambridge, startup Harlequin created LispWorks, a commercial Common Lisp with a graphical user interface and various tools focused on creating applications with graphical user interfaces. They targeted Unix workstations (Windows support had to wait another decade) and quickly became successful at selling the product both in the UK and abroad, including the US (where an office in "the other Cambridge" was opened). When Lucid went out of business, Harlequin acquired the technology and most of the staff and continued as a public company under the name Harlequin Group plc. At its peak, they employed over 300 staff with offices across the UK and US.

The downturn came fast, and costly investments in failed expansion plans forced the company into administration in 1999. The company that acquired the assets of Harlequin was interested in their Postscript technology and spun off the Lisp and related functions into a company called Xanalys. More acquisitions and mergers ended with a group of employees buying the rights to the LispWorks technology in 2005 and start a company called LispWorks Ltd., a UK company that markets LispWorks to this day.

Like Allegro, LispWorks is available as a restricted free (as in "gratis") edition for hobbyists and in several commercial licensing formats targeting industry and academia. One of LispWorks' more widely acknowledged contributions to the Common Lisp ecosystem is called the Common Lisp HyperSpec [46], a "hypertext" version of the Common Lisp specification first published on the Internet in 1996 and still hosted by the company. It is probably still the most widely used reference to the ANSI Common Lisp implementation, even through formatting and layout clearly show their age by now and alternatives are available.

Chapter 13

A New Style of Lisp on Java

The chapter on the AI winter and the fall-out for Lisp might have been in a somewhat pessimistic voice, but not all is lost. We now arrive at a completely new version of Lisp, called "Clojure," which runs on top of the ubiquitous Java Virtual Machine. We will get to this "Java" thing later on, but let's start with this new language itself.

Clojure is pretty much Lisp as one would design it in the 21st century. A couple of things happened since McCarthy's earliest work:

- Computers got not only much faster, but started spawning multiple cores: "multi-threading" (running multiple things at the same time in a program) is a given, not an additional exotic extension.
- Language runtimes morphed into multi-language platforms, essentially an operating system on top of the operating system. Oracle's Java Virtual Machine (JVM) and Microsoft's .NET are the most well-known examples.

A modern Lisp should take into account the learnings of the previous decades. An important one is that object orientation—which often revolves around mutable state—and concurrency don't mix well. The main attempt to marry object orientation and concurrency is called the Java Memory Model [39], which, when first released, comprised over 30 pages of dense specifications that most users of the language probably do not understand sufficiently to apply in practice. A modern Lisp should support concurrency, but use a functional approach like persistent data structures, and allow only limited and well-controlled interactions between threads.

A modern Lisp implementor probably wants to be able to leverage the incredible work that went into the major language platforms, though. Implementing a language is relatively simple if you build an interpreter or a naive compiler. But once you start diving into concurrency, garbage collection, and modern techniques like just in time compilation, things get hairy to the level that hundreds of computer science PhDs can productively spend a full career working on these topics. But if you target an existing language runtime, like the Java Virtual Machine, you get all that for free.

Computer programmer Rich Hickey wanted such a modern Lisp, and Clojure is the result of pursuing that wish. It leverages the Java virtual machine so that right from the bat, Clojure could compete with much more established players; not only that, but "runs on the JVM" also checks off an important box for many businesses. If you want to work in Clojure, there's a good chance that your IT organization already knows how to deploy, monitor, and manage your application because they know how to deal with "Java applications." Hickey's choice of platform immediately gave Clojure the suit and tie it needed to succeed in business.

Overview

Clojure describes itself as a "dynamic, general-purpose programming language, combining the approachability and interactive development of a scripting language with an efficient and robust infrastructure for multithreaded programming". That it is a Lisp dialect is only mentioned in the next paragraph.

Like Scheme, Clojure is predominantly a functional programming language, going back all the way to Lisp's lambda calculus roots. In a world of multithreading, functions provide a nice safe space for computation: a proper ("pure") function can not affect anything that is also running on the same computer, because all it can do is look at its input arguments and emit an output return value. Shared mutable state is not a concept that exists in pure functional programming and by making that the heart of a system most of the code is understandable and simple to reason about.

Transactions in memory

But pure functions make for boring programs, and functional programming languages invariably need escape hatches to actually *do* something. After all, computer programs are meant to interact with the messy world out there, but pure functions can't get us there. In Clojure's case, the big problem to solve was how to share mutable state between multiple parallel computations ("threads"). Here is a simple problem:

```
x := 42
y := 0
start_task(print(y))
start_task(y := x)
```

`start_task` starts a (parallel) process so that the last two lines execute concurrently. What is printed here? That depends on which of the two computations "gets there first", so both "0" and "42" are valid answers. Now consider a banking application.

```
account = 0.
start_task(deposit(account, 10)).
start_task(withdraw(account, 5)).
```

Assuming that `withdraw` won't allow overdrafts, will this succeed? If the deposit comes first, the account would have enough money to allow the withdrawal that follows, but if the two tasks run in the other order, the withdrawal, coming first, will fail. You won't know beforehand and each time you run this either outcome is possible. These are trivial examples, but they show how ordering becomes important when a computer can do multiple things at the same time in your program.

Having something fail is inconvenient, but the bank's rules still are adhered to: an overdraft won't happen. But now let's say that `withdraw` does this:

```
withdraw(balance, amount):
  if balance - amount < 0:
    error "Overdraft not allowed"
  else
    balance = balance - amount.
```

And we run

```
account = 10.
start_task(withdraw(account, 10)).
start_task(withdraw(account, 10)).
```

The two tasks run in parallel, let's label them "A" and "B", then this ordering is possible:

```
A: if balance - amount < 0: <-- check succeeds
B: if balance - amount < 0: <-- check succeeds
A: balance = balance - amount <-- balance is now 0
B: balance = balance - amount <-- balance is now -10
```

We allowed an overdraft where none is allowed! Java, as one of the first widely-used "multithreading-included" platforms, saw a lot of issues around just these sorts of concurrently-running programs. The "Java Memory Model" specification plugs all the holes that popped up when people tried to do multi-threading on the thus-far only informally specified Java Virtual Machine.

As mentioned before, this material is likely beyond comprehension for the average Java application developer and the common solution is often to simply not use shared objects at all. "Stateless" computing in the age of Internet web applications retrieves all data from the database, modifies it per the web request, and then writes the changed data back.

The database is where shared mutable state is kept and given that databases are a fifty year old technology by now, they have become pretty good at it: they order changes in "transactions", and guarantee that in the example above, all of A will execute before all of B will execute. Problems persist, of course (the above account example will now throw an error, which you still need to handle as a developer), but moving the problem out of the Java Virtual Machine and into the database is widely regarded as a pragmatic solution for dealing with the complexities of the Java Memory Model.

But not dealing with a problem at all has its cost: you need to go to the database, which lives on a separate machine in most instances and will want to write everything to its disk to make sure data does not get lost. A good thing, but also a slow thing. Changes in local memory are several orders of magnitude faster than changes on a disk that usually sits at the other end of a network cable, so the cost of ignoring the JMM is paid for in performance. If we're not directly interested in the durability aspect of a database, can we have our cake and eat it, too?

The answer is "yes," and Clojure's solution to the problem is to add a pretty complete transactional engine to the language so it can do what the database can do, but then in memory. The above example in Clojure would read:

```
(def account (ref 10))
(defn withdraw [account amount]
  (dosync
    (if (> (- (deref account) amount) 0)
      (alter account - amount))))
(withdraw account 1)
=> 9
(withdraw account 1)
=> 8
```

(feel free to type along by installing Clojure [36] and firing up the `clj` REPL). In a nutshell, we wrap the amount in a reference (created by `ref`), which is the material that transactions, delineated by `dosync`, operate on. And instead of operating directly on the amount, we instruct the system to dereference or alter the references; that way Clojure "knows" about all the changes we're making and can do its magic. It is hard to show in a book that this works, but it does: this minimal change will ensure that the withdraw function always does a check and change in a single transaction, and if multiple concurrent blocks are running, Clojure will try to do as much work in parallel using optimistic locking. If things fail, because the account got changed between the check and the modification, it will retry.

The careful reader will note that we're cheating here a bit: whereas the synchronization-free pseudocode started background tasks to run things in parallel, here we just check `withdraw` by invoking it twice. We'll fix that in the next section as we look at how Clojure talks to Java so we can run multiple processes.

Java interoperability

The Java Programming Language is wildly popular but much-maligned, and that has been the case pretty much since its inception. Remember James Gosling, from Gosling Emacs? We find him back a good decade later at Sun Microsystems, where he and Mike Sheridan and Patrick Naughton started a project to create a language to program devices for interactive television, like set-top boxes. It was not some lofty academic project, but a down-to-earth and practical attempt to make these devices easier to program by providing a higher level language and toolset than just a C compiler.

THE C PROGRAMMING LANGUAGE — Created at Bell Labs in the early 1970s, "C" was an attempt to create a programming language that was low level enough to be "close to the metal" and high level enough to be somewhat portable between machines. First constructed to create utilities for the Unix operating system, it morphed into one of the most widely used programming languages. The drawback of the fact that it is so low level is that a programmer needs to remember to manually deal with lots of little details, like allocating and freeing memory, and getting it wrong will result in crashes or security bugs. The widespread problems that this created prompted especially businesses to look elsewhere, and Java was one of the solutions to make programming "safer".

It took ideas from the worlds of Lisp and Smalltalk—like object orientation and a byte-code virtual machine—and married them with the target audience's expectation: a language that used C-like syntax like curly braces to delineate blocks of code. So where a C programmer would type:

```
include <stdio.h>

int main(void)
{
    printf("hello, world
n");
}
```

In Java, this became:

```
class HelloWorld {
    public static void main(String[] args) {
        System.out.println("Hello, World!");
    }
}
```

Different, but not as scary as, say, Lisp for the average C programmer. Below these superficial similarities, though, it brought a lot to the table:

- Java code was compiled to intermediate "byte code" that ran on a virtual machine. Wherever the virtual machine ran, the byte code would run—Sun called this "WORA", for Write Once,

Run Anywhere. Interactive TV was being explored on a plethora of devices, all with their own processors, memory layouts, toolchains, and so on; Java promised to make these differences go away.
- It was *safe*. No manual management of pointers, buffer overflows, crashing systems because of bad memory accesses, which is all the daily bread and butter for a C developer but problematic when it happens on a consumer device.
- It had cross-platform GUI support in the form of its Abstract Widget Toolkit library. Again, write once, run anywhere, even for applications with a graphical UI. Whether a TV set-top box or a Windows machine, the same code would do the same thing.
- It had multi-threading support built-in and it was easy to use. While C had threading libraries, they were arcane and risky to use; Java's multi-threading came with a simple interface and reasonably clear expectations and limitations.

In other words, Java was tailor-made and pretty much perfect for the development of interactive TV apps. The industry soundly rejected it, probably because the whole concept of "interactive TV" was already too new for the somewhat conservative set of corporations that formed the target audience, and introducing new technology on top of that was seen as reaching too far. Where Java *did* become popular, seemingly overnight, was when it got integrated into browsers for the budding "Web". The Internet had existed for longer, but the advent of the World Wide Web and better communication technologies made it accessible to an ever growing group of people beyond its initial scope of academia, research, and the government. Early WWW browsers were very static, they displayed the HTML markup of a document and you could click links to other documents, but forms got added early on, and that taste of interactivity made people want more.

Because "interactive TV" and "WWW" were kind of playing on the same field of "new media", web browser support was added to Java from the very first version—the library had an "Applet" package and early browsers got patched to run little snippets of Java code called applets that could greatly enhance a web page, by doing things like playing sounds and animations up to running full application user interfaces. While applets quickly got surpassed by technologies like Flash and the JavaScript programming language which was much better integrated with the browser, it did get a lot of early adopters acquainted with the language and when Sun decided to also support the server side of the World Wide Web with its "Servlet" specification and implementation, adoption was swift:

with Java on the server and a range of technologies in the browser, companies could offer applications to the whole world without having to think about the specific computer platforms that either server or browser ran on. It would always just work.

Java on the server was where people felt Java was meant to be. The language was too verbose and too cumbersome for the interactive stuff on the desktop, and "features" like "does not crash" and "can multitask" weren't seen as important differentiators there. If a webpage crashes, the user could simply reload and be on their way. Server-side though, these features were a big boon: until then, web requests were handled essentially by spawning off a process for each incoming request, an expensive operation. Java had a cross-platform threading model that was much cheaper in terms of overhead and pretty much overnight, Java became the main "back-end" programming language and Sun the absolute star player of the 1990s "dot-com" boom. Sun became pretty much the only 1980s Unix vendor to survive that era unscathed.

By the time that Hickey started on Clojure, Java was firmly entrenched. The world, however, had moved on and largely was over its love affair with object orientation, and Java did not age well. As Sun promised perfect backward compatibility—which was an important promise for conservative players like banks, who think in software lifecycles of decades, not days—its older libraries were still around and mostly "the way to do it". They were cumbersome and not popular and, in the case of things like multithreading, more complicated to use than it looked like at first face (people kept discovering edge cases in the implementation, which was informally specified until the Java Memory Model settled things). Still, Java was omnipresent and "if it exists, there is a library for it in Java" holds true to this day.

Let's use Java interoperability to "fix" the example by making it actually concurrent, accompanied by a big warning sign that this is not how you are supposed to do things in Clojure when it comes to asynchronous code (look up concepts like "agents" and "futures" in the Clojure reference documentation [13] to learn about the proper way of doing it):

```
(.start (Thread. (fn [] (withdraw account 8))))
(.start (Thread. (fn [] (withdraw account 8))))
(deref account)
=> 2
```

As you can see, the withdraw happens and it happens only once, so we can declare success with our example. Let's unpack the Java interoperability bits, though, and for those that aren't aware of the

Java threading library, let's juxtapose it with a roughly equivalent Java version.

```
class RunWithdraw {
   public static void main(String[] args) {
      new Thread(new Runnable() {
        public void run() {
           withdraw(account, 8);
        }
      }).start();
      new Thread(new Runnable() {
        public void run() {
           withdraw(account, 8);
        }
      }).start();
   }
}
```

(Note that this is not code that would execute—we did not implement the functions `withdraw` or `account` that the code invokes, but this is the shape of code to start threads in Java and that is what is important). In the Java version, we call the constructor `Thread.new` with an argument of what Java calls an "anonymous subclass"—an ad-hoc implementation of `Runnable` that implements a custom version of the run method. We need that because `Thread.new` expects a `Runnable` argument—everything in Java must be an object, so this is the way to represent "something that a thread can run", in other words, a function with zero arguments. It is a bit verbose, and Clojure does the same thing in a much more concise manner: it is a functional language, so it has first-class function objects (which we define with `fn`), and in Clojure they are automatically `Runnable` to make Java happy. This gets rid of the ugly anonymous inner class (to be fair, Java has had a simpler notation for essentially the same thing since version 8, but we're looking here at what is going on under the hood, not at the best way to write things in Java, which would be

```
() -> { withdraw(account, 8); }
```

instead of the whole `new Runnable` invocation).

Back to Clojure, `.start` says "call the method of the class of the first argument with the rest of the arguments as *its* arguments". In other words: `.method <object_or_class> <arg1>...<argn>` is the general form. Unpacking what we pass to `.start`:

```
(Thread. (fn [] (withdraw account 8)))
```

We see the Java `Thread` class followed by a dot in the position of a function call. This is shorthand for `new Thread`, and essentially Clojure made it so that when you see a dot, you are likely looking at an interaction with plain old Java code. Like in the Java example, `Thread.new()` receives a `Runnable`—here an anonymous Clojure function—and then we call `start` on the result.

Given that in Java, constructing instances of classes and calling methods is pretty much all there is, this is also pretty much all there is to the Java interoperability feature. There is a somewhat more generic "dot" special form, but that one is mostly meant for macro writers. The details can be found in the "Interop section" of the Clojure reference guide.

Making it so easy to call Java code meant that Clojure can not only use the enormous body of library code that is available for Java, but also that it is easy to integrate into existing products and projects, making for a smooth transition.

Immutable data structures

Clojure is a *functional* language, first and foremost. That means that it prefers side-effect free functions where possible, and a good way to accomplish this is to have data structures that never change. That also explains the term `ref` in the example code above: `(def account (ref 10))` defines a *reference* to the number 10. The reference can change, the number 10 can not. In the case of a single number, that is sort of obvious, but in the case of complex data structures like arrays, it is less obvious. In most languages, you can have an array in memory and add an element to it by modifying the array, and in most mainstream languages today, this is idiomatic usage. The problem of course is that every bit of code that references the array "sees" the change, and if you have multiple processes using that array they can overwrite each other's changes. What often happens is that process implicitly expects to only work on the original data and will crash when it encounters a new value. Mutable data structures can be problematic even when a single process is operating on them. This is normal Javascript code:

```
> l = [1, 2, 3]
[ 1, 2, 3 ]
> x = l
[ 1, 2, 3 ]
> x[0] = 4
4
> l
```

```
[ 4, 2, 3 ]
```

If `l` was meant to represent "the original list", say, we're in trouble. And if `l` or `x` get passed to a different thread that operates concurrently on the same data, we're likely in big trouble (imagine looping through an array that changes all the time. When are you done?).

Immutable data structures solve that problem. We've seen them before, as lists. Say we have a list (in terms of old skool Lisp CONS cells, this for example in SBCL):

```
(setq j `(1 . (2 . (3 . nil))))

(setq l (cons 0 l))
```

Then all we did in memory was to *add* something, leaving `j` intact:

```
☞ CL-USER: l
=> (0 1 2 3)
☞ CL-USER: j
=> (1 2 3)
```

Clojure extends this concepts from consed lists to arrays, maps and sets, ensuring that these are safe to pass around. If you pass a set to another process and then "modify it", the process keeps its original set and your modification results in a new set, which—like a new cons list—probably shares some memory storage with the original one but has the new values in it. The only way to share data in a mutable sense is to share a reference to the data and modify the reference in a careful and controlled manner, through transactions. There is no direct way to reproduce the Javascript behaviour in Clojure, actually:

```
☞ user=> (def l [1 2 3])
☞ user=> (def x l)
☞ user=> (update x 0 (fn [_] 4))
[4 3 2]
☞ user=> x
[1 2 3]
☞ user=> l
[1 2 3]
```

The update did not change the array in place, it created an updated copy instead. This prevents a lot of confusion and subtle bugs and forces developers to be explicit (using transactions, refs and agents) about sharing mutable state.

Differences with other Lisps

Clojure is essentially a Scheme-style Lisp: it is a Lisp-1, it heavily leans on immutable data, but it is not a "proper" Scheme in that it does not automatically implement tail call optimization (this is more a shortcoming of the underlying platform, the JVM, than a conscious design choice—there is a keyword, `recur`, to instruct the compiler to work around this). It also has a slightly different idea of `nil`—it is analogous to the Java `null` value, and does not have the Lisp concept of it being equal to the empty list, `'()`. There are more details, but probably the biggest stand-out is that Hickey opted for some syntactical sugar by calling the other parenthesis-like pairs into action:

- `(...)` creates, like in Lisp, a list—which is called a Sequence in Clojure and behaves slightly differently but overall analogously to the Lisp "cons-list".
- `[...]` creates an array, called `Vector` in Clojure. Its contents are directly addressable by number, and that makes it a good candidate for things like function arguments. In case you wondered what the `[]` in the `(fn [] ...)` did above, now you know.
- `{....}` creates an associative array, called `Map` in Clojure (with various implementations). A variation on the syntax is `#{}` which creates a Set of distinct values.

All have "pure Lisp" equivalents for those purists that balk at this modernism, but word from the field is that, overall, Clojure people like how the somewhat richer syntax helps convey what code does in a meaningful (and short-hand) way.

There is more to talk about: look in the documentation for "protocols", "records", "extensions" for how the language deals with extensibility, for example. Then there is ClojureScript [14] which lets you run essentially the same language in the browser. At this point, let's end our brief visit with the advice that if you work in an environment where the Java Virtual Machine is the norm and you have developed a taste for Lisp, this is probably an excellent spot to begin your explorations to combine the two.

Chapter 14

Your Language Is a Lisp

On various channels on the Internet discussions invariably flare up with titles like "is Ruby a Lisp?" (Ruby is a programming language that was heavily influenced Smalltalk. But given that Smalltalk's and Lisp's histories are intertwined, it is probably not surprising that people compare it to both.) These discussions are often seen as interesting because to most of the participants in these discussions Lisp is this thing they might have had for one class in college but mostly remains that mythical language that makes returning appearances in the legends of computer programming. Maybe, by declaring their language "a Lisp," they can be closer to the heroes of lore.

Any categorization of course is bound to have fringes on the edges between categories and it is no different with programming languages: if you would try and change, say, C into Lisp by changing a single feature at a time, it would be impossible to pinpoint the exact change that turns your hybrid language from "C-like into "Lisp-like."

But the very fact that the question is impossible to answer with any kind of precision does not mean that it cannot make it a good pass-time for some, it is endless fodder for arguments and parts of the Internet thrive on that.

It is more instructive, though, to see how Lisp has *informed* programming language development everywhere. And we'll probably find out that the average popular programming language can be placed on a spectrum ranging from "has taken a lot of inspiration of Lisp" all the way to "this actually is Lisp." Let's review some of the more salient aspects of Lisp and see how modern languages fare.

Dynamic typing

Let's start with a big one: dynamic typing. A lot of languages will require you to declare types of things beforehand. This usually stems from a mix of concerns: the programmer may make mistakes that the compiler can't detect easily and thus get unnoticed until run time. It might also be hard to optimize for the compiler if it does not know what types it can use. A simple example is floating point versus integers: the latter are often much cheaper to operate on so if a compiler knows beforehand that some code is going to use just integers it can spit out efficient assembly code versus more generic code that needs to use floating point operations *and* probably ensure that any integers it does encounter get transformed to floating point numbers first. We encountered an example of the difference that some knowledge about types can make in the section on Common Lisp's typing and optimization, page 162.

The oldest "high level" languages were of the kind where the programmer had to declare types. Fortran started out by making the distinction by convention: variables starting with "I" (and "J" through "N") must be integers, everything else was assumed to be floats. ALGOL 60 required full declarations of the sort we know in many languages today, for example:

```
REAL A B
INTEGER I J

... do something with A B I and J ...
```

These hints-in-the-code usually make the language classify as "statically typed," especially when it is mandatory to provide these hints. Lisp on the other hand focused on computing with symbols, not with numbers. What is the type of a symbol? That's a bit hard to specify and given the fact that originally it was all lists and atoms anyway there was no real need to make the programmer declare types ahead of time. LISP I did not even have different numeric types—just floating point numbers. The fact that "Numbers in LISP" is just a section in the LISP I manual in the chapter "The LISP Programming System" probably shows how much of an afterthought they must have been.

So where ALGOL and FORTRAN required the programmer to declare types ahead of time LISP just would read in some tokens, decide it was parseable as a floating point number, and store it that way (as a pointer to a list of all floating point constants it encountered, as you may recall from the discussion of its numbers on page 6). All we can do then is to hope that the programmer was smart enough to not use it in a position where the system expected a list or an atom. A result is that if we let the IBM 7094 run some LISP 1.5 code with a typo, say:

```
TEST  FACTORIAL

DEFINE ((
   (FACTORIAL (LAMBDA (X)
                (COND ((EQUAL X 0) 1)
                       (T (TIMES X (FACTORIAL (SUB1 X))))))
    )
))

FACTORIAL (())

STOP
FIN      END OF LISP RUN
```

The invocation of `FACTORIAL` should have `(10)` or something like that as its argument, not the empty list. Things will hum along ingesting the function definition right up to where we do the bad invocation:

```
FUNCTION   EVALQUOTE   HAS BEEN ENTERED ARGUMENTS..
FACTORIAL

(NIL)

*** ERROR NUMBER *I  3* INDEX 4 =   14405 OCTAL. ***
```

And off to the manual it is to figure out what that error means (in this case: "I3" is "Bad argument—numval" and the explanation that this error "will occur when numerical functions are given wrong arguments"). A modern Lisp is a bit nicer to the user—feeding the analogous code to SBCL:

```
(defun factorial (n)
  (cond ((equal n 0) 1)
        (t (* n (factorial (- n 1))))))
```

will result in the following interaction:

```
☞ CL-USER: (factorial ())
  ...
  The value
    NIL
  is not of type
    NUMBER
  ...
```

For all practical purposes this is mission accomplished: the programmer makes a mistake, they are duly informed, and for Lisp people that was good enough. We've seen that Common Lisp allows optional type declarations to help it emit tight code but that's something that is of concern at the very end of a process when everything is working but the programmer wants to make it go faster. It is neither needed nor typically used at the beginning of the development process when nothing is working anyway, the programmer is sketching out a solution using charcoal, as it were, and the last thing on his mind is feeding the compiler the information to emit tight code. Performance can come later.

Dynamic typing is quite prevalent in the industry. Languages like JavaScript, Python, and Ruby are very popular and they all belong to this category. And if you're using one of these or similar ones (PHP, Perl, Elixir, ...; it is a long list) then you can trace your language's roots straight back to the ideas behind LISP I, developed in 1958.

Symbols and high level datastructures

McCarthy's idea was to elevate programming to the level of thought by making symbols stand front-and-center. While internally these were just pointers to memory locations and the name of symbols was—and is—mostly meaningless to a computers it *feels* like they are something different. They are rich. Try the FORTRAN equivalent of

```
DEFINE ((
  (CHANGE (LAMBDA (A)
    (MAPLIST A
      (FUNCTION (LAMBDA (J) CONS (CAR J) (QUOTE X))) )))
))
```

as a function that takes a list say `(A B (C D))` and changes it into a list `((A . X) (B . X) ((C . D) . X))`; in other words it changes each element of a list into a cons cell of that element and the symbol 'X'. Not that useful, but if we start associating *concepts* like "color" or "size" and so on with symbols than such an operation could easily be interpreted to mean "set the color of A B C ... to 'blue' ". Moreover, because these concepts would be expressed as symbols and translated as fast pointers to memory locations, operating on such concepts isn't much slower than operating on raw integers. And for the computer it *isn't different*. It just feels different to us. At least it should feel different.

```
(make-animals '(cat dog))
```

(where `make-animals` would return a datastructure, say `((cat . animal) (dog . animal))`) should feel different from

```
AREA = LENGTH * WIDTH
```

Still high level but we're operating the computer in Fortran as a calculator and in Lisp as a thinking/reasoning machine of sorts.

A lot of languages have picked up on these concepts and it is normal these days to manipulate complex data structures as if they are the things themselves. Of course the concept of a structured piece of data like a record in a database isn't Lisp's but the concept of manipulating it in a symbolic matter? That is very much down to McCarthy and his work already predicts something that we now call "object-oriented programming". The idea that computers could easily transcend numbers and be more than just a record keeper and calculator: it is not too far-fetched to trace that back to a professor and his students doing some work on a lambda-calculus based language in the 1950s.

A language to create languages

By far the most powerful contribution of Lisp is the idea that if you have a problem, one way to solve that problem on a computer is to create a language specifically geared towards that problem and then solve the problem in that language.

That approach is usually a scary proposition because creating programming languages is hard. The successful ones, even when originally created by a single person or a small team, have dozens or even hundreds of people working on it discussing things to include and to reject; endlessly tweaking it and honing it for the specific application in mind.

And yet there is the lonely Lisp hacker doing pretty much that. While the approach is never as explicit as "identify problem -> create language -> solve problem," working in Lisp invariable entails building a little language specific to the problem domain at hand; Lisp is just so good at that that it never feels that way.

It should not come as a surprise that Lisp can operate this way: extensibility was one of the core requirements that McCarthy had in mind when starting out. Let's dive into a couple of features that make it easy in Lisp to build domain-specific languages.

Homoiconicity

One of the harder parts of creating a programming language is to make the computer understand what you mean. And often you also want to go the other way around: generate code or at least manipulate it. Say that you have a description of an application programming interface to some service or library you need to use and the description is structured so a computer could read it. You could take the description and painstakingly type in the equivalent code or you could take the description, read it in, and then let the computer generate code. Whether you read program code in your own newly developed language to parse it or generate code from machine-readable descriptions: it is code but for the time being, you are treating it as data. And, as we have seen, in Lisp it is extremely easy to go back and forth between the two.

Homoiconicity is a term that did not originate with Lisp but describes it very well. A programming language is considered "homoiconic" when code and data have the same or similar shape and are manipulated in the same way (homo = 'the same' and icon = 'representation'). It means that code like

```
(defun plus-one (x) (+ x 1))
```

and data like

```
(cat ((claw-count . 20) (sheds . a-lot)))
```

are essentially the same thing, just s-expressions. It is only when we feed the first one to a compiler that it morphs into a function we can call. Still, it is just a bunch of linked of cons cells, exactly like the structured description of a cat's essential features that follows it.

So if we want to create a specific language and we're ok with Lisp's syntax then the job becomes simple. Say we want to work with an API and there is a machine-readable description of the API. You read in that definition, massage it into s-expressions and then massage the s-expressions into other s-expressions that happen to represent the code you want to generate. Feed it to the Lisp compiler, done. Technically, you just wrote a compiler; but it didn't feel that way. And similarly for working on code or data you create yourself to describe something domain-specific: It is just a bunch of s-expressions so you can let the Lisp parser read it in and then do whatever you want with it to emit the equivalent Lisp code to make your language execute. You just wrote another compiler and again it didn't feel that way.

"But," some will argue, "you can do that in every language!" Indeed, since the dawn of time people have written code that generates code. A great example is Sun Microsystem's RPC library, which had an "Interface Definition Language" to describe message formats, and C code would read that and emit new C code. There is a big difference though: the C code needs to *parse* the IDL into an ad-hoc in memory data structure, and then (most likely) starts printing out strings. After that one step, it is done: you can't further work on these strings (not without writing another parser, now for the C Programming Language), and not much in the code will be useful for other "external" domain-specific languages. In Lisp, it is s-expressions all the way so everything that knows how to operate on s-expressions (which is "everything" in Lisp) can be roped in to help. It is a bit like the old argument about "can this language do X?" where a lot of people will smugly answer "yes, if it is Turing-complete," an answer that is correct but not helpful. The question of course needs to be phrased as "is it *easy* to do X in this language?" Now we're talking about qualitative differences, but of the sort that make a huge impact on the daily life of a programmer in a language, and qualitatively, Lisp makes it trivial to define little languages tailored to solve specific problems.

There are other languages that took a page out of Lisp's playbook and adopted the ability to morph into something problem specific language. A popular and modern example is Elixir; it does not feel "Lisp-y" at all:

```
for i <- 1..10 do
  IO.puts("Hello #i!")
end
```

but that's just superficial. The first thing that the Elixir parser does is to convert this code into:

```
{:for []
 [
   {:<- []
    [
      {:i
       [
         if_undefined: :apply
         context: Elixir
         imports: [{0 IEx.Helpers} {1 IEx.Helpers}]
       ] Elixir}
      {:.. [context: Elixir imports: [{0 Kernel} {2 Kernel}]] [1 10]}
    ]}
   [
     do: {{:. [] [{:__aliases__ [alias: false] [:IO]} :puts]} []
      [
        {:<<>> []
         [
           "Hello "
           {:"::" []
            [
              {{:. [] [Kernel :to_string]} [from_interpolation: true]
               [
```

```
                {:i
                 [
                   if_undefined: :apply
                   context: Elixir
                   imports: [{0 IEx.Helpers} {1 IEx.Helpers}]
                 ] Elixir}
              ]}
             {:binary [] Elixir}
           ]}
          "!"
        ]}
     ]}
  ]
 ]}
```

and if we clean this up and get rid of the special syntax (square brackets indicate lists and curlies indicate "tuples" which are, if you squint a bit, just a special kind of list):

```
(:for ((:<- ((:i (:.. 10))))
   (do:
     ((:<<>>
       ("Hello "
        (:"::" (((:. ((:i)))))
        "!"))))))
```

It's not *exactly* Lisp, but—apart from the extra annotations to help Elixir's compiler resolve things like `i` to the correct value—it is very close to just a set of s-expressions. And, indeed, Elixir comes with a macro facility that is pretty much a straight lift from Lisp, including things like `defmacro`, `quote`, and `unquote`. Macros aren't anything special, they are just code that operates on code as if it is data in Lisp-like languages; it's the homoiconicity that makes the thing work nicely.

You may recall that McCarthy wanted a LISP 2 that would look more like ALGOL but still had the power of Lisp under the hood: Elixir comes quite close to realizing that idea.

If your language has a macro facility that operates on what we call "the AST level" (where "AST" stands for "Abstract Syntax Tree", essentially the simple transformation from source code to something s-expression like that the Elixir compiler did above), then you have a language that likely traces this bit of ancestry back to Lisp.

THE TERM "MACRO" — The term "macro" did not originate with Lisp but with early assembler programs. Assembler has a lot of repetitive code. For example, most assembly code comes with conventions about how functions call each other (pass arguments on the call stack, or in registers, or a combination of these) and these conventions are the start and end of any function call and function implementation, always exactly the same and invariably multiple lines of code. It was obvious that having some code generation facility where you could say "define the start of a function body as these five assembly instructions under the name ENTER" and then just type "ENTER" everywhere would be both a time-saver and a bug prevention device. Lisp borrowed the term, but its manipulation of s-expressions really is on a different level than the simple text-level pre-processing that assembly languages (and related languages like C) still employ. But we call them both "macros". Naming is hard.

First-class functions

Another explicit design goal of McCarthy, and we encountered it earlier, was the ability to use whole functions as data in computer memory. Not just the source code, but the compiled version: to be able to refer to it and pass it around as if it were just another piece of data. It is what allows us to say, in a modern Lisp:

```
☞ > (mapcar #'factorial '(1 2 3 4 5))
(1 2 6 24 120)
```

We invoke the Common Lisp standard function `mapcar` (map over the CARs of the list) with two arguments, one of which is a literal list and the other happens to be a reference to some implementation of the factorial function.

Without it, extending the language with custom constructs is hard or even impossible. It is often seen as a defining feature of "functional languages"—languages with deep roots in the lambda calculus, like Lisp—versus "object-oriented languages." Classifications of programming languages is hard, though. What to make of this Smalltalk example (it does the same as the Lisp code above)?

```
#(1 2 3 4 5) do: [:i | i factorial].
```

It is *slightly* different, but essentially what we do here is send the array `#(1 2 3 4 5)` a message `do:`. The argument: a block of code in the form of an in-line function with a single argument, or a lambda expression if you wish. Something so essential as iteration is implemented in what people consider the language that is the pinnacle of OO using, well, functional-style code. Smalltalk can't even decide to go left or right without resorting to passing blocks of code around as data:

```
(indicator = 'left')
  ifTrue: [car goLeft]
  ifFalse: [car goRight].
```

What happens here is that the expression that compares the variable (indicator) to the value `'left'` results in an object of class *Boolean*. Depending whether the two are the same, the object is an instance of one of two subclasses: *True* and *False*. Yes, in Smalltalk, *everything* is an object, even Boolean values like "true" and "false"!

Here is the fun bit: the Smalltalk class *True* implements the message `ifTrue:ifFalse` as:

```
ifTrue: trueBlock ifFalse: falseBlock
  ^ trueBlock value.
```

while the class *False* implements it as:

```
ifTrue: trueBlock ifFalse: falseBlock
  ^ falseBlock value.
```

In these to methods, `value` is the message you send to a "block" of code to evaluate it and the caret is Smalltalk's way of saying `return`.

Putting it all together: we have a comparison which returns the object "true" or "false", instances of their respective classes, and Smalltalk's dispatch mechanism invokes the corresponding method for the message `ifTrue:ifFalse`.

Without higher-order functions, this most object oriented language of them all, which even does boolean logic using polymorphic dispatch, would look different indeed!

Treating code as data and having references to functions to pass around is not new, and in fact, *any* "Von Neumann" style computer, where bytes that represent code and bytes that represent data are mixed together in the same memory space, may be considered homoiconic (and it is a good bet that if you are reading this electronically, you are reading this on a Von Neumann style computer). Assembly programmers have used "jump tables" for a long time, where you calculate somehow an offset into a list of addresses, and then jump to that address. However, many "high level" programming languages, like Fortran—the very reason that McCarthy started his quest that resulted in Lisp—do not allow for this of trickery. It was Lisp that showed the way and the feature was deemed too powerful and important that Alan Kay and his people felt it necessary to make it a core feature of the OO language they were inventing.

Lambda expressions and references to functions are all but a standard feature of modern computer programming languages, and you can probably thank McCarthy and his band of students for that.

HARVARD: THE OTHER ARCHITECTURE — As the text says, most computers you will encounter in the wild are "Von Neumann" style computers, which have a unified memory space for code and data (and thus can be considered homoiconic on the machine language level). This is not the only way to build computers, and a lot of microcontrollers work differently. They have separated memory areas for code and for data, and this is called the "Harvard architecture". It has some benefits: code can be "burned" in cheaper and permanent read-only memory, then there is often somewhat persistent battery-backed memory—a little bit of it—for certain configuration parameters, and finally volatile memory for working data. This makes the part cheaper to build and, to some extent, safer as well: a lot of attack vectors on regular computers rely on being able to modify code or make a program jump into what really should be considered as data, and Harvard architecture computers simply don't have that capability. Of course, with losing that capability you also lose a lot of strengths that require mixing of code and data which is why this architecture has proven less popular for general computers.

As usual, in real life, the dichotomy is not as strong and a modern computer is a mixture of architectures anyway, having numerous embedded systems supporting the central processing unit. The complexity of the modern computer makes a "pure" implementation of a single architectural model infeasible and probably unwise.

Your language is a Lisp

Is it? Well, unless it is *called* "Lisp" (or "Scheme"), probably not. But your language is likely to have a lot of features that trace back straight to work initially done in Lisp. Sure, other languages have had their impact as well, we should not underestimate the contributions of the likes of Algol and Simula, but if you look at modern software development, where terms like "Domain Specific Languages" are bandied about whether people work in Lisp or not; where an OO language like Java had "first-class functions" as one of the most celebrated updates in its history; and where large-scale symbolic manipulation of data is probably the job definition of a majority of developers, the impact is outsized.

It does not matter, of course, whether your language "is a Lisp". Let's end our journey with a well-known passage by physicist Richard Feynman to help us realize that what your language can and cannot do (and where it came from) is much more important than how you name or categorize it.

> [...] and one kid said to me, "See that bird, what kind of a bird is that?"
>
> And I said, "I haven't the slightest idea what kind of a bird it is."
>
> He says, "It's a brown throated thrush," or something, "You father doesn't tell you anything."
>
> But it was the opposite: my father *had* taught me. Looking at a bird he says, "Do you know what that bird is? It's a brown throated thrust; but in Portuguese it's a ... in Italian a ...," he says "in Chinese it's a ..., in Japanese a ...," etcetera.
>
> "Now," he says, "you know in all the languages you want to know what the name of that bird is and when you've finished with all that," he says, "you'll know absolutely nothing whatever about the bird. You only know about humans in different places and what they call the bird."
>
> "Now," he says, "let's look at the bird."
>
> – Richard Feynman, *What Do You Care What Other People Think?* [21]

Lasting Autograph

– Richard P. Gabriel

In the late two thousand aughts my friend and colleague Robert Hirschfeld asked me to ask John McCarthy to autograph a copy of the Lisp 1.5 Programmer's Manual. Robert is a Smalltalker, and because Alan Kay, Smalltalk's creator, admired Lisp and in particular the Lisp-in-Lisp interpreter, eval, he wanted the signature to be on that page in the Manual. By that time, John was in poor health, mostly bedridden, and with declining mental clarity—perhaps dementia, perhaps Alzheimer's. Over the past few years I had been visiting him occasionally, just to talk and keep him alert; sometimes I'd read a chapter from a novel he enjoyed. He had a caregiver, and a wife—Wife #3, Carolyn Talcott—quietly looking after him.

I don't remember much about the visit. The entrance to his home was dark and his bed was down another hallway to the left in a living area, not a bedroom. As I arrived he was sitting up on the edge of the bed in red & black pajamas. He seemed to recognize me. We talked a bit, and then I asked him about signing the book. He said he would and then put it on his knee and with the pen I brought he very ...slowly ...signed it.

This was the house where I would also sometimes go to explain how I repaired the programs he sent me to help him with. Surprisingly—perhaps—he was a lousy Lisp programmer. None of the programs of his I saw was more than a few pages long.

We chatted a little more, then he grew tired and got properly into bed. That was the last time I saw him. He signed at the top of page 13 above the definitions of the functions `apply` and `eval`:

> *I used to understand all this. I'm sure you can.*
> *John McCarthy*

I used to understand all this. I'm sure you can
John McCarthy

if either side of the equation is defined at all.

Example

```
f:      λ[[x;y];cons[car[x];y]]
fn:        (LAMBDA (X Y) (CONS (CAR X) Y))
arg1:      (A B)
arg2:      (C D)
args:      ((A B) (C D))

evalquote[(LAMBDA (X Y) (CONS (CAR X) Y)); ((A B) (C D))] =
    λ[[x;y];cons[car[x];y]][(A B);(C D)]=
    (A C D)
```

evalquote is defined by using two main functions, called eval and apply. apply handles a function and its arguments, while eval handles forms. Each of these functions also has another argument that is used as an association list for storing the values of bound variables and function names.

```
evalquote[fn;x] = apply[fn;x;NIL]
```

where

```
apply[fn;x;a] =
    [atom[fn] → [eq[fn;CAR] → caar[x];
                 eq[fn;CDR] → cdar[x];
                 eq[fn;CONS] → cons[car[x];cadr[x]];
                 eq[fn;ATOM] → atom[car[x]];
                 eq[fn;EQ] → eq[car[x];cadr[x]];
                 T → apply[eval[fn;a];x;a]];
    eq[car[fn];LAMBDA] → eval[caddr[fn];pairlis[cadr[fn];x;a]];
    eq[car[fn];LABEL] → apply[caddr[fn];x;cons[cons[cadr[fn];
                                                caddr[fn]];a]]]

eval[e;a] = [atom[e] → cdr[assoc[e;a]];
    atom[car[e]] →
              [eq[car[e],QUOTE] → cadr[e];
              eq[car[e];COND] → evcon[cdr[e];a];
              T → apply[car[e];evlis[cdr[e];a];a]];
    T → apply[car[e];evlis[cdr[e];a];a]]
```

pairlis and assoc have been previously defined.

```
evcon[c;a] = [eval[caar[c];a] → eval[cadar[c];a];
              T → evcon[cdr[c];a]]
```

and

```
evlis[m;a] = [null[m] → NIL;
              T → cons[eval[car[m];a];evlis[cdr[m];a]]]
```

Appendix A

Retro hardware

This book is about software, but software is defined by the hardware it runs on. We have therefore highlighted some important hardware bits, like how much memory the IBM 704 had, or what its processing speed was. That sort of stuff directly defined what you could do with it, so it's important.

In this appendix, we'll take a look at some random bits of hardware technology that are just interesting in their own right. Old hardware is getting more and more attention, for a whole string of reasons: Studying the computers of the past is a great way to learn about the craft of operating and programming computers and it is important to preserve some of that old hardware; There is a yearning, as usual in many trades, to the simpler days of the past; And finally, maybe, because there's something very tactile and awesome and robust about the old electronic and electromechanical stuff.

As said, this is a random selection, nothing more, and it's in random order.

Core memory

Today we still sometimes use the term "core dump" to signal that a computer, or a piece of software, got so confused that the best it could do was to dump its entire memory contents to persistent storage (like a hard disk) for humans to puzzle over. But where does this term come from? Core memory consisted of tiny ferrite "cores", doughnut-shaped beads made of a magnetically impressionable material. Data was stored by having the cores magnetized one way (representing a 0) or the other (for a 1). Interestingly enough, this memory is write-only—you can't read it directly. What you can do is try to write it and measure whether an opposing current got induced because of the bead's current magnetic field orientation—if so, you

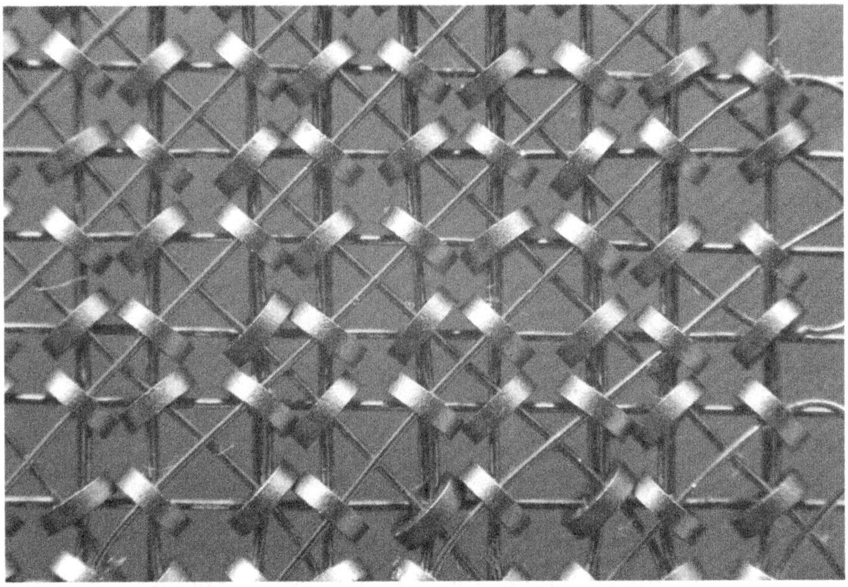

Figure A.1: A small piece of core memory
(Source: *Konstantin Lanzet, via Wikipedia*[1])

were trying to overwrite a 1 (say), if not, a 0. After this "destructive read," the value obtained can be written back.

Figure A.1 shows a macro photo of a small piece of core memory (each bead is maybe a millimeter in diameter here). It is woven together with wires that fulfill different functions. Two wires "address" a particular ferrite bead's X and Y location by running current through the respective wires that is, in each, well under the threshold for changing the bead's magnetic state but together comes close to it. This sort of "activates" the addressed bead for the write wire: the X + Y + write wires together have enough current to change the addressed bead's state, so while the write line may be zig-zagging through many beads, only one bead will reach the current threshold to change state. A fourth wire is used to sense the presence or absence of a counteracting magnetic field and is used for the destructive read. In the picture, the horizontal and one of the two veritcal wires are the X and Y addressing wires, the other vertical wires are the sense wires, and the zig-zagging wire is the write wire. The ferrite beads in this picture can store 54 bits, so imagine this times 20,000 (all hand-made) to get to the amount of memory the IBM 704 sported.

Core memory is resilient: data is essentially kept forever. It is reasonably fast (cycle times at the end of the technology's practical

[1] `https://en.wikipedia.org/wiki/File:KL_Kernspeicher_Makro_1.jpg`

life were below a microsecond), and it is incredibly resistant against electromagnetic interference, be it from purposely-caused electromagnetic pulses or the radiation from space. Because of these characteristics, the military and space agencies used core memory well into the 1980s—the Space Shuttle, for example, used the technology in many mission-critical areas.

Core memory can also be used as read-only memory in a simple way: have your read line go through or bypass each core location to represent an unchangeable 0 or 1 value. For the Apollo guidance computer, for example, Navajo women painstakingly wove the pattern of 0s and 1s that represented its programs in core memory modules using microscopes, fine copper wire, and what must have been extremely steady hands. These and other intriguing factoids have made core memory receive renewed attention in hacker and maker circles: at the time of writing, for example, in exchange for the paltry sum of $160 you can buy a small 64 bit core memory module to experiment with. But it should not be too hard to roll your own, if you're so inclined.

Punched cards

Everybody who had more than a five minute introduction on the history of computers has encountered the concept of punched cards, and the story invariable starts with Jacquard's programmable weaving loom, then goes on to discuss Hollerith and finally lands at the "modern" punched card that can hold 80 columns of text, and was used exclusively at the beginning and still extensively in the 1970s and even throughout the 1980s. Figure A.2 shows a typical card of this style, in this case containing a line of Fortran code.

This card is lacking one thing: the human readable version of what is on the card. In the illustration, the card contains what looks like Fortran code:

```
12    PIFRA=(A(JB,37)-A(JB,99))/A(JB,47)
```

Usually, the "keypunch" device would not only punch out a column of holes, but also have a little dot matrix printer to print the character represented by the holes on top. This would make it easier to "read" the cards, important when a stack of cards got dropped. In one of the funnier remarks about punched cards, Professor Brailsford of Nottingham University dryly obseves that dropping a stack of cards was a really good way to learn about the factorial function [69]. The card shown here, though, has "insurance": the very rightmost column has a number, and this most likely was a serial number for the cards

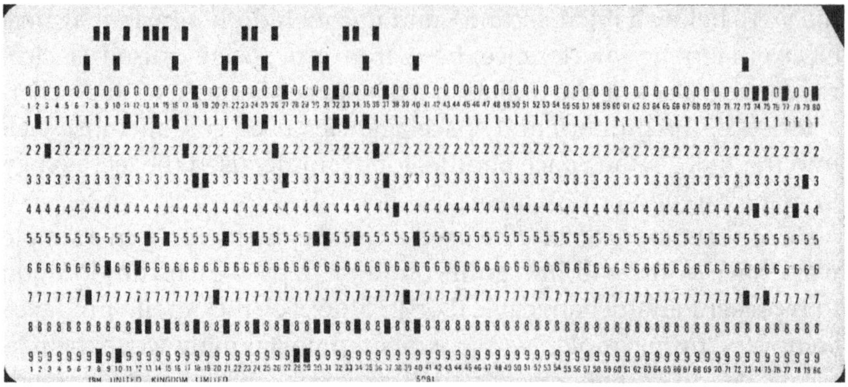

Figure A.2: A punched card
(Source: *Pete Berkinshaw, via Wikipedia*[2])

in the program. This is card 430, and when dropped, all you needed to do is to stack them up again and drop them into a card sorter, an electromechanical contraption that would use the data in these last columns to re-stack your cards in the correct order.

One interesting thing you will notice is that never you will see more than two holes in a single column. This is to preserve the structural integrity of the cardstock material: if you'd punch a bunch of columns with lots of holes then the card would have areas with more air than paper and it would be too easy to damage the card.

Punched cards were an eminently practical input device for the early computers. Teletypes were invented and in use, but having a programmer type in program code directly into the computer, before time sharing was invented, hogging that expensive machine just to type in code at human speed was a silly idea. Here is a fun quote on how people were thinking about how to protect computers from programmers, in this case in the context of the IBM 704 installed at General Motors in Detroit:

> We threw the programmers out of the machine room, hired professional computer operators, and standardized the communication between the programmer and the operator. The programmers caught on to the new mode of operation rather quickly since we instructed the operator to proceed to the next job when there was confusion or something didn't work out. [61, p. 9]

It was clear: the machine had to run, the programmers' job was to not interfere with that, and a stack of punched cards could be read in

[2] `https://commons.wikimedia.org/wiki/File:Used_Punchcard_5151286161.jpg`

Figure A.3: The IBM Model 26 keypunch
(Source: *leighklotz, via Wikipedia*[3])

at a speed of dozens per second so that program entry time was kept to a minimum. Punched cards were fast and efficient, at least from the computer operator's point of view. And punched cards were not just input: the computer could output them as well. This way, if one program did a computation step, the results could be punched out and then mixed in with the program for the next computation step as input. Everything revolved around punched cards. In MIT's internal manual for the IBM 704 [19], there is a hardware list that includes half a dozen keypunch terminals, a card sorter, a duplicator, and off-line equipment to exchange code and data between magnetic tape and cards. All of these were usable without taking up valuable computer time.

So there you are, as a programmer, sitting behind the IBM 26 keypunch (see Figure A.3). Every keystroke you type immediately is made permanent by fresh holes in the current card, every time you hit enter, a new card is put in place, and as you progress, slowly a stack of cards builds up at your left. A typo means a card can go into the shredder and you can start over. Ninety-four cards later, you have your code for an implementation of Wang's algorithm for propositional calculus ready, one card per line of code. You grab the stacked cards from the keypunch, then get the standard deck of cards that goes before it: It contains instructions to tell the computer

[3] `https://commons.wikimedia.org/wiki/File:IBM_26_Keypunch.jpg`

to load LISP 1.5 (from magnetic tape and not from a truly enormous stack of cards), load your code from the card deck, and finally print the results. You walk over to the operator, only to find that there's a queue of jobs so you drop the cards off and go out for a smoke (everybody smoked these days, and now you know why). Next comes the fun bit: the read-out shows you missed a closing parenthesis, so you take that card out, carefully splitting the deck so you put the new one back in the right spot, re-type it, stack everything up again, and back to the operator's queue it is.

Punched cards are awesome: all of the punched cards that have been physically preserved are still readable, and it shares that robustness aspect with core memory. Programs on punched cards last for centuries, and reading them is trivial; they're a great boon to computer historians in that way. But for programming a computer? Let's be glad that McCarthy insisted on pushing through timesharing.

Appendix B

Retrocomputing

There has been a realization in the last few decades that the old systems we studied in this book are about to be lost forever, and retrocomputing—the art of running old systems—has seen a huge surge because of that. It not only allows authors to be more precise when talking about history by letting them work on the actual environments of the past, it is also really cool to get a good feeling for the sort of environments that the Hackers Of Lore used.

While this book is not a scientific publication, we think it's important that every code example in here is reproducible by you. Lisp is a very hands-on system and we want you to try things out; and maybe experience a bit of how it would have been to code on a late 1950s IBM mainframe. This appendix, therefore, explains how to run every system used in the book. All code is open source and freely available from various places on the Internet; the versions and references used here are just those that happened to have worked for the author, newer versions are likely available by the time you read this.

The main tool is SIMH [60], the Computer History Simulation Project, which implements simulators for an impressive array of historical machines. Emulating a complex system like a PDP-10, finding the original ITS tapes, converting them to modern ASCII, and packaging it all up to run on a modern Linux, Mac, or Windows system is no small feat. We are truly standing on the shoulders of giants here and we can't thank the people behind efforts like SIMH enough. A lot of the more interesting bits of this book would not have been possible without their work.

The instructions below have been tested on Linux systems running the Debian 12 distribution. The author's repositories also contain support for Nix-based systems, which were tested on NixOS 23.11.

LISP 1.5 on the IBM 7094

The starting point to learn more about LISP 1.5 is the page on the LISP 1.5 family on the site of the Software Preservation Group [16]. There is a reference to downloadable tarball [43] on that page that contains a quick way to get things up and running. A repository based on that tarball which adds some patches to make things work on current systems can be found at [44] and is probably a better starting point than the bare tarball.

However, the quickest way to get going is to use Docker. We'll assume some terminal skills and the availability of a Docker setup that can run x86-64 containers from here; please refer to your operating system's documentations for details on how to set this up. Once you have it all setup, open a terminal, and run:

```
☞ $ docker pull cdegroot/i7094-lisp15
 docker.io/cdegroot/i7094-lisp15:latest
Trying to pull docker.io/cdegroot/i7094-lisp15:latest...
Getting image source signatures
Copying blob 9bde31704b79 done   |
Copying blob b0a0cf830b12 done   |
Copying blob eed97612fb79 done   |
Copying blob b83c0b624aaf done   |
Copying blob 395782bc29a5 done   |
Copying blob e1dde6b67431 done   |
Copying blob 59b138853080 done   |
Copying blob c388622290eb done   |
Copying config eca66c2a46 done   |
Writing manifest to image destination
eca66c2a460ce0ff48670593dee119b098c63529254ed768d9e975de8910ed78
$
```

(The details in the output may differ, but as long as you don't get any error messages, you're good to go). One of the simpler programs, and bundled as an example with the emulator code, is a recursive factorial program. Fire up an editor and create `factorial.lisp`:

```
       TEST  FACTORIAL

DEFINE ((
   (FACTORIAL (LAMBDA (X)
                (COND ((EQUAL X 0) 1)
                       (T (TIMES X (FACTORIAL (SUB1 X))))))
    )
))
```

```
FACTORIAL (10)

STOP
FIN
END OF LISP RUN
```

A couple of things of note: `DEFINE` is a bit of an odd duck—modern Lisps will have `(DEFINE ...)` (or `DEFUN`, or `DEF`, or any variation of that). And there's some non-LISP code wrapping the actual definition of factorial and its implementation; this is the code to tell the supervisor process what the job name is, and where the code starts and ends; if you experiment with your own code, just consider it boilerplate and wrap your code in it as well. Once you have the file, go back to the terminal:

☞ **$ docker run -i cdegroot/i7094-lisp15 <factorial.lisp**

```
=== Starting i7094 run ===


IBM 7094 simulator V3.8-1
MTA: unit is read only
MTA: unit is read only
MTA: creating new file
MTA: creating new file
MTA: creating new file
CDR: creating new file
CDP: creating new file
LPT: creating new file

HALT instruction, PC: 10524 (TRA 10523)
Goodbye

=== Run done, output follows ===

             TEST  FACTORIAL



  THE TIME ( 0/ 0  000.0) HAS COME, THE WALRUS SAID, TO TALK OF MANY THI
NGS .....   -LEWIS CARROLL-
 EVALQUOTE OPERATOR AS OF 1 MARCH 1961.    INPUT LISTS NOW BEING READ.


  THE TIME ( 0/ 0  000.0) HAS COME, THE WALRUS SAID, TO TALK OF MANY THI
NGS .....   -LEWIS CARROLL-
  FUNCTION   EVALQUOTE   HAS BEEN ENTERED, ARGUMENTS..
 DEFINE

 (((FACTORIAL (LAMBDA (X) (COND ((EQUAL X 0) 1) (T (TIMES X (FACTORIAL (
SUB1 X)))))))))

 END OF EVALQUOTE, VALUE IS ..
 *TRUE*

  FUNCTION   EVALQUOTE   HAS BEEN ENTERED, ARGUMENTS..
```

```
FACTORIAL

(10)


END OF EVALQUOTE, VALUE IS ..
3628800



  THE TIME ( 0/ 0  000.0) HAS COME, THE WALRUS SAID, TO TALK OF MANY THI
NGS .....   -LEWIS CARROLL-
 END OF EVALQUOTE OPERATOR
      FIN

 END OF FILE ON INPUT -OVERLORD- *0  6*
$
```

The Docker container takes the Lisp code on its stdin using a small wrapper script; this is because Docker containers can't (by default) access file on your filesystems. There are solutions for this but they are all more complicated than simply piping the file into the container—just take care to specify `-i` and to not forget the < redirection.

The wrapper script writes your code to its local filesystem, and then invokes the IBM 7094 emulator with two emulated tapes: one with your Lisp code on it, converted on-the-fly first in BCD from ASCII and then wrapped with tape headers and footers, and one with Lisp 1.5 on it. The run completes, the mainframe halts, and then the wrapper script prints the output from the run on the terminal.

This not only emulates the computer, but also the workflow: if you make a typo, the system will loudly complain and you get to find the error, fix it, and try again. The only step left out is walking back from the mainframe room to your office with a print-out, and having to punch the correction on a card and insert it in the right spot in your deck before trying again.

The tarball and corresponding repository come with an example program in the file `propcal.txt` which has code for the Wang propositional calculus from the LISP 1.5 book, and this is a nice starting point for trying out some beefier Lisp code on the IBM 7094 with LISP 1.5.

Maclisp on the DEC PDP-10 under ITS

Where LISP 1.5 runs, essentially, on "bare metal", Maclisp is expecting a much more complex environment. The most accessible environment is MIT's ITS—Incompatible Timesharing System—which was a response on MIT's official efforts at timesharing systems that did not make the average MIT hacker happy. ITS is well-supported on the SIMH PDP-10 emulator, and it comes with Maclisp. And you don't only get a famous version of Lisp, but also early versions of Scheme, Emacs, and a ton of utilities and games. Essentially, it will transport you right back to the MIT AI Lab of the '70s and its associated hacker culture. This machine deserves a deep dive if you're into retrocomputing so we will not only show Maclisp, but also some other interesting bits and pieces.

First, credits where credits are due: a big thank you to all the contributors to the PDP-10 ITS repository on GitHub [62]. They deserve thanks not only for the emulator and operating system itself, but also for the awesome job of chasing down backup tapes, digitizing print-outs, and assembling all that into a reasonable facsimile of what was used in the 1970s.

Where the LISP 1.5 emulation was a "one-shot" run of the mainframe computer, ITS requires a bit more work and will need to you actually work "on" the computer. It is not hard to learn, but it will take some adjustment and especially, for those used to work on the command line, to unlearn some things because, well, pretty much everything worked differently back then.

If you're well-versed with the command line, build tools, tweaking things, and so on, by all means checkout the repository above and follow build instructions. It will give you the most flexible setup and you will end up with all sorts of updates. You need MacOS, FreeBSD or (Ubuntu/Debian) Linux for this, although if you are a Windows user, the Windows Subsystem for Linux should work just fine. If you just want to give ITS a quick spin, continue reading and follow the Docker-based instructions below; they're a bit more involved than the simple "batch-mode" LISP 1.5 setup, but not too hard to follow.

Start by pulling the image so you know you're all set.

```
☞ $ docker pull cdegroot/pdp10-its
Trying to pull docker.io/cdegroot/its:latest...
Getting image source signatures
...
Writing manifest to image destination
0490b593acd6abdf93bc58505d5394f660dd58211fd017149f747f2c8bd0a035
```

Again, ignore the numbers, as long as the output matches you're good to go. One problem with Docker images that require complex interaction is that you need to learn long and complicated command lines, but this image comes with a little helper embedded. Simply running the image will tell you what to do:

```
☞ $ docker run cdegroot/pdp10-its
As a first step, we need to copy the bundled disk image to a place
```

```
outside the container. Please re-run this container as follows:

docker run -it -v pdp10-its-out:/its/out  \
    cdegroot/pdp10-its:latest ./runit.sh copy
```

ITS comes with state stored on a disk, like a modern operating system. Docker containers are bad at managing state, so you need to run the container with an external Docker volume where the emulator can write the PDP-10 disk images. This also means that anything you change to "your" PDP-10 will be preserved across reboots. Go ahead, and enter the command—it will mount a Docker volume in the container and instruct the script to write initial (clean) disk images to it:

```
☞ $ docker run -it -v pdp10-its-out:/its/out cdegroot/pdp10-
its:latest ./runit.sh copy

This will copy the distribution disk image into the working directo
mounted into the container. Only do this if you're doing a new setu
or are fine losing the data you currently have.

Hit [Enter] to continue or [Ctrl-C] to abort.
☞ Enter

'./gt40' -> '/its/out/./gt40'
'./pdp10-ka' -> '/its/out/./pdp10-ka'
'./pdp10-ka/aplogo.ptp' -> '/its/out/./pdp10-ka/aplogo.ptp'
'./pdp10-ka/bootvt.bin' -> '/its/out/./pdp10-ka/bootvt.bin'
...
'./pdp10-ka/syshst/h3text.2018' -> \
    '/its/out/./pdp10-ka/syshst/h3text.2018'
'./pdp10-ka/system' -> '/its/out/./pdp10-ka/system'
'./pdp10-ka/system/config.202' -> \
    '/its/out/./pdp10-ka/system/config.202'

Volume setup. You can now use the start program with

docker run -it -v pdp10-its-out:/its/out -p 10002:10002 \
  cdegroot/pdp10-its:latest ./start
```

As you see, the script gives you the option to bail out with Ctrl-C. You can use the copy command to re-create your PDP-10 from scratch, which is handy if you messed things up, but less so if you didn't mean to. In this case, we're starting, so hitting Enter will show a list of files that are copied and the next command to run. We're almost in business! Copy the command it output and watch the magic happen:

☞
```
$ docker run -it -v pdp10-its-out:/its/out -p 10002:10002 \
cdegroot/pdp10-its:latest ./start
```

```
KA-10 simulator Open SIMH V4.1-0 Current  \
    git commit id: 20fa16ec
/its/out/pdp10-ka/run-18> set dpy disabled
%SIM-ERROR: Non-existent device: DPY
/its/out/pdp10-ka/run-20> set stk enabled
%SIM-ERROR: Non-existent device: STK
/its/out/pdp10-ka/run-22> at -u tk 10000 speed=300
%SIM-INFO: Listening on port 10000
/its/out/pdp10-ka/run-23> at -u tk line=2,10012
%SIM-INFO: Line 2 Listening on port 10012
/its/out/pdp10-ka/run-26> at -u dpk 10002 speed=4800
%SIM-INFO: Listening on port 10002
/its/out/pdp10-ka/run-27> at -u dpk line=11,10019 speed=4800
%SIM-INFO: Line 11 Listening on port 10019
/its/out/pdp10-ka/run-28> at -u dpk line=15,10020 speed=4800
%SIM-INFO: Line 15 Listening on port 10020
/its/out/pdp10-ka/run-30> at -u mty 10003 speed=50000
%SIM-INFO: Listening on port 10003
/its/out/pdp10-ka/run-31> at -u mty line=9,10018 speed=9600
%SIM-INFO: Line 9 Listening on port 10018
/its/out/pdp10-ka/run-32> at -u mty line=8,10017 speed=9600
%SIM-INFO: Line 8 Listening on port 10017
/its/out/pdp10-ka/run-33> at -u mty line=7,10016;notelnet speed=50000
%SIM-INFO: Line 7 Listening on port 10016
/its/out/pdp10-ka/run-34> at -u mty line=6,10015 speed=9600
%SIM-INFO: Line 6 Listening on port 10015
/its/out/pdp10-ka/run-36> at -u ten11 line=0,10011
%SIM-INFO: Line 0 Listening on port 10011
/its/out/pdp10-ka/run-37> at -u ten11 line=1,10021
%SIM-INFO: Line 1 Listening on port 10021
/its/out/pdp10-ka/run-39> at auxcpu 10006
%SIM-INFO: Listening on port 10006
/its/out/pdp10-ka/run-42> set imp ip=192.168.2.101/24
%SIM-INFO: IMP DHCP disabled
/its/out/pdp10-ka/run-45> at imp tap:tap0
%SIM-ERROR: Eth: open error - No such file or directory
/its/out/pdp10-ka/run-60> set wcnsls enabled joystick
%SIM-ERROR: Non-existent device: WCNSLS
/its/out/pdp10-ka/run-61> set ocnsls enabled
%SIM-ERROR: Non-existent device: OCNSLS

 DSKDMP
```

Ignore the errors and don't "touch" anything. You're now looking at the PDP-10 console, and here is where things get weird. You want to start ITS, and you can do that by entering [i] [t] [s] [Enter] [Esc] [g]. The latter keystrokes will be echoed by the system as `$G`, so when you see:

```
DSKDMP
```

Enter the magic sequence:

its Enter Esc g

and watch your PDP-10 start into ITS:

```
$G SALVAGER.317

IT IS NOW 3:40:06 PM EDT, SATURDAY, MAY 18, 2024

KA ITS 1652 IN OPERATION AT 15:40:06 KA ITS 1652 SYSTEM JOB USING THIS
CONSOLE. TV 11 WENT DOWN -- 15:40:06 LOGIN TARAKA 0 15:40:06 TOP LEVEL
INTERRUPT 200 DETACHED JOB # 4, USR:TARAKA CNAVRL 15:40:07 IT IS NOW
3:40:39 PM EDT, SATURDAY, MAY 18, 2024 LOGIN .BATCH 0 15:41:08
```

The date will, of course, differ and after you are done wondering how this '70s system survived Y2K, you can login. Enter "Ctrl-Z" to login:

☞ Ctrl + z

```
KA ITS.1652. DDT.1548. TTY 0 You're all alone, Fair share = 99% Welcome to ITS!

For brief information, type ? For a list of colon commands, type :? and
press Enter. For the full info system, type :INFO and Enter.

Happy hacking!
```

That's it. Welcome to the ITS "shell", called DDT, which is more of a debugger than a shell (some of you may remember MS-DOS' `DEBUG.COM`, and this is reminiscent of that) and it serves as both: you can do the expected things like file manipulation, starting programs, but also set interrupts and inspect registers. Needless to say, we'll declare the debugging bits out of scope here and limit our exploration to strictly the "user level".

Before we continue, you may have spotted the `-p 10002:10002` on the Docker command line. This opens up a network port to the PDP-10, behind which a terminal emulator server (to be precise, the "Datapoint kludge") is listening. You can continue as you are and things will work, but ITS has various background jobs running that will output to the console and will then mess up your Emacs session or similar. Therefore, it's recommended you open another window, ensure you have `telnet` installed, and continue through there, again logging in with Ctrl + z :

```
☞ $ telnet localhost 10002
Trying ::1...
Connected to localhost.
Escape character is `^]'.

Connected to the KA-10 simulator DPK device, line 0
```

```
☞ Ctrl+z
KA ITS.1652. DDT.1548. TTY 21 You're all alone, Fair share = 99%
Welcome to ITS!

For brief information, type ? For a list of colon commands,
type :? and press Enter. For the full info system,
type :INFO and Enter.

Happy hacking!
```

And we're back were we were, but now hopefully undisturbed. You may have noticed a little thing: these days, when you login to a computer, or a website, or pretty much *anything*, it wants to know who you are and prove that you are who you say you are, for example by asking for a username and password. ITS was built in the '70s, hippie culture was everywhere, and the idea was that this computer should be for everybody so it put up the lowest possible barrier towards participation. You can, therefore, just login and start working, without a need to identify yourself. For casual exploration, this is enough and we won't go into details of the user registration process, but let's at least set a username and create a home directory. For `CEES`, below, use your preferred username (or "handle" if you want to sound oldschool cool), which can be up to six characters.

> THE LIMIT OF SIX — A limit of six characters sounds arbitrary, but remember that the PDP-10 is a 36-bit machine, partially with such a word size to be able to store both elements of a Lisp CONS cell in a single word. The machine used a character encoding scheme with six bits per character (which gives room for encoding the uppercase letters, digits, and four special characters Space, Period, Percent, and Dollar sign). Six bits per character in a 36 bit word gives six characters that can be efficiently stored in a single word, and that's how usernames and file names are stored on the PDP-10.

```
☞ :login CEES
  KA: CEES; CEES MAIL - NON-EXISTENT DIRECTORY
☞ Ctrl+r CEES; ..new. (udir) Enter
  DSK: CEES; ..NEW. (UDIR) - FILE NOT FOUND
  DSK: DIR CEES CREATED BY CEES HACTRN 17:07:22
```

With these two commands you are signed in and have created your "home" directory (ignore the "non-existent directory", it is there). Time to explore, and let's dive right in with creating a quick Maclisp file using Emacs. Start Emacs, using `:emacs[Enter]` and type in a little "Hello, world" style program:

```
(defun hello ()
  (print "Hello Maclisp!")
  (terpri))
```

Ask Emacs to save (Ctrl+x Ctrl+s) and on the prompt type `hello lisp`. Then exit Emacs (Ctrl+x Ctrl+c). If you now do Enter, you should see the file appear:

```
KA   CEES
FREE BLOCKS #2=370 #3=1664 #0=571 #1=1684
  1   HELLO  LISP   1 ! 5/18/2024 17:11:50
```

ITS DOES NOT LIKE MODERN KEYBOARDS — If you were in Emacs and tried to move around using the cursor keys, chances are that all that happened is "A", "B", "C", "D" being displayed on screen, messing up your code. This is because most modern terminal emulators send VT-100 escape sequences and ITS expects VT-52 ones (even when it emits VT-100 compatible controls. Yes, it is confusing). The quick work-around, as long as you are not doing a lot of full-screen editing, is to use "[Ctrl-F]" and "[Ctrl-B]" to move a character right (forward) or left (backward), and to use "[Ctrl-N]" and "[Ctrl-P]" to navigate to the next or previous line.

Let's load it in Lisp:

```
☞ :lisp
  Alloc?
☞ n
```

```
*
☞ (load "hello")
T
☞ (hello)
"Hello MacLisp!"
```

ITS has job control, which allows you to switch quickly between multiple programs. If you hit Ctrl + z, you will be back in DDT (and it will print some stuff you can ignore—use Ctrl + l to refresh your screen). Say you do that from Maclisp, in order to edit some more:

```
☞ :job emacs
☞ :continue
```

And you're back in the editor (if nothing seems to happen, use Ctrl + l to refresh the screen and Emacs should repaint its state). You can save, exit Emacs, attach to Maclisp, reload the code, and re-run it again making for a quick development cycle (and for the real hackers under you, there are shortcut keys for all that to make it *really* fast). Try it!

Scheme and other programs

From DDT, `:SCHEME` will drop you in a pretty early version of Scheme, one that is still written as a bunch of Maclisp macros. The source code is available, in the `SCHEME;` directory (directories on ITS are indicated by a terminating semicolon). `:listf scheme;` will give you a listing of files—the `FASL` files are compiled Lisp, but the code you really want is in `NSCHSY 99`—use `[Ctrl-R]scheme;nschsy 99` to display the source code on the terminal or browse it with Emacs.

You stand to learn a bit about Maclisp and Scheme in one go. The numeric extension is normal on ITS, it denotes a version number and ITS has special shortcuts to say "save this file with the next version number" which would write this particular file as `NSCHSY 100`. Revision control systems were not invented yet, but this probably worked well enough.

Another program that some of you will recognize (as it is still around and installed by default on most Linux systems), and the cornerstone of ITS' help system, is `INFO`. You can use it to browse documentation on pretty much anything installed, like `:info emacs` from DDT. Navigation is limited, hit "H" in info to go through a quick primer.

A full list of installed software can be found in the Git repository [48], and another worthwhile thing to explore are emulators for all the hardware at MIT, including early video displays ("MAZE" will run on a vector video display and is a first-person perspective of a maze you can walk through); however, that requires a full local installation and we'll leave you to explore the Github repository all by yourself. There's a lot to find (Eliza, early Logo implementations, Macsyma, Conway's Game of Life, it is a long list), but please don't shutdown the machine without this:

```
☞ :games;adv448
  Is this a restarted game?
☞ n
  Welcome to Adventure!! Would you like instructions?
☞ n
  You are standing at the end of a road before a small brick building
  Around you is a forest. A small stream flows out of the building an
  down a gully.
```

...

Happy exploring!

Shutting down

If you want to save work, it is advised to do an orderly shutdown. Logout everywhere using `:logout`, and then on the "console"—the terminal window where you started Docker—do:

```
☞ :lock
  LOCK.156

  _
☞ 5down
```

And follow the prompts, then logout. You can use "Ctrl +] quit" to power off the machine and exit the console, or simply kill the container at this point.

Medley Interlisp

The final stop on our quick journey through history brings us to the US West coast, where at Xerox' famous Palo Alto Research Center (PARC) an incredible amount of innovation happened in the 1970s. One of the products to come out of this was Interlisp, and this system of lore has been revived in the Medley Interlisp project [81].

With the addition of a graphical user interface, Medley can't be wrapped in a container, so you need to go out to the project's download page [55] and download a package for your operating system, then follow the instructions to start. If you have problems getting things working, there is also the option to run Medley "online" in your browser, this requires user registration[56].

In either case, you should be greeted by this screen:

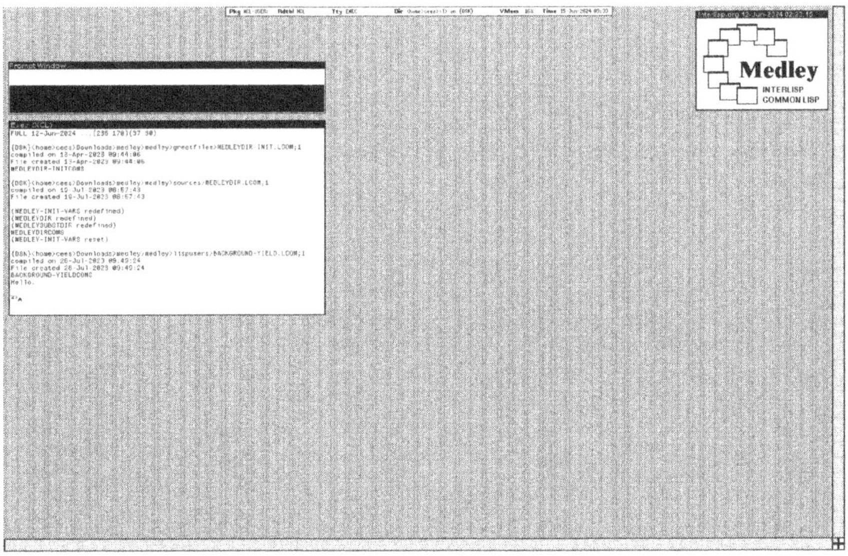

There are a couple of things to mention here: we're in the 1970/1980s, and operating systems were not really a thing on smaller computers (the PARC projects very much invented the idea of "personal computer"). Both systems out of PARC (Smalltalk and Interlisp) therefore came "nuts and bolts included", meaning that they run their own desktop, window manager, mouse handling, and so on. The mouse that Interlisp used was the same three-button mouse that Smalltalk used, with bindings to all of them. For example, on the standard Medley desktop, the right mouse click will bring up a context menu. If you don't have a three-button mouse, consult the documentation on potential alternatives. A final remark is that GUIs over the last fifty-odd years have advanced a lot in shininess and resolution, but little in interaction: you should feel reasonably at home for the basic operations of interacting with this little desktop environment.

Medley is a rich environment, and reasonably easy to use once you get over the—to our modern taste—somewhat ugly raster fonts. The system is worth exploring, but we won't tediously replicate the excellent primer called "Medley for the Novice", which is the best way to get acquainted with this system [54].

Medley is a great way to explore "Lisp as it was back in the day", but development on these Lisp machine style systems has not completely halted. A commercial version of Symbolic's Genera system is still available, and a more modern effort can be found in the form of experimental systems like Mezzano, a full operating system with graphical front-end pretty much completely written in SBCL Common Lisp [57].

Appendix C

A Tour of Current Lisps

In this appendix, we'll do a quick tour of current Lisp implementations. Nothing fancy, just what makes them special and where to find them, in the hope that you will find something to your liking. Each "kind" of Lisp will also come with some pointers on learning resources.

Lisp was implemented by a grad student on a 1950's mainframe pretty much overnight, and grad students and others have been following the example ever since. This means that there are *a lot* of Lisp implementations out there (Wikipedia lists around three dozen Common Lisps alone!), and that also means that the editorial sharp instruments had to come out to whittle down the list to something manageable. The list below tries to contain versions that see some threshold of use and that are "of interest", either because they are a standard Lisp or they are interesting in their own right. If you feel like following into the footsteps of all the Lisp implementors the world has seen, we got you covered as well: *Make a Lisp* [49] and *Build Your Own Lisp* [33] should keep you busy for a bit.

For all Lisp versions, we will reference the official site for details and downloads, but do note that more often than not, your operating system's package manager may already have it available.

Common Lisp

Before touring implementations, a little word on how to set things up. There are essentially two main ways to interact with Common Lisp these days: the commercial Lisps come with their own Integrated Development Environments (IDEs), while the Open Source ones expect you to bolt on your own. The latter is pretty much always Emacs talking to a running Lisp through the SLIME or SLY protocols, although support is available for Visual Studio Code, the

IDE by Microsoft that is, at the time of writing, very popular.

To get started, Portacle [64] is a decent "batteries included" choice if the free/personal editions of the commercial providers are not what you want (usually because of the limitations in these products). Portacle is a well-polished bundle of Emacs, SBCL, and some other tools to get you up and running in no time on any of the three supported platforms (Windows, Mac, Linux/x64).

There was a time where finding a tutorial on Common Lisp was hard. A lot of the learning materials were locked away by commercial vendors, courses often eschewed the rich and complex language for the simpler Scheme, and the material that was available seemed to be aimed at post-grads in Computer Science.

Luckily, that's been fixed and there are a number of introductory texts available. Two stand out:

- *Practical Common Lisp* [74], an excellent introduction to Common Lisp by Peter Seibel, which is starting to show its age in the "practical" bits (not sure that many people still operate an "MP3 Database"), but otherwise is still a great starting point.
- *The Common Lisp Cookbook* [80] is a very hands-on collection of pages that range from how installing Common Lisp to using the Win32 API, and many topics in between.

Armed with these two resources, you should be able to conquer the world, one set of parenthesis at a time.

Steel Bank Common Lisp (SBCL)

The main free implementation of Common Lisp these days is Steel Bank Common Lisp, or SBCL. It is a descendant of Carnegie Mellon University Common Lisp (CMU Lisp, which is still around but does not see as much effort as SBCL), and the name is a nod to banker Andrew Mellon and steel barron Andred Carnegie.

SBCL runs on all modern operating systems (the usual suspects: macOS, Windows, Linux, plus a handful of Unix derivatives like Open Solaris and BSDs) with the Linux version targeting a wide range of processors.

You can get SBCL from the SBCL website [70].

ECL

Emeddable Common Lisp is an implementation of Common Lisp that compiles down to C code, and therefor runs pretty much everywhere a C compiler is present. As the name says, it is specifically targeted at embedding a Lisp into larger applications, enabling the use of Lisp as an application extension language, for example.

As mentioned, ECL runs on pretty much anything that has a C compiler, which includes platforms like Android and iOS.

ECL's official website has downloads and documentation [18].

ABCL

We visited Clojure in the book, but what if you both have "runs on the JVM" and "is Common Lisp" on your wish list? Armed Bear Common Lisp has got you covered. One of its strong use cases is for those that still want to write "classical" GUI applications: they can make use of Java's Swing user interface toolkit and write cross-platform applications with a native look and feel. In fact, the documentation mentions this as a core benefit.

However, it is also a great way to extend an existing Java code base with a Common Lisp, just like ECL does for "native" applications. Needless to say, it will run wherever Java runs, so refer to Java Virtual Machine availability for your favorite platform.

All the details can be found on ABCL's website, but once you get it going, it should not be too different from other Common Lisps [7].

LispWorks

LispWorks is a proprietary implementation of Common Lisp by LispWorks Ltd. As mentioned above, in contrast with the free Lisp versions, it comes with its own IDE and is thus a good way to get started without having to think about lining up multiple moving targets. While commercial and thus coming with the expectation that money changes hands at some point, they have a Personal Edition that has some restrictions that should be fine for the hobbyist and is free of charge.

LispWorks runs on Windows, Macintosh, Linux, FreeBSD and Solaris/x64 and can be obtained from the product's website [47].

Allegro Common Lisp

Allegro Common Lisp is the second main proprietary Common Lisp product. It leans a bit more towards knowledge management and AI research, but is a complete Common Lisp that also comes as a full product, including IDE (which runs in your web browser).

Allegro runs on Linux, Macintosh, Windows and FreeBSD, comes with a restricted personal use edition that is gratis, and can be obtained from the company's website [5].

Scheme

Except for Racket, most Schemes don't come with an IDE, and there is also no standard to hook an implementation into Emacs like Common Lisp has. But pretty much all Scheme languages come with editor plugins, be it for Emacs, Vi, or Visual Studio Code. For the "batteries included" experience, install DrRacket; for those that already use Emacs, Guile is well integrated.

While not normally important when getting started, there's one caveat with Scheme: while "Common Lisp" is a very well defined concept and code written in Common Lisp can be expected to run unchanged on all implementations, Scheme is a bit messier. For starting out, you probably won't notice any differences, but once you get deeper, you want to take into account what language revision (revision 7 is current at the time of writing) and what "Scheme Requests for Implementation"—in a nutshell, extensions to the base language—you require.

For learning Scheme, Racket and its official toturial [23] are probably the simplest starting point. That tutorial ends with a link to *How to Design Programs* by MIT which is more in-depth and should keep you occupied for a bit [20]. MIT's famous course book, *Structure and Interpretation of Computer Programs* [4] can also serve as a Scheme primer, albeit for a somewhat older dialect. Racket supports the language used in that course using a language "pragma" and thus makes an excellent platform to work through the book.

Racket

We discussed Racket in the chapter on Scheme, so we'll leave it at that. It's a powerhouse of an implementation, is available on Linux, Macintosh and Windows, and can be downloaded from the project's website [67].

Guile

Guile is the official Scheme of the Free Software Foundation's GNU project, and as such an important building block, providing the implementation language for one of the operating system packaging models (GUIX) and the initialization/management system (The GNU Shepherd). It works extremely well as an embeddable Scheme, but is a fully mature Scheme in its own right. Those on Linux probably do well to pick this version for general use.

Guile can be found at the GNU project's Guile page [27].

Get-Scheme

A meta-entry, as there are so many Scheme versions to choose from and they all have something in favour of them. If "none of the above" is your answer, visit `get.scheme.org` [72] and browse the official list of implementations. There surely will be something there that matches your needs.

Other Lisps

While Common Lisp and Scheme often feel like the dominant implementations, the list hardly stops there so let's visit some other Lisps.

Emacs Lisp

Emacs Lisp is mainly used to create an editor, but there is nothing that prevents you from using Emacs Lisp as a full-fledged programming language. It can do pretty much all you need, comes with a built-in IDE, and even knows tricks like switching between lexical scoping and dynamic scoping on a per-file basis. Since Emacs version 29, just-in-time compilation is part of the standard builds, so the classical argument "Emacs Lisp is slow" does not hold water anymore. The official site for Emacs is the GNU project site [26], where you can download the product for its various officially supported platforms.

For most, learning Emacs Lisp is a thing that happens while staring at others' code that gets included with Emacs. It's more of a lifestyle choice than the previous three, because if you are a Vi or Visual Studio user, you can pick up any of them while still staying in your comfy editor.

That will not fly with Emacs. The only way to learn Emacs is to retire your current IDE and become an Emacs user. It's unique in this sense, in that you can use it (if you are so inclined) as an application programming language that is the same language as what your editor is written in. Everything is integrated to a level not otherwise experienced since the 1980s.

With that out of the way:

- Install Emacs, the vanilla version. There is a link in there, "Emacs Tutorial", that you can click and which you should click. Learning Emacs Lisp starts with knowing how to navigate Emacs.
- Emacs comes with *An Introduction to Programming in Emacs Lisp* [6], which you can not only find online, but also in the docu-

mentation bundled with Emacs. Just hit `M-x info` and "Emacs Lisp Intro" should appear in the table of contents.

From there on, think what you want to make Emacs do, read other people's code, and make Emacs your own. There are not too many limits - even an X11 Window Manager written in Emacs exists. It's probably just that kitchen sink that's unattainable.

Clojure

To recap: a modern Lisp on the JVM for those that are either bound to the platform or want to reap the benefits of newer ideas like software transactional memory to handle concurrency. While it started on the JVM, the language has grown in popularity since then and ports to other run-times are available, including .NET, the browser, and even Erlang's BEAM VM.

In order to learn the language, the site has an overview of how to learn the language, including an online tutorial and links to some excellent books [79].

Lisp Flavoured Erlang

An odd duck worth a mention, Lisp Flavoured Erlang, or LFE for friends, is a powerful Lisp implementation that runs on top of the Erlang virtual machine, the BEAM. It is in flavour a bit like Common Lisp, but very well adapted to its host platform, which comes with some restrictions (Erlang does not have global or mutable data, an important cornerstone of the design that makes Erlang into what it is) and a whole list of advantages (the Erlang platform is famously fault tolerant and scalable, and can do concurrency at levels other platforms only dream of).

If building robust and scalable server-side systems is your thing and you want to explore a Lisp for doing that, LFE should be your first stop.

LFE runs everywhere where Erlang runs, which includes the usual list of Windows, Linux, Macintosh and various BSD flavours [45].

uLisp

All the Lisp implementations so far target "real computers", the things with keyboards and screens that run the complex modern operating systems we all know and sometimes love. uLisp, however, targets the world of computing devices that don't have these luxuries, the small world of microcontrollers. It is a great platform for makers that want to build their next project with Lisp instead of, say, Arduino's C++ dialect.

It supports all the usual suspects in the microcontroller world: AVR, ARM, ESP and RISC-V, with various levels of support for features like floating point, graphics, and Wi-Fi (a lot there depends on whether the platform at hand even offers these features).

So, if you're planning to finally build that ESP-32 based weather station and want to explore Lisp, the project's site is as good a place to get started as any [86].

Other learning resources

Let's wrap this appendix up with a list of well-known books in the Lisp community that are likely to help you in your travels regardless of which Lisp you use (although they're all somewhat Common Lisp heavy):

- *On Lisp* [29], is a classic and these days available for free online. It is very well written and covers a wide range of topics, from functional programming and macros to how to add simple continuations to Common Lisp.
- *Let over lambda* [34] goes deep into the woods of a certain style of macros that is very much its own style, but you're bound to pick up on a couple of useful concepts. Around half the book is available for free, and if you're serious about learning Lisp, the full version is well worth the price.
- Finally, the probably weirdest (in a good way) Lisp book of all times, *Land of Lisp* [10]. It has quirky comics and lots of fun little games are implemented along the way. It will happily serve as a tutorial for Common Lisp at the same time.

List of Figures

Bibliography

[1] Hal Abelson et al. "The Revised Revised Report on Scheme, or An UnCommon Lisp". In: (1985). URL: https://standards.scheme.org/official/r2rs.pdf.

[2] Hal Abelson et al. "The Revised[3] Report on the Algorithmic Language Scheme". In: (1986). URL: https://standards.scheme.org/official/r3rs.pdf.

[3] Hal Abelson et al. "The Revised[4] Report on the Algorithmic Language Scheme". In: (1991). URL: https://standards.scheme.org/official/r4rs.pdf.

[4] Harold Abelson and Gerald Jay Sussman. *Structure and Interpretation of Computer Programs*. MIT Press, 1984.

[5] *Allegro Common Lisp*. URL: https://franz.com/products/allegro-common-lisp/.

[6] *An Introduction to Programming in Emacs Lisp*. URL: https://www.gnu.org/software/emacs/manual/html_node/eintr/index.html.

[7] *Armed Bear Common Lisp (ABCL)*. URL: https://abcl.org.

[8] *Awesome Common Lisp*. URL: https://awesome-cl.com/.

[9] *Awesome Lisp Companies*. URL: https://github.com/azzamsa/awesome-lisp-companies.

[10] Conrad Barski. *Land of Lisp - Learn to Program in Lisp, One Game at a Time!* No Starch Press, 2011, pp. I–XVIII, 1–482. ISBN: 978-1-59327-281-4. URL: http://landoflisp.com/.

[11] Stefan Bauer-Mengelberg. "Kurt Gödel. On Formally Undecidable Propositions of Principia Mathematica and Related Systems I". In: *Journal of Symbolic Logic* 30.3 (1965), pp. 359–362. DOI: 10.2307/2269629.

[12] Alonzo Church. *The Calculi of Lambda-Conversion*. Princeton University Press, 1936. URL: https://archive.org/details/AnnalsOfMathematicalStudies6ChurchAlonzoTheCalculiOfLambdaConversionPrincetonUniversityPress1941.

[13] *Clojure Reference Documentation.* URL: https://clojure.org/reference.

[14] *ClojureScript.* URL: https://clojurescript.org/.

[15] *Comprehensive Perl Archive Network.* URL: https://www.cpan.org.

[16] Computer History Museum. *Lisp 1.5 family.* URL: https://softwarepreservation.computerhistory.org/LISP/lisp15_family.html.

[17] B.J. Copeland et al. *The Essential Turing.* Oxford University Press, 2004.

[18] *Embeddable Common-Lisp.* URL: https://ecl.common-lisp.dev.

[19] editor F. Helwig. "Coding for the MIT-IBM 704 Computer". In: (1957). URL: https://bitsavers.org/pdf/mit/computer_center/Coding_for_the_MIT-IBM_704_Computer_Oct57.pdf.

[20] Matthias Felleisen et al. *How to Design Programs, Second Edition.* 2014. URL: https://htdp.org/2024-11-6/Book/index.html.

[21] Richard Feynman. *What do you care what other people think?* 1988.

[22] *Fixed-point combinator/Y combinator.* URL: https://en.wikipedia.org/wiki/Fixed-point_combinator#Y_combinator.

[23] Matthew Flatt. *Quick: An Introduction to Racket with Pictures.* URL: https://docs.racket-lang.org/quick/.

[24] Richard P. Gabriel and Kent M. Pitman. "Endpaper: Technical Issues of Separation in Function Cells and Value Cells". In: *LISP Symb. Comput.* 1.1 (1988), pp. 81–101.

[25] Steven Ganz et al. "The Revised^7 Report on the Algorithmic Language Scheme". In: (2021). URL: https://standards.scheme.org/official/r7rs.pdf.

[26] *GNU Emacs.* URL: https://www.gnu.org/software/emacs/.

[27] *GNU's Programming and Extension Language.* URL: https://www.gnu.org/software/guile/.

[28] Kurt Gödel. "Über formal unentscheidbare Sätze der Principia Mathematica und verwandter Systeme I". In: *Monatshefte für Mathematik und Physik* (1931). Translation to English in [11]. URL: https://web.archive.org/web/20180411113347/http://www.w-k-essler.de/pdfs/goedel.pdf.

[29] Paul Graham. *On LISP: Advanced Techniques for Common LISP*. Prentice Hall, 1993. URL: https://paulgraham.com/onlisp.html.

[30] Cees de Groot. *The Genius of Lisp*. Berksoft Publications, 2026.

[31] Carl Hewitt, Peter Bishop, and Richard Steiger. "A Universal Modular ACTOR Formalism for Artificial Intelligence". In: *Proc. International Joint Conference on Artificial Intelligence* (1973).

[32] Philip Hilts. *Scientific Temperaments - Three Lives in Contemporary Science*. Sands, 1982.

[33] Daniel Holden. *Build Your Own Lisp*. CreateSpace, 2014. URL: https://www.buildyourownlisp.com/.

[34] Doug Hoyte. *Let Over lambda*. Lulu.com, 2008.

[35] IBM. *IBM 704 Data Processing System Reference Manual*. 1958.

[36] *Install Clojure*. URL: https://clojure.org/guides/install_clojure.

[37] Guy L. Steele Jr. *Common LISP: the language, 2nd Edition*. Digital Pr., 1990. ISBN: 0131556649. URL: https://www.cs.cmu.edu/Groups/AI/html/cltl/cltl2.html.

[38] Guy Lewis Steele Jr. and Gerald Jay Sussman. "The Revised Report on Scheme, A Dialect of Lisp". In: (1978). URL: https://standards.scheme.org/official/r1rs.pdf.

[39] *JSR 133: Java Memory Model and Thread Specification Revision*. 2004.

[40] Gregor Kiczales, Jim des Revières, and Daniel G. Bobrow. *The Art of the Metaobject Protocol*. MIT Press, 1991.

[41] J.C.R. Licklider. "Man-Computer Symbiosis". In: *IRE Transactions on Human Factors in Electronics* HFE-1.1 (1960).

[42] VLadimir Lifschitz. *Artificial Intelligence and Mathematical Theory of Computation: Papers in Honor of John McCarthy*. Academic Press, 1991.

[43] *Lisp 1.5 distribution tarball*. URL: https://web.archive.org/web/20070711004603/http://www.informatimago.com/develop/lisp/lisp15-0.0.tar.gz.

[44] *Lisp 1.5 repository by the author*. URL: https://git.sr.ht/~cdegroot/lisp15.

[45] *Lisp Flavoured Erlang*. URL: https://lfe.io/.

[46] LispWorks Ltd. *Common Lisp HyperSpec*. URL: https://www.lispworks.com/documentation/HyperSpec/Front/.

[47] LispWorks Ltd. *LispWorks*. URL: https://www.lispworks.com/.

[48] *List of programs included in the PDP-10 ITS emulator*. URL: https://github.com/PDP-10/its/blob/master/doc/programs.md.

[49] Joel Martin. *The Make-A-Lisp Process*. URL: https://github.com/kanaka/mal/blob/master/process/guide.md.

[50] John McCarthy. "Memorandum to P.M. Morse Proposing Time Sharing". In: (1959).

[51] John McCarthy. *LISP I Programmer's Manual*. MIT Press, 1960. URL: https://bitsavers.org/pdf/mit/rle_lisp/LISP_I_Programmers_Manual_Mar60.pdf.

[52] John McCarthy. "Recursive Functions of Symbolic Expressions and Their Computation by Machine, Part I". In: *Communications of the ACM* (1960).

[53] John McCarthy. *LISP 1.5 Programmer's Manual*. MIT Press, 1962. URL: https://archive.org/details/lisp15programmer00john.

[54] *Medley for the Novice, Release 2.0*. 1992. URL: https://interlisp.org/documentation/Medley-Primer.pdf.

[55] *Medley Interlisp Install and Run*. URL: https://interlisp.org/software/install-and-run/.

[56] *Medley Online - IDE for Interlisp and Common Lisp*. URL: https://online.interlisp.org/user/login.

[57] *Mezzano*. URL: https://github.com/froggey/Mezzano.

[58] Marvin Minsky and Seymour Papert. *Perceptrons: An Introduction to Computational Geometry*. Cambridge, MA, USA: MIT Press, 1969.

[59] Janneke Nieuwenhuizen and Ludovic Courtès. *The Full-Source BOotstrap: Building from source all the way down*. URL: https://guix.gnu.org/en/blog/2023/the-full-source-bootstrap-building-from-source-all-the-way-down/.

[60] *Open SimH - Bringing Antiquities back to life*. URL: https://opensimh.org/.

[61] Robert L. Patrick. "General Motors/North American monitor for the IBM 704 computer". In: (1987). URL: https://www.rand.org/content/dam/rand/pubs/papers/2008/P7316.pdf.

[62] *PDP-10 project ITS repository*. URL: https://github.com/PDP-10/its.

[63] Roger Penrose. *The Emperor's New Mind*. Oxford University Press, 1989.

[64] *Portacle - A Portable Common Lisp Development Environment*. URL: `https://portacle.github.io/`.

[65] *Quicklisp beta*. URL: `https://www.quicklisp.org`.

[66] *Racket Downloads*. URL: `https://download.racket-lang.org/`.

[67] *Racket, the Programming Language*. URL: `https://racket-lang.org/`.

[68] John C. Reynolds. "Definitional Interpreters for Higher-Order Programming Languages". In: *ACM Conference Proceedings* (1972).

[69] Sean Riley. *Punched Card Programming - Computerphile*. URL: `https://www.youtube.com/watch?v=KG2M4ttzBnY`.

[70] SBCL Contributors. *Steel Bank Common Lisp*. Originally CMU Common Lisp, created and published by Carnegie Mellon University. When CMU's attention wandered, SBCL got forked. 1999. URL: `https://sbcl.org`.

[71] *SBCL: the ultimate assembly code breadboard*. 2014. URL: `https://pvk.ca/Blog/2014/03/15/sbcl-the-ultimate-assembly-code-breadboard/`.

[72] *Scheme Implementations*. URL: `https://get.scheme.org`.

[73] *Scheme Requests for Implementation*. URL: `https://srfi.schemers.org/`.

[74] P. Seibel. *Practical common Lisp*. Apress, 2005. URL: `https://gigamonkeys.com/book/`.

[75] C.E. Shannon et al. *Automata Studies*. 1956.

[76] Raymond Smullyan. *To Mock a MOckingbird: and Other Logic Puzzles*. Oxford University Press, 1982.

[77] Gerald Jay Sussman and Guy Lewis Steele. *Scheme: An Interpreter for Extended Lambda Calculus*. Tech. rep. AI Memo No. 349. Cambridge, UK: Massachusetts Institute of Technology, Dec. 1975.

[78] Warren Teitelbaum. *PILOT: A Step Toward Man-Computer Symbiosis*. MIT Press, 1966.

[79] *The CLojure Programming Language*. URL: `https://clojure.org`.

[80] *The Common Lisp Cookbook*. URL: `https://lispcookbook.github.io/cl-cookbook/`.

[81] *The Medley Interlisp Project - a retrofuturistic software system.* URL: https://interlisp.org/.

[82] Ken Thompson. "Reflections on Trusting Trust". In: *Commun. ACM* 27.8 (1984), pp. 761–763. DOI: 10.1145/358198.358210. URL: https://users.ece.cmu.edu/~ganger/712.fall02/papers/p761-thompson.pdf.

[83] *Truth Table.* URL: https://en.wikipedia.org/wiki/Truth_table.

[84] Alan Turing. "Computing Machinery and Intelligence". In: *Mind* LIX.236 (1950).

[85] Alan M. Turing. "On Computable Numbers, with an Application to the Entscheidungsproblem". In: *Proceedings of the London Mathematical Society* 2.42 (1936), pp. 230–265. URL: http://www.cs.helsinki.fi/u/gionis/cc05/OnComputableNumbers.pdf.

[86] *uLisp - Lisp for microcontrollers.* URL: http://www.ulisp.com/.

[87] Alfred North Whitehead and Bertrand Russell. *Principia Mathematica.* Cambridge University Press, 1925.

[88] Sam Williams. *Arguing AI: The Battle for Twenty-first Century Science.* Random House, 2002.

[89] Terry Winograd. *Procedures as a Representation for Data in a Computer Program for Understanding Natural Language.* AI-TR–17. Excerpts and images reproduced with permission. M.I.T. AI Laboratory, Feb. 1971.

[90] Terry Winograd. *SHRDLU.* URL: https://web.archive.org/web/20250328093213/https://hci.stanford.edu/winograd/shrdlu/.

Index

Made in the USA
Monee, IL
13 September 2026

63176214R00162